An Introduction
to the
Sociological
Study of Deviance

The Wrong Stuff

DESMOND ELLIS

Collier Macmillan

Collier Macmillan Canada, Inc.
1200 Eglinton Ave. East, Suite 200
Don Mills, Ontario M3C 3N1

Acknowledgement is due to the Metropolitan Toronto
Library for providing the illustration on the frontispiece
from the first (1651) edition of *The Leviathan*, by Thomas
Hobbes.

Macmillan Publishing Company
866 Third Avenue, New York, New York 10022

CANADIAN CATALOGUING IN PUBLICATION DATA
Ellis, Desmond
    The wrong stuff

Bibliography: p.
Includes index.
ISBN: 0-02-947020-X

1. Deviant behavior.   I. Title.

HM291.E44   1987   302.5'42   C86-094971-0

Designed by Brant Cowie/Artplus Ltd.
Typesetting by Computer Composition of Canada, Inc.
Printed and bound in Canada

  2 3 4 5 6   92 91 90 89 88 87

CONTENTS

CHAPTER TWO

CHAPTER FIVE

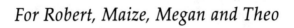

For Robert, Maize, Megan and Theo

PREFACE

BEFORE LEAVING England for Canada during the early 1960s, I attended Leicester University where I obtained a B.A. In the process, I received a fine undergraduate education in sociology. For this, Norbert Elias, John Goldthorpe and Percy Cohen were mainly responsible. They inculcated in students an appreciation of history, of the contributions made to the discipline by classical sociological theorists, and of the relevance of the wider societal context for an understanding of social phenomena such as crime and deviance. Implicit in their approach to teaching was the idea that good specialized work in sociology is usually done by students who are, first and foremost, good sociologists.

What I learned at Leicester has stayed with me. I hope that some of it is reflected in *The Wrong Stuff*.

In its manuscript form, this book was reviewed by a number of sociologists. Three of them in particular, Bernard Hammond, Richard Henshel and Laureen Snider, did an excellent job. Their criticisms and suggestions were most helpful. I would also like to thank the person who edited *The Wrong Stuff*, Conrad Wieczorek. His contribution went beyond editing, important as this task is. Penny Butcher did a splendid job of typing the manuscript. I would like to thank her. Finally, the La Marsh Research Programme on Violence and Conflict Resolution (York University) deserves a vote of thanks for providing funds to undertake research projects (e.g., wife abuse, vandalism, corporate violence) that eventually became chapters in the book.

DESMOND ELLIS
York University

INTRODUCTION

OBJECTIVES

THE PRIMARY OBJECTIVE of *The Wrong Stuff* is to introduce students to the sociological study of deviance. This involves a two-step process. The first step is to show the influence of classical and general sociological theories on four major, contemporary theoretical perspectives on deviance. The second step will be the application of all four of these theoretical perspectives to *each* of the following topics: Corporate Crime, Police Deviance, Wife Abuse and Vandalism.

Strain, Control, Interactionist and Conflict are the names given to the four theoretical perspectives included in this text. These are regarded as standard theoretical perspectives because each one is well established in the sociology of deviance. Most sociologists who study deviance either use one of them or some combination of elements borrowed from more than one. This does not mean that all sociologists who study deviance would place any given theoretical perspective under the same general title I have selected. Here, as elsewhere, there is a lot of room for differences in judgement.

The specific topics to which the four theoretical perspectives are applied were selected for a number of reasons. First, these topics provide an alternative to the usual array of relatively powerless, lower class (e.g., winos, bums) and exotic (e.g., nudists, group sexists, swingers) deviants included in many deviance texts. Certainly, the relatively powerless are included in *The Wrong Stuff*, but so are those who possess a great deal of power (corporate executives) and authority (police officers).

Second, in this text the "cafeteria concept" — a little bit of many kinds of deviance — is replaced (to preserve the food analogy) with the concept of *table d'hôte* — a few selected offerings. The offerings are limited in number so that each topic can be covered in some depth. This seems necessary for the acquisition of a more than superficial knowledge of them. Third, in addition to a limited offering, topics offered *table d'hôte* also constitute a *set* of topics based on an integrating idea or theoretical notion. Thus, corporate executives, police officers, wives and youth are included because they stand in a different power/authority relation to the state, to men and to adults respectively. These differences are not trivial. They help explain why crime is endemic in business corporations, why police officers and husbands can use unauthorized force with relative impunity while youthful vandals cannot.

Finally, each of the topics included in *The Wrong Stuff* (Corporate Crime, Police Deviance, Wife Abuse and Vandalism) represents a sociological grouping of enduring significance to sociology in general and to the sociology of deviance in particular, i.e., class, gender and age. Specifically, corporate executives constitute a property owning/controlling class; police officers constitute a working class group whose job is to maintain law and order. Abused wives and the men who abuse them are grouped as members of the feminine and masculine genders. Youth constitutes a social category segregated by age. Membership in these groupings has important implications not only for the kind and amount of deviance members perpetrate, but also for the way in which the state acts and reacts to their deviance. A theoretical perspective that simultaneously embraces class, gender and age-induced reasons for deviance *and* state reactions to deviance, will probably contribute more towards understanding deviance than one that embraces one and neglects the other.

PLAN OF THE TEXT

This book is about deviance. Some sociologists define deviance objectively. Others offer subjective definitions. In Chapter 1, these two kinds of definition are described. Their strengths and weaknesses are then discussed in the context of defining terrorism. An alternative definition of deviance, one that rejects the subjective-objective dichotomy, is also presented.

In Chapter 2, four major theoretical perspectives are identified. These are Strain, Control, Interactionist and Conflict. Each perspective is described in relation to the classical/general theory from which it was, more or less directly, derived. Where Chapter 1 dealt with the question, "What is Deviance?", Chapter 2 describes the way in which each of the four theories answers why and how questions relating to deviance and deviants. A brief summary concludes this chapter.

All four of the perspectives described in Chapter 2 are applied to each of four substantive topics. Each topic has a chapter to itself. Chapter 3 is devoted to Corporate Crime; Chapter 4 covers Police Deviance; Chapter 5 deals with Wife Abuse; and Chapter 6 with Vandalism. Each of these four chapters commences with objective and subjective definitions of the topic being covered. Then all four theoretical perspectives are sequentially applied to the topic. A summary concludes each chapter.

The final chapter, Chapter 7, is reserved for conclusions.

CHAPTER ONE

DEFINITIONS OF DEVIANCE

THREE CLASSIC TALES OF DEVIANCE

THIS BOOK IS ABOUT deviance. But what is deviance? Do deviance and the deviant refer to the same thing? And what about crime and criminals? Are they the same as deviance and deviants? Then, where does conformity fit into the picture? Is it simply the opposite of deviance, in the sense that deviance is bad, harmful and unusual, while conformity is good, helpful and usual in societies? Is it possible for the same behaviour to be both conforming and deviant?

One way of giving preliminary answers to these questions is to provide examples that deal with them. For this purpose, three fairly well-known cases have been selected. In one, a career outlaw hung around Nottingham Forest; in the second, a hunchback in love made his high-rise home in Paris; and in the third, a career murderer lived in London.

Robin Hood, as you may recall, "stole from the rich and gave to the poor." Does his conduct constitute deviance? Was he a deviant, a criminal or both? What about the Hunchback of Notre Dame? He looked funny, lived in a cathedral bell tower and fell in love with a young woman who lived in a suburban home with her mom and dad. Consider next, Dr. Jekyll and Mr. Hyde. Here the same individual is as nice as Kermit the Frog by day and a serial killer by night. Does what these individuals did constitute deviance? Are they deviants, criminals or both?

To these questions, sociologists have formulated a number of answers. Some would remind us that Robin was a criminal, an outlaw because he violated laws made by the state, i.e., King John. Others would regard King John as a criminal, because he arbitrarily changed the customary law of the land regarding deer killing by local, rural residents. Under customary law they were permitted to kill forest deer. Rural residents were quite law abiding with respect to deer-killing. When the law was changed to legally limit deer hunting to the land-owning aristocracy, formerly legal behaviour suddenly became illegal. Rural folk, generally, regarded this change as illegal and immoral. Robin was actually conforming with widely held social norms when he continued to hunt deer. For this reason, the Inlaws (the state) declared him an Outlaw. He then became a career outlaw, stealing from the rich and giving to the poor. To local rural residents he was a hero because, at some risk to himself, he conformed with social norms relating to helping others whose access to food had been unfairly restricted.

The Hunchback of Notre Dame elicits answers of a different kind. As in the previous example, social norms or rules constitute the basis for judgments regarding conformity and deviance. However, sociologists such as Goffman (1965) identify not one, but two sets of rules which apply in this case. The first of these is "body norms." Insofar as most of us deviate from ideal North American body norms (Mr. and Mrs. Universe), most of us are deviant. However, a few individuals deviate quite markedly and in obvious ways from norms defining normal bodies. These deviations are referred to collectively as stigma. The large hump on his back is the Hunchback's stigma. Because Quasimodo did not conform with widely held norms regarding how the body ought to look, he was labelled a deviant.

In addition to these body norms, there are also widely held social norms relating to how stigmatized persons ought to behave when interacting with normal people. Above all, they must demonstrate that they know their place. They should not push too hard in the direction of getting normals to regard and treat them as normal, that is, as a person without the stigma they obviously display. Falling in love with a beautiful gypsy girl contravenes social norms that apply to stigmatized individuals. The Hunchback of Notre Dame, then, is a double deviant. He violated body and behavioural norms. However, as neither set of norms constitutes a law, i.e., a rule made by the state, he is not a criminal.[1]

However, Quasimodo, ugly on the outside but a beautiful person inside, became a criminal when he killed a number of citizens, including his former companion Frollo, the archdeacon of Notre Dame, who intended to harm his beloved Esmeralda. It was Esmeralda, the beautiful, innocent gypsy girl, who offered water to the bound and beaten Quasimodo, while righteous Christians stood by and celebrated his pain. Who is the deviant? Follo, a person of learning and a holy, righteous man on the surface, kept his involvement in necromancy and alchemy a secret. Was he deviant? Of all the main characters in the book *The Hunchback of Notre Dame* (1831), only the surface ugly Quasimodo; Esmeralda, a member of a stigmatized social group, gypsies; and surface ugly Notre Dame, the cathedral, emerge as beautiful inside. They conform with norms, social and aesthetic respectively, that Victor Hugo believes human beings everywhere should share.

The third case, Jekyll and Hyde, elicits answers of a radically different kind. Dr. Jekyll is a normal person by day. During the night, however, a radical transformation takes place. Nice Dr. Jekyll becomes Mr. Hyde, a serial murderer. So long as no one knows of Dr. Jekyll's secret, can we call him a criminal or a deviant? Some sociologists would answer, no. They believe that these labels can only be applied if and when others, e.g., family members, neighbours and/or the police become aware of and react to Jekyll/Hyde as a murderer or weird or both.

In contrast to this, other sociologists provide more traditional and common sense answers. There is, they would say, a law prohibiting murder as well as rules regarding mental health. Because he violated the former, he is a criminal and because he violated the latter, he is a deviant. The difference between these two labels arises because of differences in the kinds of norms that were violated. Deviants violate the non-legal norms of the groups to which they belong. Criminals violate legal norms. Norm transgressions are common to both.

Returning now to the questions with which we began, these case studies suggest the following answers. Deviance appears to refer to behaviour that violates social norms. Crime is a sub-category of deviance. It refers to behaviour that violates legal norms. A deviant is an individual (or group) that has been publicly labelled as deviant by a social group. A criminal is an individual (or group) that has been officially labelled as a criminal by the state. Alternatively, deviants are individuals (or groups) that contravene social norms, criminals are persons who violate that sub-set of social norms called laws. Behaviour that conforms with one group's norms may violate the norms of another group and vice versa. Conformity is not the opposite of deviance. Both can be harmful or helpful to society. Moreover, as members of groups with different or conflicting norms use their own group's norms as a standard of judgement, the presence of conformity entails the presence of deviance.

The answers given to the questions raised by these case studies represent two major ways of defining deviance. One is objective. Objectively defined, deviance refers to behaviour that violates rules or norms. The existence of these rules constitutes objective standards used by group members in making judgements. That is why this definition is referred to as being objective. The other way of defining deviance is subjective. Subjectively defined, deviance denotes the reactions of others that result in the successful application of the label deviant. It is because these reactions involve such subjective processes as interpretation and assigning meaning to behaviour, that the definition emphasizing reactions is called subjective.

Objective and subjective conceptions have a history. Contemporary formulations of them are characterized both by similarities and differences, strengths and weaknesses. The primary goal of this chapter is to describe these in greater detail. The second task is to locate the first goal within the broader and conceptually prior goal of clarifying the relation between conformity and deviance.

CONFORMITY AND DEVIATION

A discussion of the relation between conformity and deviation is important for a number of reasons.[2]. One of the most significant of these is that it will show the need for giving conflict a more prominent place in sociological attempts to explain both conformity and deviation.

Conflict, Conformity and Deviation

Moral evaluations are central to definitions of conformity and deviaton. Group members who do what the group says or believes they "ought to do" are conformists, while those that do what they "ought not to do" or not do what they "ought to do" are deviants.[3] These judgements apply not only to individuals but also to groups themselves. Thus the Toronto branch of the Humane Society and the Animal Liberation Front use their own values – animals have a right to be treated properly – as the standard for judging researchers who mistreat animals for research purposes as deviant. These scientists respond by calling their accusers "radicals" and "animal nuts." The standards they use to justify their work and buttress their own name-calling are the scientific value of the quest for knowledge and/or the medical value of healing the sick (*The Toronto Star*, July 14, 1986).

From the perspective of the sociologist of deviance, the significant thing about these group differences is that they are not merely differences. Instead, they are quickly converted into a moral hierarchy. Hierarchy is the result of differential moral evaluations of group differences because the process of evaluation is "zero-sum."[4] This means that morally upgrading one's own group invariably involves morally downgrading others. We climb up by "planting our boots on the faces of others." According to Douglas: (1970, 6-7) "The more effective any... group is in getting the categories of deviance and crime imputed to others, the more effective it is in getting the categories of morality and law-abiding citizen imputed to itself. Others must be degraded, if it is to be upgraded."[5] Conflict, in short, is endemic to the relation between conformity and deviation.

General Theories

The example of group differences in the preceding segment points to a general phenomenon in society: one group's deviance is often another group's conformity. Thus, members of street gangs who vandalize property or shoplift may be conforming with delinquent subcultural norms. In the process, they are almost certainly violating the norms of property owners, store owners and perhaps of society in general. The relevant point is that the same behaviour is called different things by members of different groups. A general theory would be one that would attempt to explain both why young persons engage in "conformist" acts and also why members of other groups call these acts deviant and do something about them.[6]

In addition to representing different sides of the same coin, conformity and deviation share four additional attributes. Both are universal, variable, instrumental and contribute to social order.

Universality

Conformity and deviation exist in all known human societies. In any society, both are to be found during the entire period of that society's history. Conformity and deviation also exist in all the social groupings and organizations that are present within any society. Both are present, then, in such "saintly" organizations as monasteries and in such "sinful" ones as penitentiaries, in such upper class places as the Toronto Stock Exchange or Granite Club, as well as in such working class places as pool halls and public housing estates.

The basis for these claims is partly empirical and partly logical. The logical argument goes like this. Organized social life depends upon the learning and acceptance of two basic sets of social norms. The first, or existential set, tells us "what is." The second, or normative set, tells us "what ought to be." Both are constitutive of the society's culture. Existential norms help us understand each other and so make social interaction more predictable. Normative norms regulate (minimally) sex and violence. The very existence of these rules or norms makes deviation possible because deviation is defined in terms of actual or potential rule transgressions. Since these rules exist in all societies, deviation is universal. Conformity, too, is universal. There are two reasons for this. One is logical, the other practical. If deviance is universal then conformity must be too because some individual or group must uphold the rules whose violation constitutes deviation. Furthermore, without at least minimal conformity to such things as language rules and rules regulating force and fraud, organized social life would not be possible (Hobbes 1963/1651; Levy 1952; Parsons 1937).

Empirical support for the universality of conformity and deviation is provided by Edgerton. Having defined deviants as "people who make trouble by breaking socially accepted rules," Edgerton goes on to identify eight universal forms of trouble-making behaviour. These are: theft and refusal to share, suicide, violence, sexual deviance, inter-generational conflict, drug abuse, mental retardation and mental illness. Although deviance is universal, Edgerton finds that "conformity, people behaving as their cultural rules would have them do, . . . is the dominant fact of life, everywhere." (1973, 5).

Variability

Across different societies, the same society at different points in time, and different social groupings within the same society, there is considerable variation in the kinds of behaviour that are labelled conforming and deviant and also in the kinds of persons labelled conformist and deviant.

As was true for universality, this claim is also based on logical and empirical grounds. On logical grounds, one should expect diversity because conformity and deviation are defined in terms of social norms, and social norms vary across societies, across groups within them, and in the same society at different times.

Research findings cited by Edgerton also indicate that for each of the eight universal forms of deviance there is a great deal of variability in the kind and amount of deviance that is permitted. For example, among the Pokot in Kenya, East Africa, married women who did not enjoy sex were considered deviant. Among the Gusii, their neighbours to the south, married women who did enjoy sex were deviant. In the former society, women who beat their husbands were not considered deviant, while men who raped their wives were. Among the Gusii, rapists appear to be conformists and husband-beaters are rare and deviant.

Within any society, definitions of even such universal forms of deviance as violence are highly variable. For example, Webster's Dictionary (American edition) defines violence as "intended forceful action which leads to injury or abuse." However, among a national sample of American men, actions considered deviant or illegitimate were more likely to be labelled violent than were actions defined as violent in Webster's dictionary.Thus 59 percent of blacks but only 23 percent of white union members defined "police shooting looters" as violent. Conversely, an apparently peaceful act of protest, the "sit-in," was defined as violent by 40 percent of white union members, but by only 4 percent of the university students included in the sample. Finally, 74 per cent of whites who felt they were being discriminated against defined "draft card burnings" to protest the Viet Nam War," as violent. This compares with 26 percent of university students who defined this behaviour as violent (Blumenthal et al. 1975, 75-76).

In sum, cross-cultural evidence indicates that behaviour that is labelled deviant in one society may be regarded as conformist in another. What was labelled conformist before the "white man" came may become labelled deviant after colonization. The same explanation of deviance may be accepted as an excuse in one society but not in a neighbouring one. Indeed, the excuse itself may be regarded as an additional form of deviance.

Instrumentality

Variations in the amount, patterning, and forms of conformity and deviation across different societies, different groups in the same society and the same society at different times, are a function of differences in the meanings of these forms of behaviour and in the consequences that are associated with them.

This conclusion is based, at least in part, on the following theoretical rationale. In addition to certain biological needs possessed by everyone, social life instills in the human being certain wants. Conforming and deviant behaviour are ways of satisfying these wants (Walker and Heyns 1962). The relative frequency of these forms of behaviour depends upon their success as instrumental, means-to-an-end, acts. For example, delinquent subculture researchers such as Miller (1958) describe the association among subcultural meanings, patterns of rewarding and punishing, and the "focal concerns," such as toughness among lower class youth. Another example: among the Mohave Indians, suicide is regarded as being highly deviant. It is also relatively rare. Among the Bena Bena of Highland New Guinea, suicide is a frequent occurrence. It is not considered deviant. Where it is met with an intermediate response, such as the "mild regret" of the Tikopia of the Solomon Islands, the rate of suicide is higher than that of the Mohave but lower than that of the Bena Bena (Edgerton 1973; 13-14).

In this connection, it is also relevant to note that the frequency and patterning of apparently impulsive or irrational behaviour is also influenced by the consequences associated with them. This is as true of "going berserk" as it is of "drunken behaviour." For example, among the Truk Islanders, Marshall found that young men who are drunk often throw stones at houses, breaking windows in the process. An examination of the houses attacked in this manner reveals that windows in the homes belonging to individuals in a position, or thought to be in a position, to punish stone throwers severely, are rarely broken. Houses on either side may have their windows broken, but not the one in the middle because it belonged to a white man (Marshall 1979).

What is defined as deviant by the state or other authorities also influences the amount and patterning of deviance in a society. That which the state defines as deviant is also influenced by the consequences attached to introducing the changing definitions of criminal deviance. Shortage of money may have more than a little to do with such changes. Thus, prior to 1960, a Canadian resident was considered dead, "when he stopped breathing or his heart stopped beating." Since then, individuals whose brains are dead can be kept breathing, their hearts pumping, for years afterwards. This costs a lot of money. Governments are finding it increasingly difficult to meet the demands for health-care resources. Hence there is a movement afoot to introduce a cheaper definition of legal death, i.e., brain death. At present, definitions of death vary across U.S. states and Canadian provinces. Thus, it is possible for the same individuals being transported from east to west to be alive in some provinces and states, dead in others and alive again in, where else? California. In some of these provinces and states then, a deviant death is the cheaper one; in others, it is the more expensive one (McLaren 1982).

Contribution to Social Order

Both conformity and deviation make a contribution to order in society. The theoretical rationale for this conclusion was stated by the French sociologist Emile Durkheim in *The Division of Labour in Society*. Although his argument was framed with crime in mind, it also applies to deviance. Society, says Durkheim, is held together, in part, by values shared by its members. These values are learned during the process of socialization, especially during childhood. To function effectively, these values have to be brought out "into the open," as it were, so that we can all be reminded of them and of what we have in common as members of the same society. Crime and deviance, normal products of social life, are detected and made public, precisely because public accusations, blame, shame and punishment all infuse shared values with new life. Strengthening the collective conscience, crime and deviation "play a definite social role in (an orderly) social life."

In more recent times, Durkheim's argument has been elaborated and explicitly formulated as a critique of theories of deviance in which deviance is regarded exclusively as an indicator of disorder or disorganization. Actively promoting the Durkheimian thesis are sociologists Dentler and Erikson (1959). In their functionalist account, social groups routinely produce deviants because deviants make a number of positive contributions to the group.[7] One of these is "to help maintain group equilibrium." That is to say, they keep the group together, doing the things it normally does and sharing sentiments important to the group. For this reason, among others, groups do not kick deviants out of the group.[7] Instead, they keep them as participants.

It should be noted that individual members of a social group may be branded as deviant by the group, and thus make a contribution to group identity, whether or not they actually behaved in the specific ways denoted by the deviant label. Elmer Johnson (1961), for example, studied the "prison rat." A prison rat is an inmate who snitches on other inmates. Johnson found, however, that some inmates could become friendly with prison guards without being labelled a rat while others could not. Moreover, regardless of its actual relation to snitching behaviour, the inmate labelled a rat fulfilled a number of important functions for the inmate group, including providing a target for inmate violence. Violence in turn dramatized loyalty to the inmate code, strengthened inmate ties and warned potential snitches.

Taken together, the evidence relating to universality, variability, instrumentality and contribution to social order may assist in the formulation of more general theories, that is, theories that can explain both conformity and deviation. In addition to sharing these four attributes, conformity and deviation turn out to be opposite sides of the same coin. Thus, a theory that explains one group's conformity can also explain another group's deviance. Since the usual relation between conformity and deviance is one of conflict, such a theory may well be one in which conflict and instrumentality are given prominence.

The inclusion of both conflict and instrumentality would still leave open the question as to whether objective or subjective definitions make a greater contribution towards the sociological understanding of deviance. The essentials of these two definitions will be described next. This will be followed by a brief review of the debate between supporters of each definition.

OBJECTIVE DEFINITIONS

Objectively defined, deviance refers to rule-breaking behaviour. In any given group, these rules or social norms are given; they exist, and group members uphold them. Group members who violate these objective standards or norms, are deviants, their rule violations constitute deviance. Thus, homosexuality, even in private and between consenting adults, violates the social norms of some people and is therefore defined as deviant by them. Jumping ahead in a line-up, telling lies and asking your grandmother to "pass the fucking butter" at the dinner table are all deviant because they violate social norms.

Legal norms, norms backed up by the coercive power of the state, constitute a sub-set of social norms. Often, but by no means invariably, legal norms regulate conduct thought to be either most harmful to society and/or to threaten its major values. Thus murder is a crime because if everyone did it, either to get what they wanted or in retaliation, life would soon become "brutish and short." Moreover, murder challenges the value of respect for life. Murder, then, is a crime because it violates legal norms. Non-hospital abortions violate legal norms and are therefore criminal, but they do not violate the social norms of a significant number of individuals. Evidently, social norms not shared by everyone can become laws. Just as laws constitute a sub-set of social norms, crime is a sub-set of deviance.

Durkheim and Merton

These objective definitions of crime and deviance have a history. Important contributors to their history include Emile Durkheim and Robert Merton. According to Durkheim, "the only common characteristic of crimes is that they consist . . . in acts universally disapproved of by members of society . . . strongly engraven . . . in all healthy consciences" (1947, 73). Laws embody "universally approved" and "strongly engraven" social norms. Suicide is a crime because it violates legal norms. Influencing his objective definition of crime as norm-violative behaviour is Durkheim's functional conception of crime. Crime is normal, exists in all societies, because it helps keeps society stable by maintaining moral boundaries. Crime reinforces moral values supportive of conforming behaviour. Thus, when a thief is publicly punished, the punishment reinforces the value of honesty and makes people feel good about their commitment to this value. To conceive of crime as functional, then, is to regard it as contributing to the maintenance of a "public temper" supportive of law-abiding behaviour (Durkheim 1947, 102).[8].

As did Durkheim, Merton also defined deviance as behaviour that violated legal or social norms. In addition, both of them formulated definitions that enabled them to explain deviance sociologically. They wanted to demonstrate that *social* causes explain variations in rates of deviant behaviour.

In offering an objective sociological definition of deviance, Durkheim and Merton were opposing *individualist* definitions formulated by psychologists, psychiatrists and biologists. Individualist definitions enabled psychiatrists and psychologists to formulate explanations that emphasized the pathological disposition of the individual. Thus, an abnormal state of mind or condition such as kleptomania, leads the individual to shoplift. Durkheim and Merton helped to legitimate the sociological study of deviance by providing a sociological alternative to individualist definitions of deviance. Because they were relatively successful in achieving this objective, they influenced generations of sociologists.

Contemporary Objective Definitions

Contemporary objective definitions of deviance fall into two major groups. Into the first go those that more or less reproduce the

Durkheim/Merton definition. Including among the sociologists who have formulated these definitions are Albert Cohen (1955), Richard Cloward and Lloyd Ohlin (1960), Jack Gibbs (1966), John Hagan (1984), Travis Hirschi (1969), Paul Tappan (1947) and Taylor, Walton and Young (1973). Tappan is recruited because he defines juvenile delinquents as "juveniles who have committed offences which would constitute criminal behaviour if perpetrated by an adult" (1947, 23). Gibb's inclusion is guaranteed by the fact that he "identifies deviant acts by reference to norms" (1966, 14). Hirschi is included because he defines delinquency as "acts, the detection of which is thought to result in punishment of the person committing them by agents of the larger society" (1969, 47). Albert Cohen clearly belongs in this group, for he defines deviant behaviour as "behaviour which violates institutionalized expectations – that is, expectations that are shared and recognized as legitimate within a social system" (1955, 62). Cloward and Ohlin's claim for inclusion is also strong. They define crime and delinquency as "behaviour that violates basic norms of the society, and, when officially known, evokes a judgement by agents of criminal justice that such norms have been violated" (1960, 3). Hagan is included because he defines deviance as "variation from a social norm" (1984, 12).

Finally, Taylor, Walton and Young, the Marxist-inspired, "new criminologists" are included because they maintain that "most deviant behaviour is a quality of the act" (1973, 147). At the same time, they separate themselves from others in the group by offering an avowedly political definition. For them, the quality inherent in "most deviant behaviour" is political. Thus, they contend that "much deviance is a political act . . . a struggle or reaction against . . . normalized repression" (1973, 221 and 169). "Normalized repression" by capitalists and their agents (policemen, judges, legislators, etc.) may also be political and deviant. However, it is not explicitly included in their definition. Quinney, another sociologist who has been influenced by Marx, does include it in his classification of crime (1974, 18).

The second major group of contemporary objective definitions includes those that are also typologies. Here, different objective definitions are offered for different types of crime and deviance. Typological definitions are based on the view that crime, delinquency and deviance are not homogeneous categories. Each is made up of different types of kinds of activity, and different theories may be required for different types of crime and deviance.[9] Sociologists who have contributed objective typological definitions include Chambliss (1966), Clinard and Quinney (1967),

Gibbons (1965), Hagan (1984), Pearce (1978), Quiney (1980) and Spitzer (1975). Motivated partly by theoretical concerns and partly by the principle of parsimony, Chambliss (1966), Pearce (1978) and Spitzer (1975) offer dichotomies. For Chambliss, crimes are either "expressive," i.e., ends in themselves or "instrumental," i.e., means to an end (1966). Pearce also divides crime into just two types, "crimes of the powerful" or corporate crime and "crimes of the powerless" or street crime. Spitzer (1975) uses the evocative terms "social junk" and "social dynamite" to refer to two major types of deviants created by social control agents in a capitalist society. Sociologist Gibbons (1965) is far less economical. He constructs 24 different types of crime: 15 adult and 9 juvenile. Clinard and Quinney fall in between. Their "behavioural system typology" contains 8 constructed types of criminal behaviour systems. These are: violent personal, occasional property, occupational, political, public order, conventional organized and professional crime (1967, 15-17). Whereas non-typological definitions, for example, those of Gibbs and Cohen, would simply define murder, car theft, embezzlement, treason, prostitution, robbery, racketeering and shoplifting as crimes, Clinard and Quinney locate each of these offences under a *different* criminal behaviour system (1967, 14-18).

John Hagan's (1984) classification of crimes into "consensus" and "conflict" crimes is interesting because it represents an attempt to delimit the applicability of consensus and conflict explanations of crime. In Hagan's classificatory scheme, three types of deviation are identified. These are crimes (conflicts and consensus), social deviations and social diversions. Predatory behaviour such as rape, robbery, kidnapping and premeditated murder constitute consensus crimes because most citizens identity these forms of behaviour as criminal.

The second type of criminal deviance identified by Hagan is called "conflict crimes." The characteristic feature of these crimes is normative disagreement or conflict. People are divided as to whether conflict crimes (abortion, prostitution, gambling, marijuana use, pornography) should be called crimes and therefore liable to punishment by the state.

Non-criminal forms of deviation include social deviations and social diversions. Social deviations include "status offences" which can be committed only by juveniles. Thus, smoking, drinking and being out alone after 10:00 at night are all status offences. A juvenile who does these things can be found to be "in a condition of delinquency." Social diversions include nudism and membership in the Macintosh Society. Members of this society spend their lives dressed entirely in rubber. They are rubber fetishists.[10]

To more radically inclined Marxist conflict theorists such as Quinney, Hagan's typology suffers from its failure to take into account the context in which crime, in a society like Canada, occurs. According to Quinney, Canada is a capitalist society. It is divided into two major groups. One consists of corporations and officials who administer that state's apparatus of social control and co-ordination. The other group is made up of the rest of society. The former group dominates the latter. In the course of maintaining its dominant position, by hook or by crook, various crimes are committed. Quinney (1980) identifies these as "repressive" or "reactionary" crimes. The rest of society must live under conditions created by capitalists. They adapt to these conditions by trying to get ahead in ways defined as legitimate. They work at jobs. They also try to get ahead illegally. They engage in a variety of "accommodative" crimes (e.g., theft). Some reject the idea of getting ahead in what they define as an immoral, that is, capitalist, society. Instead, they try to change society by engaging in "crimes of resistance." Quinney's typology is set out in Table 1-1.

TABLE 1-1 *Quinney's Typology of Crimes Under Capitalism*

Type of Crime	Class Location	Class Motive
Representative/[a] Reactionary	Own/manage capital or control the state's coercive apparatus	Dominate
Accommodative[b]	Neither own or manage capital nor control the	Survive
Resistance[c]	state's coercive apparatus	Change

Notes: a. e.g., illegal corporate donations to politicians, illegal surveillance.
b. e.g., mugging, burglary.
c. e.g., industrial sabotage.
Source: R. Quinney, *State, Class and Crime*, (London: Longmans, 1980), 65

Quinney's attempt to define forms of domination as criminal has a more sophisticated parallel in the definition of delinquency offered by a modern English (neo) Marxist scholar, Colin Sumner. According to Sumner, delinquency consists of social censures (accusations and sanctions) initiated by the state and derived from a pro-capitalist, anti-youth ideology. Thus delinquency consists in, "a series of flexible ideological terms of abuse or disapproval which are used with varying regularity and precision in the practical networks of domination" (1981, 3). Although they are flexible, these anti-youth networks of domination are objectively present.

Hence, Sumner's definition remains objective, with the referent being the state rather than youth. He is quite explicit about this. For him, delinquency is "not best defined as a set of distinguishable behaviours offending collective norms" (1981, 3).

Gordon West was quite taken with Sumner's definition and decided to use it in his book, *Young Offenders and the State* (1984). At the same time, West reminded himself to remain "sensitive to issues raised in other definitions (especially the legal interactionist ones)" (1984, 14).

SUBJECTIVE DEFINITIONS

Subjectively defined, deviance is a name or label that is not "in" behaviour but is external to it. The label becomes attached to behaviour during the course of social interaction. Violation of legal or social norms may be one good reason why the labels crime or deviance may be applied but it is not the only reason. Furthermore, there is nothing automatic about the relation between violating norms and being labelled deviant. Behaviour has to be interpreted and meanings assigned before labels are applied. Because audiences vary in the meanings they attach to even the same kind of behaviour, any given deviant act can be associated with a variety of labels. No act automatically defined as criminal (murder, abortion) or deviant (homosexuality, queue jumping) because it violated legal or social norms, is immune from the mediating effects of the subjective processes of interpretation and assigning meanings. These influence the way in which audiences react to behaviour. Just as norm violations are central to objective definitions, audience reactions are central to subjective definitions.

Tannenbaum

Like objective definitions, subjective definitions also have a history, albeit a somewhat shorter one. An important early contributor to their history was Franklin Tannenbaum. Almost alone among his contemporaries, Tannenbaum was among the first to provide a definition of deviance that directed attention away from rule breakers alone and towards the interaction between rule breakers and rule-enforcers. When they arrested and convicted mainly law-abiding juveniles for relatively minor adolescent pranks, policemen and judges "dramatized evil." The "dramatization of evil" that took place in courts changed the way in which juveniles viewed themselves. They now tended to regard themselves as evil, as young criminals, and to behave in ways consistent with their changed self-concepts (Tannenbaum, 1938).

Tannenbaum's contribution is important because, like Durkheim before him and Merton afterward, he helped make the study of deviance social. Indeed, Tannenbaum made it even more social, because he emphasized the *interaction* between deviants and rule-making in his formulation. Next, his conception of social was different. Durkheim and Merton emphasized social causes that preceded deviant behaviour in time. In Tannenbaum's conception of deviance, social processes that *followed* deviant behaviour were made central. Finally, Tannenbaum helped provide an alternative focus for sociological inquiry by doing something Durkheim and Merton did not do: he identified deviance with *reactions* and not with the behaviour reacted to.

Contemporary Subjective Definitions

Major contemporary formulators of subjective definitions include Becker (1963), Erikson (1962), Kitsuse (1962) and Lemert (1951). They have all included the three elements identified above in their own subjective definitions of deviance. At the same time, there are important differences among them.

In 1951, Lemert published his now well-known definition of primary and secondary deviance. Primary deviations are deviations that are "rationalized or otherwise dealt with as functions of a socially acceptable role." An example of a primary deviant is a school teacher who occasionally shoplifts and feels very guilty about doing this. Deviation becomes secondary "when a person begins to employ his deviant behaviour or a role based upon it as a means of defence, attack, or adjustment to the overt and covert problems created by the consequent societal reactions to him" (1951, 76). A teacher who becomes a full-time career shoplifter, who dresses in a manner that facilitates shoplifting (large pockets), who regularly sells what he steals to fences and who regards himself as a shoplifter, but one whose behaviour is justified by his opposition to being ripped off by "big business," this individual is a secondary deviant (1951, 75-78).

In his book, *Social Pathology* (1951), Lemert was primarily interested in distinguishing between the original and random causes of single or occasional acts of deviance and effective causes of career or regularly recurring acts of deviance. He went on to identify societal reactions to an initial act(s) of deviance as a major effective cause of career deviance. Societal reactions (e.g., media publicity, arrest, conviction, imprisonment), were called an effective cause, but they systematically changed occasional deviants into career deviants. Lemert's early definition (1951, 76) suggested a fairly close relation between deviant behaviour and deviant label. In a later article, Lemert offers a definition that weakens this link. Here, a formal definition of types of deviance is replaced with the concept of "deviance matters,"[11] or "deviance data." Deviance data are produced "whenever persons and their actions mutually differentiate through processes of stigmatization, rejection, isolation, segregation, punishment, treatment or rehabilitation" (Lemert 1982, 238).

In addition to attenuating the deviant behaviour-deviant label link, the 1982 definition is more fully social than his own earlier one and the definitions of Becker, Erikson and Kitsuse. Note the word "mutually" in his definition. This is included because Lemert wants to emphasize that reacting to deviance also has consequences for *the reactors*. Lemert's later definition is more fully social, then, because it requires the student to study the effects that stigmatization, rejection and so on have on both deviants and rule-enforcers and not just on the former.

The definitions offered by Becker, Erikson and Kitsuse are more similar to Lemert's earlier definition than to his later one. According to Becker, "deviance is *not* a quality of the act a person commits, but rather a consequence of the application by others of rules and sanctions to an "offender." The deviant is one to whom the label has been successfully applied: deviant behaviour is behaviour that people so label (1963, 9). For Erikson, "deviance is not a property *inherent* in certain forms of behaviour: it is a property conferred upon these forms by the audiences which directly or indirectly witness them" (1962, 308).

While these two definitions are quite similar, they are influenced by different conceptions of deviance. Erikson conceives of deviance as being functional for society. This means that deviance "plays an important part in keeping social order intact" (1962, 308). Deviance, in other words, is not invariably harmful to society. By contrast, in Becker's conception, deviance seems either unrelated to the wider society or possibly harmful.[12] Deviance for Becker, then, is either just another way of behaving or is socially injurious (1974a, 41).[13]

OBJECTIVE V. SUBJECTIVE DEFINITIONS

To include "versus" in the subheading is to indicate that competition characterizes relations between the proponents of each definition. Prior to the 1960s, objective definitions were more numerous and more influential.[14] Since the 1960s, an effective challenge to objectivists has been posed by subjectivists led by Edwin Lemert and Howard Becker. Details of the subjectivists' challenge and objectivists' response are contained in a number of articles and books.[15] Instead of reproducing these debates, a few of the major points will be discussed in connection with a socially significant contemporary phenomenon, international terrorism.

What is a Terrorist Act? Who is a Terrorist?

An objective definition of "terrorist incidents" has been formulated by the U.S. Federal Bureau of Investigation. According to the FBI, a terrorist act is "a violent act or an act dangerous to human life in violation of the criminal law of the U.S. or of any state to intimidate or coerce a government, the civilian population or any segment thereof in furtherance of political or social objectives" (FBI 1982, 87).[16]

Subjectivists offer this alternative definition: An act successfully labelled as "terrorist" is a terrorist act. They maintain that this definition is more useful than the FBI's objective definition for the following two reasons. First, the fact that the same acts have had different labels applied to them and that different acts have had the same label applied to them, means that there is nothing inherently "terrorist" about the acts defined as terrorist by the FBI.[17]

The same thing can be said for terrorists themselves. History provides numerous examples of yesterday's terrorists becoming today's statesmen and prime ministers of their respective countries (e.g., Castro of Cuba, Begin of Israel and Mugabe of Zimbabwe).

Secondly, the definition excludes the possibility of "state terrorists" and diverts attention from an examination of the processes that generate government statistics on terrorist acts.[18] Objectivists are led by their definitions to take official statistics as a more or less accurate measure of the amount and nature of terrorist acts. They do not treat the production of such statistics as a *theoretical* problem in itself. Subjectivists do. Their definitions require it. Thus, they feel that they are in a far better position to examine the degree to which statistics on terrorist acts vary with whether the group that is responsible for them supports a Christian capitalistic or an atheistic communist regime, is winning or losing its struggle to replace one capitalistic regime with another, is supportive of trade and/or military links with capitalistic countries and so on. (Bell, 1979; Schreiber 1979 and Greisman, 1977).

Objectivists respond to these criticisms by recognizing that they do have some merit (Gibbs, 1966). At the same time, they counter with two major criticisms of their own. First of all, subjective definitions entail (not merely imply) acceptance of the proposition that societal reactions are the effective causes of career terrorism. Yet, there is ample evidence to support an opposing proposition: societal reactions have very little to do with the choice of terrorism as a career. This choice is usually a matter of commitment to political, religious, or social values or ideals (Bell 1979; Rapaport 1984). Frequently, a commitment is made prior to any kind of societal reaction to their activities. More than this, terrorists, as individuals, are often secret deviants. No label is applied to them as individuals because as individuals, they remain unknown. In short, a definition that ignores terrorists and focusses on societal reactions to them cannot generate an adequate perspective on, or theory of, career terrorism.

The first criticism is part of a second, more general, one. Subjective definitions divert attention away from a socially and sociologically significant set of questions. These have to do with explaining why, in any given society, some groups are more likely to engage in terrorist activities than others, why rates of terrorism vary across societies and in the same society in different historical periods, and why states themselves vary in their commitment to terrorism. The explanation entailed by a subjective definition leads one to conclude that only one factor – different state reactions – explain all these variations.

In reacting to this criticism, subjectively oriented sociologists would probably admit that their perspective does neglect the ideological and other factors that motivate terrorists prior to any official reaction to their terrorist acts. At the same time, they would maintain that the variations in terrorism across societies and time periods can be explained by pointing to variations in the law-making and name-calling activities of different state authorities.[19]

A review of this debate yields the weak but true conclusion that each major definition has both strengths and weaknesses. One clue pointing to a major strength of each was furnished by Becker himself. Thus he observes: "It might be worthwhile to refer to (behaviour that violates rules) as rule-breaking behaviour and reserve the term deviant for those labelled as deviant by some segment of society" (1963, 9)

Becker's suggestion preserves the objective/subjective dichotomy while apparently regarding both definitions as equally useful. Some conflict theorists, however, appear unwilling to maintain this dichotomy. They prefer to make processes that embrace both definitions central to their definitions.

In this connection, consider Austin Turk's group conflict definition. Confining his interest to criminal deviance, Turk defines criminality as "the state of having been officially defined as punishable" by a legally constituted political authority. Criminality, in short, is a legal *status* (1969, 18 and 10). Given a conflict between legal/political authorities, criminalization refers to the process whereby "deviates . . . will be officially treated as criminals" (1969, 64), i.e., defined as punishable. Here criminal laws are objectively given, and they may be violated, but whether law violators will actually be criminalized is the result of an indeterminate, flexible conflict-relational process. Turk goes on to identify factors that influence this process.

For some Marxist conflict theorists, criminal deviance is part of a much more general societal process.[20] For example, in their *Policing the Crisis*, Hall et al. define mugging (a crime) neither subjectively nor objectively. Instead, mugging is defined as a "sociocriminal phenomenon" involving a conflict relation between young blacks on the one hand and the police and the government of Margaret Thatcher on the other. Viewed both historically and in a specific historical and societal context, mugging turns out to be a political resource that the Thatcher government could use to solve its "crisis of hegemony," i.e., its ability to rule by relying on its educational and moral resources. Thus, for Hall et al., an impoverished objective/subjective dualism is replaced by situating mugging "in relation to the state, the political juridical apparatuses, the political instance, the modes of consent, legitimation, coercion and domination — the elements which contribute to the maintenance or disintegration of a specific mode of hegemony" (1978, 196). In sum, Hall et al. use mugging to analyse the production of consensus by the state.

For sociologists who accept and work within the objective/subjective dichotomy, a definition that focusses on both the social causes that precede single or occasional acts of deviance (original causes) and social reactions to deviance (effective causes), would seem to be one that combined the major strengths of each definition. To this end, the following definition is offered. *Social deviance refers to norm-violative behaviour that is more or less strongly associated with reactions intended to inhibit its future occurrence.* When the norms violated are also laws, we may refer to the behaviour as criminal deviance.

Sociologists who work outside the subjective/objective dichotomy will provide useful definitions to the degree to which their definitions require, not merely permit, large-scale structural and historical analyses.

SUMMARY

Sociologists who study deviance differentiate between social norms and a sub-set of these called laws. They also differentiate between deviance and a category within deviance called crime. Two major definitions of deviance, objective and subjective, were identified. Norm violations are central to the first; reactions based on interpretation and the assignment of meaning are the essence of the second. Deviance entails the presence of conformity. Conformity refers to compliance with norms (objective) or reactions that successfully label behaviour as conforming (subjective). Conformity and deviance obviously differ from each other. Less obviously, they share certain attributes. Both are universal, variable, instrumental and contribute to social order. Objective and subjective definitions of deviance are also characterized by similarities and differences. These exist not only between but also within each definition. A third alternative for defining deviance is one that rejects the objective-subjective dichotomy. Instead, deviance is located within large scale societal structures and processes and is defined as a resource that is used by the state to achieve such objectives as the production of consensus and the prevention of social change.

SUGGESTED READINGS

Jack Gibbs, "Conceptions of Deviant Behaviour: Old and New," *Pacific Sociological Review* 9 (Spring, 1966): 9-14

Stuart Hall, C. Critcher et al., *Policing the Crisis: Mugging, The State, Law and Order* (London: Macmillan, 1978), 1-28 and 181-194.

Gordon West, *Young Offenders and the State* (Toronto: Butterworth and Co., 1984), chapter 1.

NOTES

1 It is possible that in falling in love, the Hunchback was conforming with idealized romantic norms. One of these is that love conquers all. It seems that this norm was not strongly held by the residents of Paris, the Romantic City, for the Hunchback's love cost him his life.

2. See R. Merton (1957, chap. 4). For a discussion of crime as a normal feature of society, see Durkheim (1947) and K. Erikson (1962).

3. Hollander and Willis (1967, 63) define conformity as "behaviour intended to fulfill normative group expectations as presently perceived by the individual." For a more general discussion of conformity and deviance, see Campbell (1961) and Walker and Heyns

(1962). For a discussion of different kinds of subcultural deviance, see Yinger (1960).

4. This comes from game theory and refers to social interactions in which one person's gain is another person's loss. See Rapaport (1966).

5. See also Jock Young, Thinking Seriously About Crime, in M. Fitzgerald, G. McLennan and J. Pawson eds., *Crime and Society* (London: Routledge and Keagan Paul, 1981), 288.

6. In this connection, see also Prus and Irvine (1980, 239); Stinchcombe (1964, 73).

7. In its essentials, a functionalist theoretical perspective rests on the assumption that any recurrent activity (e.g., crime) or established institution (e.g., law) has consequences for society as a whole or for certain social groupings within it. A functionalist analysis focusses on discovering and analysing these consequences. For a good example of this kind of analysis, see R. Merton's treatment of political corruption (1957, 71-82).

8. Although they influence definitions, conceptions of crime are not the same as definitions. A conception emphasizes a predominant aspect or view of phenomenon. A definition delimits a field of study by saying what the phenomenon is. Thus, it is possible for different conceptions to yield similar definitions. For a useful discussion of the relations among conceptions, definitions and theory, see Gibbs (1966, 9-11).

9. Criminal/deviant typologies are constructed or grouped according to certain theoretically or empirically derived (research findings) criteria. Clinard and Quinney, for example, use four characteristics to generate their typology of criminal behaviour systems. These characteristics are: criminal career of the offender, (is crime a full-time or part-time endeavour), group support (to what extent is the offender's behaviour supported by a subculture or group), correspondence between criminal and legitimate behaviour patterns (to what extent is the criminal behaviour consistent with legitimate patterns of behaviour, e.g., gambling on football games and on the stock exchange) and societal reaction (variations in type and severity of informal and criminal justice system reactions). M. Clinard and R. Quinney (1967, 15-17).

10. Hagan (1984) classifies deviations into these three forms on the basis of scores they receive when his index is applied to them. The index contains three items: perception of harm to society, agreement about the norm and severity of punishment for infractions.

11. Deviance matters are defined as dealing with, "the process of differentiation, how people become differentiated and what moral significance is attached to their differences" Lemert (1982, 238).

12. The first option is suggested by this statement: "We ought to see it (deviant behaviour) simply as a kind of behaviour some disapprove of and others value. ..." (Becker 1963, 176). He also makes this statement: "Our theoretical interest in the nature of social order combines with a practical interest in actions thought harmful to individuals and society to direct our attention to ... crime, vice, nonconformity, aberration, eccentricity or madness" (ibid., 177).
13. In Kitsuse's definition, "Forms of behaviour per se do not differentiate deviants from non-deviants." What does? "The responses of the conventional and conforming members of society who identify and interpret behaviour as deviant transform persons into deviants." (1962, 253). Kitsuse's conception of deviance aligns him with Becker. His definition is very similar to Becker's.
14. See Sagarin and Montanino (1976); Cullen and Cullen (1978) and Gibbs and Erickson (1975).
15. The central figures in this debate were Becker (1974) and Gibbs (1966), Hirschi and Lemert (1975) and Gove (1975), Scheff (1975) and Schur (1971). Alvin Gouldner's (1968) critique of the labelling perspective is one of the most polemical in sociological print.
16. There is no officially published definition of terrorism or terrorist acts by Canadian authorities. Still, the National Intelligence Section of the Royal Canadian Mounted Police must know terrorists when they see them, because in 1985 they identified 178 international terrorists in Canada. Others who have formulated objective definitions include Jerome Corsi (1981, 48). He defines terrorism as "those violent acts wherein the perpetrators articulate goals or purposes which relate to grievances against the policies or actions of some identifiable political actor(s) or state(s)." In Rapaport (1984, 676) terrorism entails "extranormal violence."
17. Examples are legend. Here are a few. Both the Palestinian Liberation Organization (supported by Libya) and the Contras in Nicaragua (supported by the U.S.A.) kill and injure innocent civilians in furtherance of political objectives, but only the former organizaton is labelled terrorist; only its members engage in terrorist acts. The Contras are called "freedom fighters" and presumably engage in "freedom acts." Conversely the same label, "terrorism," has been applied by the Ontario Medical Association to the Liberal government's attempt to ban extra billing by Ontario doctors. Johnson and Johnson define the act of putting cyanide in their Tylenol capsules as "an act of terrorism, pure and simple." The Palestinians who killed and injured numerous civilians in the Rome and Vienna airports in December 1985 were engaging in terrorist acts as were Japan's Middle Core Faction (Chukahuha) when they sabotaged Tokyo's rail system in November 1985.

18. For a discussion of state terrorism, see Greisman (1977) and especially Herman (1982).
19. For a very different conception of terrorism, one that stands outside of traditional objective-subjective conceptions, see the International Socialist's publication *Socialist Worker* 113 (February, 1986).
20. Critical criminologist Brian Maclean defines crime as, "a social process which includes a number of social events each of which is inextricably bound up with the other" (1986, 4).

CHAPTER TWO

THEORETICAL PERSPECTIVES ON DEVIANCE

INTRODUCTION

A PERSPECTIVE ON DEVIANCE is a way of looking at deviance. A theoretical perspective is a disciplined way of defining, analysing and explaining deviance. In addition to a number of specific differences, the perspectives described in this chapter also differ in two rather general ways. One is a process/structure difference, the other has to do with micro and macro levels of analysis. As these are relevant to the descriptions that follow, they will be discussed briefly at the outset.

Among sociologists, social structure refers to relatively stable elements that constitute a sort of fixed framework for social interaction. Thus, a differentiated set of occupational roles or jobs, to which different amounts and types of authority are attached, constitute an important part of the social structure of a penitentiary. This structure identifies, guides and co-ordinates the goal-oriented activities (e.g., custody, therapy) of guards, psychologists, social workers, classification officers and so on. In the same way, important structural parts of a whole society – social classes, gender groups, ethnic groups, values (conceptions of the desirable, e.g., democracy or monogamy) and norms (rules) – identify, guide and co-ordinate the interaction of its members.

Social process refers to the subjective experiences of individuals in large and smaller-scale social settings. These processes mediate the effects of social structural factors on social interaction. A concrete example may help clarify the meaning of these two concepts.

One important structural fact about Canadian society is the existence of social classes – lower, working, middle and upper. Delinquency rates – the number of delinquent acts per 100 000 juveniles – is another structural or group property. A structural hypothesis is one that links social class and delinquency rates. The hypothesis may take the form of stating that delinquency rates will be higher for lower and working class youth than for those in the middle and upper classes. If this hypothesis is supported by re-search findings, the structural theorist is satisfied. The same thing cannot be said for the process theorist.

In a process account, the sociologist would want to know what it is about membership in these different classes that influences the delinquent conduct of members in different ways. He or she may believe that social control processes have something to do with it. So, parents and children in different social class groupings are observed and/or interviewed and it is discovered that lower and working class parents cannot adequately supervise their children because they have more children and because both parents have to work. Here, social control mediates the effect of group mem-bership (social class) on delinquency. In other words, the process theorist discovers that middle-class juveniles are adequately su-pervised by their parents, and that is one reason why they are less likely to engage in delinquent acts. Conversely, lower- and mid-dle-class children are more delinquent because their class position impairs parental supervision.

In this text, examples of stuctural perspectives are provided by Hirschi and Spitzer. Howard Becker and Albert Cohen furnish examples of process perspectives. You will also discover that Becker's process (labelling) perspective is meant to be applied in relatively small-scale social settings (e.g., bars, jazz clubs, nudist camps, police stations), while Spitzer's perspective applies to the whole of society. These different levels of application and analysis are referred to as micro and macro theoretical perspectives, respectively.

Some of the theorists whose work is described in this book, for example, Box, try to link micro and macro perspectives. Thus, being at the top of a business corporation in a capitalist society changes the way in which top corporate executives think and feel about conforming with social and legal norms. Other theorists neglect such linkages, preferring instead to formulate micro or macro theoretical perspectives. Becker is an example of the first kind, Marx and Greenberg are examples of the other.

FOUR PERSPECTIVES ON DEVIANCE

The theoretical perspectives described in this chapter are grouped under four general headings: strain, control, interactionist, and conflict. Because elements or parts of one perspective are combined with elements of others, these groupings only roughly separate the four perspectives from each other.[1] Still, they are sufficiently different from one another to warrant their groupings under the headings indicated above. On a consensus - conflict continuum, strain would be located at the consensus end and conflict at the opposite end. If, in strain theory, the deviants are "frustrated strivers," in control theory they are "loners." In the interactionist perspective, they tend to be "hollow and malleable," and in conflict theory they are "fighters."[2] If, in strain theories, individuals become deviants because of "legitimate desires that conformity cannot satisfy," in control theory, the same result obtains because individuals are "free to commit delinquent acts because (their) ties to the conventional order have been broken" (Hirschi 1969, 3). In the interactionist perspective individuals become career deviants because of the stigmatizing or punitive reactions of others, while criminals in conflict theory are either forced into crime by capitalists, or have made crime part of their struggle against them. Finally, each perspective has been influenced to varying degrees and in different ways by four major figures, Durkheim, Hobbes, Mead and Marx.

Emile Durkheim, Thomas Hobbes, George Herbert Mead and Karl Marx differ from each other in a number of ways. They are nationals of different countries, France, England, the U.S., and Germany respectively. They lived and worked in different time periods, the late 19th, 17th, early 20th and 19th centuries respectively. They formulated different kinds of social theories. At the same time, they are similar to each other in one important respect. The questions they asked and the theories they formulated have significantly influenced the development of sociological theory generally and sociological theories of crime and deviance in particular. For this reason, the description of strain, control, interactionist and conflict theories will commence with a brief introduction to Durkheim's anomie-functional, Hobbes' control, Mead's symbolic interactionist and Marx's conflict theory.

FUNCTIONAL STRAIN THEORY: THE CONTRIBUTION OF EMILE DURKHEIM

Four ideas are central to Durkheim's sociology. First, human beings are essentially egoistic. Their wants always exceed the means available to satisfy them. Because they are exclusively interested in satisfying their own individual wants and will do anything to satisfy wants that are always increasing, it is not possible to have a stable society composed solely of rampant egoists. They will routinely rob, deceive and kill each other in order to satisfy escalating psychological and material wants. Imagine what society would be like if it were composed solely not of patient, trouble-free Maytag salespersons, but only of infants whose every psychological and material want must be instantly and continuously satisfied without regard to the wants of others.

Second, the basis of social order is shared values and norms. That is to say, egoism is effectively regulated only among interacting individuals who believe that life ought to be preserved, who believe in honesty, trust and so on. Moral regulation, then, is the basis of a relatively peaceful, orderly society. In such a society, these rules are obeyed because they are right and not because of the material benefits such obedience may confer.

Third, in more or less obvious ways, most, if not all, regularly recurring activities, as varied as religious worship, sports, crime and work continue to exist in society because they contribute to the stability of society. They are, in other words, functional or good for society as a whole. This is why they continue to exist.

Fourth, society can be viewed as an organism made up of interdependent parts in equilibrium. Change one part and you change other parts. The direction of change is usually towards restoring stability or dealing with the disturbances caused by social change. As crime and social control are both regularly recurring, interdependent activities, each must be studied in relation to the other if we wish to obtain an adequate sociological understanding of either.

The centrality of these ideas for Durkheim's functional theory of crime and social control is clearly evident in his treatment of crime in *Rules of Sociological Method* (1950/1895) and of anomie in *Division of Labour in Society* (1952/1893) and *Suicide* (1951/1897).

Behaviour that is defined as criminal is a regularly recurring feature of all known societies that have criminal laws. This indicates that crime is a normal feature of social life. Crime is normal and keeps recurring in these societies because it is functional for them. That is to say, it makes a positive contribution to social life. More specifically, a certain amount of crime, not too little and not too much, is functional for society. It keeps society healthy. Thus criminals draw members of society together by providing a target for their self-righteous moral indignation. Crime reminds the "good guys" that they are good, are morally praiseworthy and therefore different from the "bad guys." In the process, norms and values are reinforced. Their shared character is emphasized.

Anomie or normlessness is central to Durkheim's work on crime. In his theory, Durkheim uses the concept of anomie in two different ways. In *Rules*, anomie is associated with social change and refers to the economy. An anomic or pathological economy increases egoistic behaviour because it "frees individuals from the moderating action of (moral) regulation" and places the individual "in a state of war with every other." In *Suicide*, anomie refers to an agitated state of mind induced by the fact that the norms or rules that formerly regulated behaviour are no longer appropriate to changed circumstances.

Anomie in the first usage is a characteristic feature of industrialized societies. An industrialized economy provides a context in which egoistic behaviour flourishes. Individuals use any means, not just proper or morally appropriate means, in attempting to satisfy their wants. At the same time, and partly as a consequence of industrialization, people become more individualized. The society-wide, shared moral system that, in pre-industrial societies used to be able to effectively regulate egoistic behaviour, is no longer capable of doing so. Industrialization, in other words, has weakened the hold of the "collective consciousness," the hold of widely shared values and norms. In this formulation of anomie, the economy, social control and deviance are interrelated.

Anomie in the second or social psychological sense, also results from "normlessness." This means that the norms and values held by the individual are no longer appropriate to changed circumstances. Thus, economic crises *and* periods of prosperity are charaterized by high rates of suicide. In the rapidly changed circumstances, created by industrialization, normally operative regulatory influences become ineffective. Individuals experience societal weakness in this respect as deregulation. Made weary, despondent and angry at themselves by experiencing a lack of any relationship between their changed economic circumstances and the regulatory power of existing values and norms, they commit suicide. Anomie, in both senses then, is associated with psychological stress or strain.

Durkheim's functionalism, his consensual assumptions, definitions, theory and positivistic methods have been subjected to a number of criticisms (e.g., Taylor, Walton, Young 1973; Ratner 1985). At the same time, his work has been praised by a number of respected contemporary sociologists of deviance. Included among these are David Downes and Paul Rock (1982). According to these sociologists, Durkheim's work remains important for at least three reasons. First, when compared with contemporary formulations, Durkheim's model of social control and deviance is as, if not more, "sophisticated and subtle." Second, the implications for deviance of a "pathological economy" are magnified under capitalism because this form of industrial enterprise thrives upon the creation of insatiable wants among consumers of its goods and services. This state of affairs is central to anomie theory. Third and more generally, Durkheim's functional conception of crime and his theory of anomie has been central to the development of sociological theories of deviance.

Functional Theory: A Contemporary Example – Davis, Polsky

Included among the best known sociological examples of the use of functional theory to interpret recurring forms of deviant behaviour is Kingsley Davis' (1937) work on prostitution and Polsky's theory of pornography (1969).[3] The starting point for both is this paradoxical finding: in most societies in which they exist, prostitution and pornography are regarded as stigmatized, illegitimate forms of sexual expression. How can they continue to exist when they are condemned? Because they perform a very important function for society. They permit the expression of anti-social or illegitimate sex.

Their functional argument proceeds as follows. Men's sexual urges are not inherently social. Quite the reverse. They cater to *individual* satisfaction. Left to themselves, men would flit from one woman to the next, and, with each woman, they would engage in all manner of sexual acts that would produce pleasure for them, but not necessarily children for society. Children mean responsibilities. Responsibly-cared-for children ensure the continuance of society. If children are to be properly socialized, something has to be done about regulating man's egoistical sexual inclinations.

The societal solution is to connect sexual inclinations and social, familial responsibilities. This is done by making a broad distinction between legitimate and illegitimate sex. Legitimate sex is confined to a married partner and (within marriage) to sexual activities that are most likely to lead to procreation. But, man's quest for new bodies and novel sexual experiences remains as strong as ever.

These illegitimate forms of sex also need to be expressed. They help "drain off" anti-social sexual urges and in this way enable men to bear the social burdens imposed upon them by confining legitimate sex to the "missionary position" with a married partner. While prostitution provides directly for sex with other women, pornography provides for the vicarious enjoyment of various kinds of forbidden but desired sexual activities. In sum, prostitution and pornography are functional for society because, by permitting the expression of anti-social sex, they act as a safety valve and so help keep families together.

This analysis, offered by two male sociologists, might suggest that prostitution and pornography are not really functional for society as a whole, but only for half of it, the male half. This may be true. However, feminists have themselves extended the functional analysis of pornography to include women. According to Anna Gronau (1985), feminists should not support censorship of pornography, even its violent forms. They should be against it. Why? Because pornography is functional for women. It serves to remind them of the rampant sexism that victimizes and exploits them. If pornography is censored, the evidence of sexism is hidden. It is more difficult to mobilize women to fight against hidden sexism than it is to fight the obvious and extreme form of sexism manifested in pornography. Pornography then is functional for women. Censorship has harmful consequences and is therefore "dysfunctional" for them.[4]

Strain Perspective: Contemporary Formulations

MERTON'S ANOMIE THEORY   Following Durkheim, a major and novel contribution to the development of anomie or strain theory was provided by Robert Merton (1957). According to Merton, anomie is a feeling of strain experienced by individuals who are brought up to believe that the American Dream is theirs to realize but for whom ethnic origin or lower-class position means a denial of equal access to the legitimate educational and occupational opportunities necessary for the achievement of material success, a central value of this dream.

In Merton's account then, the disjunction between culture, between the norms and values that make up the American Dream and social structure, the unequal distribution of educational and employment opportunities, causes deviance by inducing strain in individuals.

In technologically well-developed, capitalistic societies, this source of strain is unlikely to diminish for two reasons. First, advertising continuously nourishes the American Dream. Second, inequality provides the motivational energy for capitalistic enterprise (Anon, 1985). This means that the disjunction referred to by Merton is likely to be an enduring attribute of capitalistic societies if not a defining characteristic of them.

To Albert Cohen, Merton's anomie theory was an important one because it accounted for the social distribution of deviance. More specifically, it explained why lower-class boys were more likely to become delinquent. They experienced more strain than did middle-class boys. At the same time, he felt that the theory could be improved by making a number of changes and additions. First, Merton seemed to regard crime and deviance as rational, instrumental kinds of activities. This may not be true for the expressive, destructive behaviour of delinquents. Second, much delinquency is a group activity. Merton's focus was on the individual as deviant. Third, it is not enough to say simply that strain causes deviance. The way in which lower-class boys create a collective or group solution to the problem of societally induced strain must also be specified. Finally, the psychological mechanism that enables such boys to accept values opposed to those American-Dream values they once believed in and shared with the rest of society must be identified.

Cohen's Strain – subcultural Theory   In Cohen's (1955) strain theory, strain results from status frustration. All adolescents are assumed to be motivated by the quest for status. They also believe that the proper way to achieve status is by using legitimate means of status acquisition. The school is a major site for status acquisition. Not all students are equally successful in achieving high social and/or academic status in school. Because of their class (family) background, working and lower-class students are, for motivational and technical reasons, not in as good a position as middle-class males to satisfy their striving for status.

Socially and academically then, middle-class students do better than working/lower-class ones in meeting the expectations of their middle-class teachers. This results in greater status frustration and, hence, psychological strain, for working/lower-class male students.[5] They react by inverting middle-class values. So, if teachers value property, punctuality and probity, they value vandalism, lateness and dishonesty.

Students whose strivings for status are frustrated tend to flock together and share their experiences and inverted values. Behaviour that is consistent with these inverted values, that is, delinquent behaviour, becomes a way of achieving status in their group, their delinquent group. In this way, the delinquent subculture helps solve the problem of status frustration.

Cohen believes his subcultural theory is important for a number of reasons. First, he extends the work of Merton by identifying the *mechanism* (reaction formation) that translates strain into delinquency. Second, it explains the *emergence* of the delinquent subculture. Third, it explains the *content* of the delinquent subculture. Fourth, it explains the *distribution* of the delinquent subculture (i.e., it tells why lower/working-class boys are more likely to create delinquent subcultures).

Building upon the work of both Merton and Cohen, Cloward and Ohlin (1960) accepted the idea that strain was associated with crime/deviance but felt that Cohen's extension of Merton suffered from three major deficits. First, Cohen over-emphasized the role of the school. For many urban lower- and working-class boys, school is not all that relevant. Being rejected by school authorities is not all that important. Much more important to street-corner kids was success in the market place. To make a lot of money was the societal goal they valued most. The status frustration they experienced most vividly was generated by the feeling that the closest they would come to achieving such a goal would be in obtaining a full-time, poorly-paid job – if they were lucky.

Secondly, Cohen failed to see that delinquent subcultures are not all the same. Instead, there are different kinds of delinquent subcultures: conflict, retreatist and criminal. The first of these engages in fighting, the second in drug-dealing/using and the third in robbery, theft, burglary and other economic crimes.

Third, the emergence of one or other of these subcultures is dependent, not simply on differential access to *legitimate* (educational or occupational) opportunities, as Merton and Cohen assumed, but also on differential access to *illegitimate* opportunities. In cities (or parts of them) where juveniles had the opportunity of becoming involved with established adult criminal rackets of one kind or another (burglary, fencing stolen property and so on) criminal subcultures were likely to emerage. Where these opportunities did not exist, juveniles would form conflict gangs. Where neither legitimate nor illegitimate opportunities were available, drug-oriented (retreatist) subcultures would emerge.

Common to the theories of Cohen and of Cloward and Ohlin is the idea that subcultures emerge as a reaction to the dominant or mainstream culture. This idea was challenged by Miller (1958) who maintained that lower-class culture developed in the same way that middle-class culture did. It developed as a solution to problems faced by lower-class people. It did not emerge as a reaction to anything. In content, this lower-class culture is characterized by a set of "focal concerns," such as toughness, that emphasize masculinity. This is due to the fact that many lower-class homes are characterized by broken, father-absent families. The absence of a father means being brought up in a female-dominated household. This state of affairs raises the problem of masculinity, a problem that is solved by a subculture emphasizing masculinity.

Both of these accounts are rejected by Matza (1964), a subcultural theorist who, in the mid-1960s, made an important contribution to the development of subcultural theory. For Matza, delinquent subcultures are not characterized by the presence of inverted middle-class values. Nor are they created reactively. Neither do they emerge as a result of experiences unique to members of the lower class. Instead, delinquent subcultures represent a *mix* of both mainstream, middle-class and lower-class values. Thus, while Miller, Cloward and Ohlin and Cohen had attempted to differentiate between delinquents and straight youths, Matza blurred the distinction. Delinquents hold both deviant and conformist values, and their allegiance to each is characterized by a "drift" in commitment from one to the other.

In addition to blurring the difference between delinquent youth and youth in general, Matza's theory of delinquent drift represented a major change in the direction taken by subcultural theorizing about delinquent youth.

First, whereas Cohen and Cloward and Ohlin seemed to suggest that being exposed to a delinquent subculture means engaging in delinquent acts, Matza introduced volition or free will into the picture. A juvenile engages in delinquent acts only when he engages his will. There is nothing automatic or determining about being exposed to delinquent subcultural influences.

Second, neither theorist seems to be aware of what members of delinquent subcultures really want. Their primary objective, says Matza, is not material success or to hit back at the middle class, but to create and experience excitement. Boredom, not a lack of funds or failure at school, is the prime instigator of "being willing" to engage in criminal/deviant, i.e., exciting-because-forbidden, acts.

Finally, the idea of societally induced strain as the major cause of deviance was central to the theories of Merton, Cohen and Cloward and Ohlin. Matza retained the idea of strain as having motivational significance, but he also introduced the process of social control into the theoretical picture. Here, he was being a more faithful follower of Durkheim than either Cohen or Cloward and Ohlin. Where these theorists had neglected the relation between deviance and social control, Matza made it central to his theory. Thus, adolescence and deviance tend to go together because adolescence is characterized by a "loosening of social controls." Again, by introducing the idea of social control, his theory can do something that neither Cloward and Ohlin's nor Cohen's theory can do: it can explain why most juveniles leave delinquent subcultures and become less deviant as they get older (Hirschi, 1969).

MATZA'S STRAIN THEORY OF MATURATIONAL REFORM   Matza starts from two well-established findings. First, delinquency, for the most part, is a group-supported activity and not a lone endeavour. Second, certain parts of cities and towns have a tradition of delinquency. In them, more than in others, delinquency has a long history. If you examine its history closely, you will discover that the juvenile's commitment to delinquency is really a mistake, a misconception. It always was. It still is (1964: 51-59 and 62-64).[6]

As a "mutually inferred, mistaken inference," the delinquent subculture is transmitted and learned in "the situation of company," that is, a group situation. The delinquent subculture is *misconstrued* from the situation of company. This is to say that each member, taking his cues from the "soundings" (swearing, barbed remarks, threats and bragging) of other members, falsely believes that they are committed to delinquency. Actually, each is as committed to a straight youth subculture as he is to a delinquent one. So, why does sounding occur? Why, if asked the date, does a member roughly reply, "No-fucking-vember, asshole"? Furthermore, why would members not just have an honest chat and clear up their false notions?

The answer to both questions is given by an examination of the Catch 22 relation between sounding and two major kinds of strain-inducing, adolescent anxieties. The first is masculinity anxiety (Am I a Man?), the second is membership anxiety (Do I Belong?). It is because of these anxieties that each member engages in sounding. Sounding helps relieve them. It convinces others that he is a man and that he does belong. At the same time, his talk provides a basis for misconstruing his own commitment to delinquency. Because he also believes that asking honest questions about his own or another member's commitment will be rebuffed and because a perceived rebuff is partly the source of his own anxieties, each member remains silent about the truth regarding the other's commitment to delinquency.

As they get older, most juveniles obtain evidence that helps reduce both kinds of anxiety and therefore the need for sounding or for an actual commitment to delinquency. First, physiological changes indicate that they are now men. Bodily hair, larger physical size, deeper voice are all relevant here. Second, they develop new attachments. A job, marriage, church membership all help solve membership anxiety. Maturational reform occurs in both cases because both kinds of anxiety are removed (for the most part) for most juveniles. The relatively few juveniles who do not develop attachments to conventional groups and institutions as they become adults and who still regard themselves as "kids at heart," go on to become adult criminals. Their twin anxieties are still as strong as ever.

If Matza locates the genesis of strain in the transient situation of anxieties generated among adolescents in the situation of company and if Cohen blames status frustration, Colvin and Pauley attempt to modernize and redirect strain-subcultural theory by viewing strain as "an outcome of contradictory, dynamic *processes* of cultural and class conflict and accommodation" (1983, 518). Strain theory is useful, but Colvin and Pauley believe that its explanatory power can be increased by doing something that earlier strain theorists did not do: try to explain the *origin* of cultural goals and unequal opportunities themselves. In the Merton, Cohen, Cloward and Ohlin formulations, these and the disjunction between them were simply treated as given.

COLVIN AND PAULEY: STRAIN/STRUCTURALIST – MARXIST THEORY
In the Colvin and Pauley formulation, workplace, family, school, and delinquency are interrelated. Strain mediates the relation between parent-child relations and the relation between school experiences and delinquency. In a capitalist society, working- and lower-class parents are usually subordinates and rarely bosses, and usually they are the lowest ranked subordinates. As such, they are subjected to coercive forms of workplace control. Bosses order them around and frequently use threats. The threats work because, being unskilled, they can easily be replaced. In difficult economic times, they are usually the first to be laid off. The experience of both unemployment and coercion in an egalitarian, fair-exchange work context induces strain in parents. One result is the reproduction of coercive forms of control in the family.

Children go to school. One important function of the school is to help reproduce the labour supply for capitalistic forms of enterprise. The usual way of doing this is to place children into tracks — academic, technical, vocational and so on. Aptitude and intelligence tests are used for this purpose. Working- and lower-class children reproduce the negative, coercive attitudes and values of their parents. As a result, they are placed into the "worker" track. At the same time, they are being taught that equality of opportunity is an important societal value. The presence of discrepancy between the value of equality and their experience of unequal treatment induces a strain, an "angry" strain, toward delinquency. So, some working- and lower-class students reject the system and engage in delinquency; others, most, are reproduced as labour for capitalist mills and factories.

Strain Theory: Critical Evaluation

Strain theory has made a number of contributions to the sociological study of deviance (Downes and Rock 1982; Colvin and Pauley 1983). Three of these stand out. First, in emphasizing strain, attention is being drawn to an important class of variables (subjective states) that mediate the relation between social position (e.g., social class) and deviant behaviour. Strain is a subjective state that motivates or pushes individuals to break rules they were taught to accept and believe in. Moreover, it provides a subjective basis upon which counter-cultural ideologies can build. This expands the theoretical uses to which strain theory can be put.

Second, by conceiving of deviation as a solution to the problem of strain or frustration, strain theories encourage us to view delinquency or deviation as more rational than we might imagine if we only focussed on the behaviour itself. Thus, even such seemingly senseless acts as vandalism may be a means to an end, a way of solving the problem of status frustration induced by schoolteachers by doing something that increases one's standing in the eyes of other members of the group.

Third, in its more recent formulations, strain theory has encouraged the development of theories that attempt to link social structure and social process. Thus, instead of simply stating that class position (a structural variable) is associated with delinquency, Colvin and Pauley (1983) attempt to describe the subjective processes that link work, family and school with each other and with delinquency.

Finally, strain theory has contributed to the development of a wide variety of sociological explanations of deviance, ranging from consensual/Durkheimian to conflict/Marxist accounts. Strain theory has also been subjected to a variety of criticisms (Hirschi 1969; Taylor, Walton and Young 1973). Most of these have been directed against the earlier versions. Three of the most salient of these criticisms are its consensual assumptions, its inability to explain maturational reform and its emphasis upon the motivations of deviants rather than the reactions of rule enforcers.

"Consensual assumptions" refers to the strain-theory assumption that societal goals valued by the middle classes are also valued by members of working/lower classes. Some evidence indicates that they do not (Kitsuse and Dietrick 1959; Lemert 1972; Miller 1958; Hyman 1953). This means that the strain induced by the disjunction between goals and means is not all that great. One may then go on to conclude that disjunction-induced strain does not play an important part in motivating working/lower-class delinquency. Additionally, if middle-class students experience no major goals-means disjunction, how does one explain middle-class delinquency?

With respect to maturational reform, strain theory cannot explain why most working/lower-class boys become more conformist as they grow older. After all, most remain in the same class grouping and presumably still experience the strains that initially pushed them towards delinquency. Yet, they get "better" as they grow older. How can a constant (strain) explain a variable (delinquent to reformed adult)?[7]

Finally, although many working-and lower-class boys may experience strain and engage in occasional acts of delinquency, a few go on to become "career delinquents." They engage in more frequent and/or more serious acts of delinquency. Strain theorists cannot explain why this happens. This is because the theoretical clue to career delinquency does not lie solely in the motivations of delinquents, but also in the reactions of school authorities, police and so on. Those students who are singled out for public punitive reactions (suspended or expelled from school, reported to the police) are more likely to become career delinquents.

SOCIAL CONTROL THEORY: THE INFLUENCE OF THOMAS HOBBES

Thomas Hobbes, an English philosopher who lived in the 17th century, presented his ideas on social control in two major works, *De Cive* (1642) and *Leviathan* (1651/1963). The three core ideas of Hobbes' social control theory are first, that human beings are assumed to be egoistic. This means that they will rely on any means of satisfying their own wants and, in the process, will be quite indifferent to the welfare of others. Second, because egoism is natural in humans, it does not need to be explained. What needs to be explained is the "unnatural" behaviour of human beings who conform with human-made rules regulating rampantly egoistic behaviour. Third, social control is a response to deviance, and coercive forms of social control can effectively regulate deviance (1651).

The theory of social control offered by Hobbes represents an attempt to answer the following question: given that human beings are essentially egoistic and if left to themselves will routinely use force and/or fraud to get what they want, how is social order possible? The answer is, because they conform with rules/ norms regulating the use of force and fraud. But why are norms able to elicit conformity? Durkheim, you may recall, answers this question by saying that widely-shared social norms, those that are essential for orderly social life, are characterized by a moral aspect. Individuals conform with them because it is the right thing to do; it is what one *ought* to do, regardless of whether gains or losses are incurred in the process. Hobbes' answer is very different. Conformity with norms is a matter of prudence, a matter of calculation. In any given social situation, individuals will weigh the positive and negative consequences of conformity and deviance and behave accordingly. For Hobbes then, conformity is a matter of rational choice. These alternative designations of the basis of social order are of more than a little significance for sociological theory in general (Ellis 1971) and, as we shall see in the forthcoming discussion of strain and control perspectives, for the sociology of deviance in particular (See Zeitlin 1984, ch. 12).

The control perspective was influenced by the fact that Hobbes answered the "How is social order possible?" question by emphasizing fear of consequences. In contrast to man's pre-civilized, civil war "natural condition," social life in a civilized society would be regulated by an all-powerful Sovereign (state) who would be in a position to punish deviations from rules that prohibited reliance on force and/or fraud in satisfying wants. Without the backing of the threat of punishment, values and norms were not capable of effectively regulating the rampant egoism of human beings. Conversely, men would curb their naturally given egoistic inclinations if the costs made contingent upon rule transgressions were made high enough. For Hobbes then, the absence of effective social controls accounted for the recurring *expression* of egoistic, deviant forms of behaviour. This idea is taken up and elaborated by a number of sociologists who are referred to collectively as social-control theorists.

CONTROL PERSPECTIVES: CONTEMPORARY FORMULATIONS

The work of social-control theorists such as Briar and Piliavin (1970), Toby (1957), Kornhauser (1978) and Hirschi (1969) is characterized by a number of attributes. The first of these is certain commonly held assumptions. Specifically, they assume that certain values shared by most members of society are reflected in legal norms or law and that behaviour labelled deviant or criminal is behaviour that transgresses these shared norms. In addition, they assume that social control is a reaction to deviance and that it operates to reduce deviance, albeit with varying degrees of effectiveness. Finally, they assume that human beings are motivated primarily by a calculation of costs and benefits associated with different ways of behaving.

Another shared attribute has to do with the nature of the question they ask. Specifically, they ask: Why do people conform with norms prohibiting deviance? Hobbes had provided an individualistic answer to this question. The sociologists referred to above converted Hobbes' theory into a sociological one by replacing individuals with group members. Groups imply social interaction. Conformist patterns of interaction are associated with the presence of social controls, while their absence makes deviant patterns far more probable. An attempt to explain conformity is also an attribute shared by social control theorists.

Finally, social control theorists tend to assume that conformity with legal norms is associated with gregariousness, that is, with attachments to others. The greater the attachment to others, the more conformist the individual.[8]

Stake in Conformity and Deviance

In 1957, Jackson Toby published an article on "the predatory behaviour of young hoodlums" (Toby 1957). It was here that a concept central to social control theories of deviance was first identified. This concept is "stake in conformity." Stake in conformity refers to investments such as status, reputation, job prospects, membership in the J.C.s, the school choir or Honour Roll, which would be jeopardized or lost if the label criminal or deviant was successfully applied to the individual. Juveniles as a social category are equally inclined to engage in deviant acts. However, lower-class, black males are most likely to actually behave in criminal or delinquent ways because they are least likely to have good reputations, good school achievement records and good job prospects to lose. They have, in other words, a lower stake in conformity.

Cohen's Social Control-subcultural Theory

Albert Cohen, the same Albert Cohen who formulated the strain-subcultural theory of delinquency discussed earlier, provided a more detailed analysis of how variations in stake in conformity are associated with social control in the family. Cohen's social control theory (Cohen, A. 1972) was published in 1972, 17 years after the publication of his *Delinquent Boys*. In addition to being far less well-known than his earlier work, Cohen's control theory differs from his subcultural theory in three major ways. First, whereas the latter theory emphasized the *presence* of a push or motivational factor (strain) to explain delinquency, his control theory emphasizes the relative *absence* of effective control in the family. Second, while Cohen's subcultural theory was limited to explaining the delinquency of lower-class males, his control theory applies to *both* lower- and middle-class juveniles. Third, his earlier theory was based on the assumption that propinquity alone was sufficient to lead to interaction patterns that were delinquent or that made delinquency more likely. What he assumed was this: juveniles hang around with others of their choice, and, usually, these others are peers they live close to, with whom they go to school and so on. In his control theory, this assumption is rejected. The social interaction patterns and peer group involvements of juveniles may be influenced by proximity, but they are also influenced by, and subject to, *social control*. A major item of family business is controlling or attempting to control the interaction patterns and peer-group membership of juveniles.

Families whose children are dependent on them have children who have a greater stake in conforming with parental rules and regulations. The dependency of children on their parents is itself a function of the salience of the rewards controlled by parents *and* their ability to make these rewards and punishments contingent upon conforming and deviant behaviour respectively. Lower-class parents do not have much money. In fact, they are usually desperately short of money. In addition, they are often multi-problem families in which there are many children and sometimes only one parent. Their economic circumstances make it difficult to provide material benefits and their "multi-problem" condition jeopardizes the provision of emotional support. As a result, lower-class children have little to lose by not listening to their parents. Their peers become the major subjects of their attachment. The greater the degree to which juveniles are subject to control by their peers, the more likely they are to become members of delinquent groups.

Middle-class families do have the material resources to maintain a high stake in conformity among their children. The fact is obvious to their children and undermines the effectiveness of parental social control. This happens because middle class parents do not seem to be able to provide their children with legitimate reasons for withholding resources they obviously possess. Parents who do withhold material benefits anyway end up with angry and alienated children. They then seek material and emotional rewards from their peers. Parents who do not withhold resources when their children behave in undesirable ways also reduce their children's stake in conformity because they will get what they want regardless of the way they behave.

To sum up, in lower-class families, the juvenile's stake in conformity is reduced by parental inability to *provide* gratifications. In middle-class families, the inability to *withhold* gratifications reduces the juvenile's stake in conformity. Juveniles with a marginal stake in conformity with parental rules are more likely to become members of delinquent groups than are those with a high stake in conformity.

Stake in conformity is central to social control theories but does not exhaust their explanatory resources. For example, the immediate situation in which juveniles are placed frequently motivates delinquent behaviour even among juveniles with a high stake in conformity. The situational stimuli responsible for this kind of outcome also need to be taken into account. This is done by Briar and Piliavin (1970).

Their "situational" social control theory starts with the following observation: "Because delinquent behaviour is typically episodic, purposive and confined to certain situations, we assume that the motives for such behaviour are frequently episodic, oriented to short-term ends and confined to certain situations" (1970, 282).

Imagine a small group of middle-class juveniles in a department store. A fire alarm in the basement of the store is set off accidentally. Customers and staff move off in the direction of the exits. A small, expensive Sony Walkman stereo is left on the countertop. One of the boys notices it and also notices that everyone is occupied in getting out of the store. So he picks it up and moves off and out into the street. When out of sight of the store, he shows the others the stereo and tells them how he "ripped it off." The others congratulate him for shoplifting such a desirable and expensive item.

This kind of outcome would not surprise Briar and Piliavin

because of the co-presence of three important situational stimuli. First, the rewards for stealing were high. Second, the chances of getting caught were low. Third, there was no adverse reaction, no assault on self-image by other members of the group. After all, only an impersonal organization was being ripped off and one that was covered by insurance anyway.

For Travis Hirschi, a major contributor to the development of social control theory, situational stimuli are not unimportant. However, he also believed that a more adequate sociological social control theory of deviance required an emphasis on the nature of the individual's bond to conventional society. As did Briar and Piliavin, Hirschi assumed that most juveniles fell into the potential/occasional delinquent group. Because of their bond to conventional society, most juveniles do not grow up to become serious or full-time criminals. For Hirschi, then, variations in conformity among juveniles are associated with variations in the strength of the individual's bond to society, for it is this bond that controls the natural inclination to deviate.

Hirschi's Social Control Theory

According to Hirschi, the individual's bond to society consists of four elements or parts: attachments, investments, involvements and beliefs.

The concept of *attachments* refers to attachments to persons. The more we are attached to others as friends, lovers, fellow human beings, the more we tend to take their feelings, wishes, and expectations into account in deciding on how to behave. The more attached we are to conventional members of society, the more likely we are to conform with rules they share and support. The lonely person, the person with few attachments to others, is less likely to respect norms that are important to others.

Although he has few friends, the lonely person may still remain largely conformist because of what he may lose if he is discovered behaving in illegitimate ways. Suppose one of the reasons why an individual is lonely is that he spends all his time in the quest for profit. Everything or much that he has acquired, all the time and effort he invested in getting rich and acquiring material goods, may be jeopardized if he engages in deviant acts and is discovered doing so. Many individuals do in fact acquire things (reputations, wives, children, jobs, club and church memberships, houses) that constitute *investments* in society. These investments constitute a "stake in conformity." The greater the individual's stake in conformity, the greater the likelihood of conforming behaviour.

Involvement refers to the sheer amount of time the individual spends doing conventional things. The individual who is lonely because he spends all his time working at a legitimate job is thus doubly controlled. Being successful, he has acquired a great stake in conformity. Being so busy, he does not have the time to enjoy riding his motorcycle, let alone joining the Hell's Angels.

Most people in society value certain outcomes (e.g., personal security) and believe that rules that support these values ought to be obeyed. Because they do hold to these *beliefs*, they tend to remain conformist. At the same time, not everyone's beliefs in the moral rightness of societal values are equally strong. Those whose beliefs are less strongly held feel less obliged to conform with societal rules. This remains true even though they accept, to some degree, the moral validity of the rules they break.

From this account, a number of control hypotheses may be derived. A few examples are presented below.

Hypotheses   The bond to society is itself made up of elements that are interrelated. For example, in the home, juveniles who, because of close parental supervision, have relatively less free (unsupervised) time on their hands are more likely to be conformist, regardless of how "happy" their home situation is. Within the school itself, attachments to conventional others (e.g., teachers) should be associated with increased control over the expression of deviant behaviour. On the street, juveniles with a low stake in conformity are less likely to be conformist and also more likely to hang around with peers who are delinquent.

Research   Evidence in support of each of these hypotheses has been presented by Wilson (1980) and by Hirschi (1971):

(a) *Parental Supervision (Involvements)*
  Harriett Wilson studied 56 intact, low-income families in which there were five or more children. All families lived in the inner-city area of Birmingham — a city in England. Using an index of chaperonage developed earlier by other researchers, Wilson gave each family a high or low score depending on the care taken by parents to ensure the safety of their children. Parents who routinely took their children to and from school, who insisted on an early bedtime, did not allow their children to roam the streets and so on, were given high scores. Parents with high chaperonage scores did not have happier homes than parents with low scores, but their children were much less likely to be delinquent.
  Wilson also discovered that parents who exercised strict supervision over their children also embraced high standards

of morality. Cleanliness, tidiness and modesty were regarded as highly desirable attributes, attributes they attempted to inculcate in their children.

(b) *Relations with Teacher (Attachments)*

According to Albert Cohen, the lower-class lad most likely to become delinquent is the one who is placed in the difficult position of liking the teachers whose expectations he finds difficult to meet because they discriminate against him in favour of middle-class boys. Opposed to this is Hirschi's social control prediction that such boys are *less likely* to become delinquent. It really does not matter how teachers treat them. So long as they value what teachers think of them, they will tend to remain conformist.

Hirschi's hypothesis was tested using data from a questionnaire administered to over 4000 junior and high-school students. "Teachers pick on me" and "Do you care what teachers think of you?" were two of the items to which students were asked to respond. The relation between answers to these questions and self-reported delinquency yielded the following finding: among the Cohen boys (those who cared a lot what teachers thought of them and felt picked on by teachers), 24 percent reported engaging in more than two delinquent acts. Among the Hirschi boys (those who did not care what teachers thought of them and who felt picked on by teachers), 52 percent reported engaging in more than two delinquent acts. Thus, those less attached to teachers were more likely to be delinquent (1969, 125).

(c) *Investments, Delinquent Peer Associations and Delinquency*

Do "birds of a feather flock together" and how are "feathering," "flocking" and delinquency related to each other?

FIGURE **2-1** *Feathering and Flocking: Cohen*

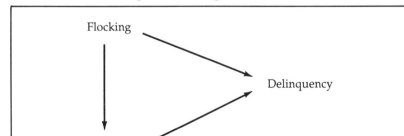

Let's say that feathering refers to stakes in conformity and flocking to delinquent peers. "Birds of a feather," then, refers to boys who have roughly the same stake in conformity. Hirschi's control theory emphasizes feathering, Cohen's strain-subculture of delinquency theory emphasizes flocking.

Figure 2-1 shows how involvement with delinquent peers leads directly to the commission of delinquent acts. Going around with "bad companions" also leads to such things as a bad reputation and poorer school grades, i.e., a decreased stake in conformity. Boys with a low stake in conformity engage in delinquent acts. Hirschi's control theory says this:

FIGURE 2-2 *Feathering and Flocking: Hirschi*

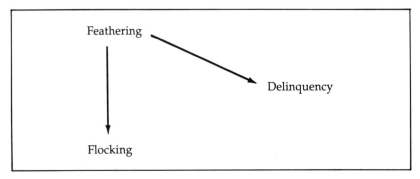

Here, stake in conformity influences the choice of friends. High stake boys are less likely to go around with delinquent boys while low stake boys are much more likely to do so. It is because of their low stake in conformity and not because of their delinquent friends that they tend to become involved in delinquent acts. Thus, an arrow is present between feathering and delinquency but absent between flocking and delinquency.

Hirschi's social control theory has been subjected to a number of criticisms (Downes and Rock 1982; Taylor, Walton, Young 1973). Two of these focus on motivation and on the consequences of social control actions and reactions. Box (1981) attempts to improve upon Hirschi's formulation by including them in his. Hirschi assumes that the motivation towards deviance does not have to be explained. We are all either naturally inclined or socially induced towards deviance. All that is necessary for humans to actually behave in deviant ways is for the social control lid (weakened bonds, nothing to lose) to be removed. In his account, however,

Box included both "situational inducements" to deviate and motivation. Thus, juveniles who have the opportunity to deviate, may or may not take advantage of it, depending upon "secrecy, skills, supply, social, and symbolic support" (Box 1981, 150). The shoplifting example given earlier describes the operaton of these inducements.

Social Control Theory: Critical Evaluation

One of the major strengths of social control theory is that it is supported by a number of research findings (Hepburn 1976; Hindelang 1973; Wiatrowski et al. 1981). Those who adopt or favour a positivistic, or quantitative, empirical approach to the sociology of deviance find this to be a significant accomplishment, especially when control theories are compared with their competitors on this specific criterion.[9]

In addition to strong empirical support, control theories seem to be especially well suited to accounting for four problems of major interest to sociologists of deviance. These are, class, race, gender and age differences in crime and deviance (Wiatrowski et al. 1981).

Finally, by taking deviance for granted and formulating a theory designed to explain conformity (Why are most people *not* deviant?) they offer a novel challenge to other theoretical perspectives. In doing this, they stimulate the development of sociological theorizing about deviance.

The challenge offered by the Hirschi-Kornhauser version of control theory was novel, but it was also flawed. The flaw, a logical one, derives from devising a theory to explain not the presence, but the *absence* of a social phenomenon, deviance. Hirschi himself admits that alternative theories that attempt to explain the presence of deviance are, on logical grounds, superior to his (1969, 32–33 and footnote 44).

Another weakness of their control theory is that it neglects the motivation or push towards deviance. Yet, delinquency often occurs in a group context and peer-group pressure is an important factor in motivating delinquent acts such as vandalism. Moreover, as Downes and Rock (1982, 199) point out, Hirschi leaves us with a very barren set of reasons for deviance. Basically, in his theory, deviance satisfies sexual, aggressive and/or acquisitive appetites. Yet, if any of these forms of deviance is examined closely, one discovers marked differences in their character. Thus, sexual deviance covers over 42 different kinds of deviance ranging from piquerism (sexual arousal associated with sticking pins or other sharp objects in people) to prostitution (Shook 1983). As sociologists of deviance, are we not interested in "models of motivation which correspond with (the typical forms) which sexual deviance takes?" Hirschi's control theory assumes we are not.

Finally, Hirschi may be criticized for his theoretical silence with respect to the processes leading to the establishment, maintenance and severance of bonds. Perhaps, if he had devoted some attention to the *relation* between authorities and subordinates in various contexts (family, school, work), his understanding of the bonding process itself would be more adequate. Specifically, he might have discovered that the individual's bond to society is influenced in important ways, not just by the absence of social control, but also by the *presence* of certain kinds of social control processes. Thus, lower-class children subjected to coercive forms of control by school authorities tend to develop hostile attitudes (ideological orientations) towards conformist authorities. Indeed, the individual's bond to society may consist, in part, of such ideological orientations (Colvin and Pauley 1983, 519).

Furthermore, if Colvin and Pauley are correct, then the effects of social control processes on conformity and deviance would be mediated or influenced by such factors as whether individuals perceive the process to be fair (e.g., punishments are administered only after a fair — due process — hearing to establish guilt and only for violations of rules that were made and publicized prior to the alleged violation) and legitimate (individuals subject to the norms enforced by authorities played some part in creating them).

Considerations such as these markedly influence the effectiveness of sanctions (rewards or punishments) studied by deterrence theorists. A study of social control in a maximum security prison, a setting that maximizes coercive forms of control, clearly illustrates the wisdom of taking such subjective factors into account (Ellis et al. 1974). Yet, those who focus on the deterrent effect of punishment do not routinely take such factors into account, even when life and death issues are, literally, involved (Erlich, 1975). Even when they do, they tend to focus on subjective processes that relate to deterring-by-punishing and not to deterring by helping ameliorate the social conditions that make deviance more probable in the first place. Thus, the capital punishment debate often focusses on how many probable victims each execution saves but rarely on how many innocent victims will be saved each year by the guarantee of a 20 percent improvement in the quality of life for ghetto residents and slum dwellers in Miami, Detroit, Toronto, or Montreal.

SYMBOLIC INTERACTION: G.H. MEAD

G.H. Mead's theory of symbolic interaction was published in 1934, in a book entitled *Mind, Self and Society* (Mead 1934). Central to symbolic interactionism as a distinctive theoretical perspective are the following core ideas. First, the Hobbesian problem of social order is redefined as a cognitive one. Whereas Hobbes and Durkheim had answered the question, "How is society possible?" by identifying the social control of rampant egoism as a necessary condition, Mead's answer emphasized shared *meanings*. A shared symbolic universe including, pre-eminently, a common language, makes social interaction predictable. Words, bodily movements and other objects in the environment mean the same thing to the interacting parties. This makes possible the co-operation necessary for the creation of society.

Second, via the process of socialization, human beings gradually learn the meanings, the descriptions and evaluations that constitute their symbolic universe. Central to this process is the emergence of the social self or "self-as-object-to-itself." Socialized individuals, individuals in whom this kind of self has emerged, have acquired the ability to describe and evaluate themselves in the same way that others describe and evaluate them. The source of the social self, then, is the reaction of others. We tend to see ourselves as others see us. Moreover, the way we see ourselves influences the way we behave. Usually, individuals tend to behave in ways that are consistent with their self-images.

Third, while the metaphor of a multi-player game, (e.g., baseball), may be applied to symbolic interaction and society, Mead's game has one very important and distinctive property: in the course of interacting with each other, self-images and the rules of the game may be changed. New self-images and rules may be created, some rules applied, others not. Thus, Mead's game is flexible and has a creative, emergent quality to it. Simply examining the game's rules as they appear in the Rule Book will not tell you very much about how the game is actually played or about the course of the game. Games have an emergent quality to them, and the process of emergence must be studied directly. The game's structure, its rules, and its competitive values should be taken into account, but the primary focus of analysis is the process of symbolic interaction. The large, many-player game called society emerges out of, and can be changed by, the symbolic interaction that takes place among individuals in such small scale settings as homes, schools, workplace, churches and so on.

Most sociologists who adopt a social psychological, symbolic interactional approach to the study of deviant social behaviour in these settings work with a set of sensitizing concepts bequeathed them by Mead. These include interaction, symbols, meanings, process, emergence and self-concept. A few have borrowed concepts formulated by other theorists and some have tried to combine Mead's micro-sociological approach with a macro-societal one. Interactionist theorists share a number of attributes. The review that follows will begin with a description of these.

INTERACTIONIST PERSPECTIVES: CONTEMPORARY FORMULATIONS

As a prelude to describing what they are for, it may be useful to identify what interactionist theorists, as a group, are against. First, they are against "absolutist, structural theories." According to Douglas (1984a, 6), this kind of theory argues that "all societies . . . have a set, but not necessarily the same set, of universally shared values that determine the basic patterns of social interaction and that produce social order." Douglas also speaks for interactionist theorists when he argues that this kind of theory should be replaced by one that assumes that "social meanings including values or rules are always problematic (or uncertain) to some degree for members of society in concrete situations."

Second, given their adoption of open, emergent, subjective definitions of deviance and their reliance on methods of study that get at meanings, at the process of interaction, interactionist theorists as a group tend to be against the use of formalized theories and quantitative, statistical methods of analysis. Direct observation including participant observation and qualitative methods of analysis, i.e., analysis using words, are more appropriate for studying the ways in which deviant selves are created, changed and/or maintained during the course of social interaction in small-scale or micro-social settings.

In addition to opposing absolutist structural theories and positivistic assumptions and methods, interactionist theorists also share the following set of assumptions and ideas. Social control is a major cause of deviance. The study of meanings will contribute more to the understanding of deviance than the study of motives. In attempting to understand deviance, the study of labels is as, if not more, important than the study of the deviant act itself. Finally, it is sociologically more interesting and important to study deviants who repeatedly engage in deviant acts than it is to study deviants who do so infrequently.

The review that yielded these conclusions also yielded this one: agreement on all of the above-mentioned points co-exists with a number of different "special interactionist theories" (Douglas 1984b, 7–12). From this number, three, the formulations of Edwin Lemert, Howard Becker and Kai Erikson, have been selected for review. These have been chosen because they reflect the diversity that characterizes interactionist approaches and because of their important influence upon the development of interactionist theories of deviance.

Interactionist-societal-reaction Perspective: Lemert

Edwin Lemert's starting point is the observation that the concept of interaction is central, not just to his perspective, but to sociology itself, insofar as sociology takes the existence of interacting individuals and groups as given. Having said this, Lemert then goes on to treat the concept of interaction as a relation involving two or more parties. This is important to him because some "interactionists" seem to forget this, focussing mainly on one or other of the interacting parties. A "full interactional analysis" means focussing on all main interactants, and this is what Lemert sets out to provide (1982, 252).

Central to Lemert's full interactional analysis is the idea that the reactions of one party to the deviance of the other constitute a major cause of an increasing involvement in deviance. Here Lemert is inverting the traditional relation between social control and deviance. In most traditional perspectives (e.g., strain and control) social control is a reaction to deviance. In Lemert's perspective, deviance (career deviance particularly) is a reaction to societal control (1967).

Lemert's full interactional analysis, then, is based upon his inversion of the usual social control-deviance relation, and it is guided by a theoretical perspective that builds upon a major distinction between random or original and effective causes of deviance. Random causes refer to the great variety of factors that motivate individuals to commit either a single act of deviance or to occasionally commit deviant acts. Effective causes refer to changes in the identity and legitimate opportunities for earning a living, brought about by societal reactions (e.g., arrest, conviction or publicity) to the original, randomly caused deviant acts. It is these reactions that transform primary or occasional deviants into career or secondary deviants.

Primary deviance is defined by Lemert as "situational" or opportunistic deviance. Not only does it occur occasionally, but it is regarded also as excusable by the individual either because it is just one of those things that sometimes happens or because it's just something that goes with the job or other perfectly acceptable social role. Thus Sherman (1974) refers to police officers who occasionally accept free coffee and meals from restaurant owners in their patrol areas. The officers know that accepting free gifts is prohibited by police rules, but they accept them anyway, because "all the guys do it." They also believe it is little enough to accept, in return for putting one's life on the line to protect the restaurant owner's property. Because these deviations "are dealt with as functions of a socially acceptable role," they constitute primary deviance.

Now, suppose a citizen and regular patron of one of the restaurants serving free meals to police officers reports the matter to the police chief and also has his complaint published in the local newspaper. As a result, three police officers are fired, and two are convicted of accepting free meals as bribes for overlooking the restaurant owner's illegally parked car and his serving liquor to minors. Their criminal conviction prevents them from obtaining jobs with other police forces or private security firms. So, they use knowledge gained as police officers to plan and execute their own burglaries and car-theft operation. Following a few arrests and trials but no convictions, they gradually come to see themselves as criminals and construct a number of justifications for their full-time, criminal careers. They are now secondary deviants. According to Lemert, their deviation is secondary because they "employ (their) deviant behaviour or a role based upon it as a means of defence, attack or adjustment to the overt and covert problems created by the consequent societal reaction to him" (1952, 77).

Sociologists interested in the study of deviance should concentrate on secondary deviance and deviants because "deviations are not (sociologically) significant until they are organized subjectively and transformed into active roles and become the criteria for assigning social status" (Lemert 1951, 75). The two successful crooked police officers referred to in the example had a very high status among professional crooks, but very low status among Rotarians and perhaps the rest of conformist society.[10]

The differentiation in status referred to here covers both social and moral aspects. In other words, conformist members of society won't socialize with career criminals because they believe it is just wrong for some individuals to make a living using criminal means while most people make a living in an honest way. The social and moral differentiation of secondary (career) deviants from primary (occasional) deviants, i.e., most of us, is the outcome of societal reactions to deviance, reactions that result in restricted educational and occupational opportunities and the acquisition of a criminal self-identity.

Interactionist-labelling Perspective: Howard Becker

Howard Becker, jazz musician and sociologist, calls himself an interactionist (1974). He calls his formulation a perspective, a disciplined point of view that helps "increase understanding of things formerly obscure." Thus, to those who believe that becoming a marijuana user simply involves smoking it, Becker's (1963) analysis suggests that this is not enough. In addition to smoking dope and interacting with others who do, the individual also engages in a number of conversations with himself. Introspective self-talk is strategically implicated in becoming a marijuana user, in labelling oneself as one.

In addition to self-labelling, the individual is also labelled by others. In both cases, Becker's labelling-interactionist perspective focusses attention on the nature, application and consequences of labels.

The participants involved in any given instance of deviance usually fall into two groups. Into the first fall various kinds of accusers and definers. The individuals being accused and labelled fall into the second group. The interaction between them involves accusations, name-calling, denials and excuses. The moral worthiness and legal status of the accused is involved here, but one cannot be sure of the outcome, i.e., we cannot always predict that the label deviant or criminal will be successfully applied. For this reason, Becker refers to the interaction between accusers and accused as a "moral drama." This moral drama is, for interactionist theorists such as Becker, *the* object of sociological study. Central to moral drama is the process of labelling.

The moral drama begins when others perceive that "something is amiss." Something about the suspect or his behaviour seems unusual or wrong. Members of the audience try to make sense of their perception by attempting to interpret the person and/or his behaviour. This is done by relating the person/behaviour to social definitions that exist in the culture and/or subculture(s). The social definitions take the form of stereotypical *descriptions* (e.g., junkie, fink, gay) that also entail *evaluation* (good/bad) and *prescription* (how should one react/what should be done).

Social definitions do two things. First, they organize interaction. That is to say, they help locate in social and moral space those whose persons or behaviour led to the perception that something was amiss. Thus, interaction becomes more predictable once a person has been defined as a "fink" or "gay." Second, the labels help create and maintain the differentiation between deviants and non-deviants. Attached to these differences are important social and legal consequences.

When they attempt to actually observe and study the process of labelling, interactionist theorists such as Rubington and Weinberg (1978, 1) focus on the following questions: What kind of breach of social norms occurred? How was the person or behaviour labelled? Whose label eventually prevailed? Why? How did the label influence social interaction? Was the label successfully applied? What were the consequences of the successful application of the label?

Successful Labelling: Career Deviants

Successful labelling refers to an outcome in which the person (or group) to whom the label is applied regards him/herself as the labellers do and regularly behaves in a manner consistent with the label. Successful labelling is, for the labelled individual, a "fateful" experience. A fateful experience is one that makes a significant difference in the life and in the life chances of an individual. It is also a difference that might otherwise not have been experienced had the label not been successfully applied.

Interactionists who have actually studied many different kinds of moral drama and their relation to deviant careers have discovered that successful labelling varies with the kinds of deviant to whom the label is applied and also with the situational conditions under which it is applied.

In this connection, it is important to make a distinction between those factors that (a) are likely to lead members of an audience to react to a person's deviant behaviour, (b) those that influence the severity of the reaction and (c) those that influence the *successful* application of the label. After all, some labels "stick." Others do not. Why the difference?

First of all, for a label to stick, it must be applied. The probability that a deviant label will be applied varies with:

- Whether a rule (norm) was broken (rule breakers vs. non-rule breakers).
- Who committed the infraction (powerful vs. powerless persons).
- When the infraction was committed (was a campaign being waged against this kind of deviance or not?).
- How frequently the rule was being broken (few vs. many infractions).
- How visible the infractions were (visible vs. secret deviance).

- What the consequences (material and symbolic) were to the labellers (gains increased/losses decreased vs. gains decreased/losses increased).

Given that a label has been applied, the degree to which the application is successful varies with:

- The severity of the reaction — the more severe, the more successful.
- The publicity attached to the reaction — the greater the publicity, the more successful.
- The degree of group support for alternative definitions — the greater the degree of agreement or consensus on the definition, the more successful.

Having identified the factors influencing the successful application of a deviant label, the next step involves applying them to a concrete case or example. For this purpose, we shall select Goffman's Desperate (1957, 1). Desperate is a young woman with a seriously disfigured face. She has no nose. Sociologists would describe her as an ascribed deviant. An ascribed deviant is a person whose body or behaviour is defined as deviant even though he/she is not responsible in any way for the condition and/or the behaviour.[11] Examples of ascribed deviants include dwarfs, giants, the very ugly and the physically handicapped. Like the Elephant Man, Desperate is an ascribed deviant.

From an interactionist-labelling perspective, Desperate is an ideal candidate for successful labelling for a number of reasons. She obviously does not conform with bodily norms (highly visible rule breaking). Although she is able to perform certain occupational and other social roles, she is denied the opportunity to do so and is avoided by normals (severe reaction). Finally, most normals agree on the social definition of Desperate as a deviant (few alternative definitions are available to her).

Interactionist-functional Perspective: Erikson

Kai Erikson's interactionist-functionalist theory of deviance differs from the interactionist-labelling perspective in three important respects. First, unlike Becker, he offers a conception of deviance that is both subjective *and* functional.[12] Thus, deviance is not only a stigmatizing label that, "is conferred upon behaviour by audiences which directly or indirectly witness them," but it is also a label that, when applied, helps bring group members together by reminding them of the dangers posed to the group by deviants in their midst. In short, a certain amount of deviance "may be an important condition for preserving stability," the stability of society (Erikson 1962).

Second, Becker's perspective tends to direct interest to the process of imputing or conferring deviant labels on behaviour in a variety of small scale settings. Erikson's theory, on the other hand, may be applied to small-scale settings such as night clubs, health spas and wrestling arenas; to society as a whole; and to the relationship or linkages between small-scale settings and the larger contexts of which they are part. Thus, applied to "becoming a marijuana user," Erikson's theory would invite an examination of the linkages among dope smoking by jazz musicians, the meaning of this activity to them, the occupation of jazz music, the structure of the music industry and the place occupied by jazz music in society as a whole.

Third, Erikson's theory invites historical scholarship. Becker's perspective is ahistorical. It is perhaps more accurate to say that time does enter into both formulations but whereas Becker's accounts deal with processes that are counted in days, Erikson deals with changes occurring over a period of years. The difference being referred to here is the difference in time it takes for an individual to become a marijuana user compared with the 30 years it took for the development, emergence, maintenance and termination of the deviance epidemics or crime wave studied by Erikson.

The latter topic is the subject of Erikson's (1966) book *Wayward Puritans*. This book provides a good example of research guided by an interactional-functionalist theory. The major problem of interest to Erikson is the relation between religious deviance and social control in Massachusetts during the 17th century. The major findings of his study are first, that deviance is, in part, a consequence of social control. Second, the kind of behaviour that is defined as deviant and the kinds of persons who are regarded as deviant depend upon the major values of a community. Communities dominated by religious values tend to produce religious deviants, those emphasizing political values, political deviants and so on. As the major values of a community change, so do its definitions of deviance. Third, a certain amount of deviance helps maintain the values that deviance threatens.[13]

Having described the essentials of Erikson's perspective and its relation to Becker's, we may now examine the various ways in which Lemert's societal interactionist perspective is similar to and different from the interactionist perspectives of Erikson and Becker.

The inclusion of "societal" in the name given to the theory espoused by Lemert indicates that it is not limited in its application to the study of deviance and social control occurring in small-scale or micro-social contexts. Like Erikson but unlike Becker, Lemert analyses *societal* reactions to deviance. This constitutes one major difference between Lemert and Becker.

The major reason for this difference is that Becker's perspective is derived from Mead's symbolic interaction theory, while Lemert's theory is derived partly from Mead's emphasis on the emergence and significance of self-identity and partly from Cooley's focus upon the influence on social interaction of groups and institutions in society. According to Lemert (1967), "Cooley's conception of social interaction is superior to Mead's for the kind of macro-sociological work" that sociologists of deviance should also do. Where Lemert derives his macro or societal orientation from Cooley, Erikson derives his from Durkheim.

Another major difference between Lemert and Becker is this. Becker's perspective tends to limit attention to the consequences for deviance of the deviant label. In Lemert's theory, the societal reaction includes the imposition of a label, but it also includes a number of other consequences. The closing of legitimate opportunities for earning a living is one obvious but not unimportant consequence of being labelled a criminal.

Third, as Plummer (1979) points out, Becker's perspective tends to confine research attention to the relation between deviance and informal agents of social control. Lemert's theory is not restricted in this way. It can and has been applied to an examination of the interrelation between crime or criminal deviance and formal agents of social control.

Finally, in place of the one-way analysis of interaction suggested by Becker's perspective, Lemert's theory invites a "full" or two way analysis of interaction. In this specific connection, Lemert makes the following observation: "By adopting the perspective of the social underdog (the member of such devalued groups as winos, bums, pimps, prostitutes, dwarfs, etc.) . . . social control is described unilaterally and social interaction takes on an asymmetrical quality that precludes appreciation of its mutuality. Full interactional analysis must show how the individual and aggregate responses of deviants through resistance, deflection, mitigation and negotiation become influences that shape the societal reaction" (1982, 253).

If Lemert's perspective holds water, then research ought to show that the legal processing of juveniles should be associated with an increased commitment to delinquency. In other words, the operation of the official (legal) social control system will inculcate or instil a delinquent identity in juveniles, an identity that increases the chances of becoming a career delinquent. This is evidently what happened to the members of the delinquent gang known as the Roughnecks.

The Saints and the Roughnecks: Chambliss

For two years, William Chambliss observed two groups of high-school students. One he called the Saints, and the other he called Roughnecks. Over the two-year period, Chambliss made these two observations. First, the rate of delinquency in both groups was roughly equal. Second, whereas not one Saint was arrested for the various delinquent and criminal activities (truancy, dangerous driving, vandalism, petty theft) they engaged in, the Roughnecks "were constantly in trouble with police and community" (Chambliss 1973).

Some years after they had graduated from high school, Chambliss returned to try to find out what had happened to members of both groups. This led to his third finding. Members of each group had followed the careers predicted for them by the police and the community. Most of the Saints were recruited to colleges and universities. Most of the Roughnecks went to prison.

How did this come about? Why were the Saints and Roughnecks morally/legally differentiated from each other when their rate of delinquency was similar?

The major reason for this differentiation is differences in the reactions of community and police to the delinquencies of members of the two groups. The delinquencies of the Saints were interpreted by the police as "high spirits," as forms of behaviour they would grow out of as they progressed towards becoming doctors, lawyers, teachers and accountants. Roughneck delinquencies were interpreted by the police in quite another way.

The invitational edge of Lemert's interactionist account stops short of inviting us to inquire into the reasons behind differences in police power to define. In the Chambliss study, social class differences explain differential police definitions and reactions. Roughneck members came from lower-class homes. The Saint's members were the children of upper middle-class parents. The socio-economic status of the family was used by the police as a vehicle or medium for interpreting and reacting differently to similar behaviour. The police were also aware of the fact that influential and knowledgeable middle-class parents are much more likely to effectively challenge legal definitions and police reactions than are uneducated, powerless lower-class parents. Ultimately, then, control over legal institutions by the middle class explains why the police react to middle- and lower-class delinquents in different ways.

Clearly, the police in Chambliss' study define similar Saint and Roughneck behaviour in different ways. Lemert's interactionist account does direct attention to these. However, the ability of police to define behaviour as criminally deviant was also influenced by differences in the social power possessed by members of different social classes.[14] Lemert's account tends to divert attention away from this possibility. His oversight suggests to Melossi (1985) the next major step in the systematic development of an interactionist account of deviance: integrate "definitions of deviance" with the "power to define."

Melossi's Grounded Labelling Theory

Melossi defines grounded labelling theory as "a theory of the social discourse about deviance and crime grounded within the social discourse about the economy and the polity" (1985, 204). He goes on to say that this theory "must have its roots in the principle that social action cannot be made intelligible if it is not set within the specific orientation of the actor, an orientation . . . expressed linguistically in a 'vocabulary of motives' " (1985, 204).[15] This set of motives is "situated in a socio-historical context and represents the mediation . . . between society, or a social group and the individual self" (1958, 205).

The starting point for the development of grounded labelling theory is the link or relation between (a) the "micro-sociological" (interpersonal) mechanisms identified in the Becker (1962) and Rubington and Weinberg (1981) accounts, mechanisms that help define situations, behaviour and people and (b) "macro-sociological" (the economy, social classes, the state) influences upon the power to define.

Mead's symbolic interaction contributed a great deal to the identification of social processes involving micro-sociological mechanisms (interaction, self, etc.). His contribution to the identification of societal factors that influence the power to define in social situations was not great (Lemert 1974; Taylor, Walton, Young 1975). It was C. Wright Mills who helped overcome this deficit by adding macro-sociological elements to Mead's micro-sociological discourse on the relation between language and social control.

What Mills added was the concept of "vocabularies of motives" and the idea of a number of audiences who collectively engage in various actions and reactions to social phenomena such as crime and deviance, and who create "vocabularies of motives" in the process. These are used to maintain and/or extend their power to define.

By far the most important influence upon the actions and reactions of state social-control agents such as legislators, policemen, judges, social workers and prison officers is the state of the economy. Changes in the state of the economy can increase or decrease their hegemony over and legitimate access to a variety of defiant, deviant and dependent populations. By constructing a "vocabulary of motives" for these populations (and their own professional efforts), the state's social control agents control them directly and indirectly. Thus, criminals may be jailed and, by "capturing" audiences (citizens generally, John Howard Society, etc.), their power to jail is accepted without question.

In Melossi's grounded labelling theory, then, the day-to-day work of social control agents in a variety of small-scale social settings is theoretically linked with the state of the economy and the vocabulary of motives. Definitions and the power to define are thus related to each other. This contribution is a useful extension of the interactionist perspective. Less easily subsumed under this perspective is the strategic significance accorded motivation in Melossi's grounded version.

Interactionists have consistently maintained that they are interested in meanings and not motives. Melossi, however, believes that the reactions of social control agents cannot be adequately understood if the "motivational constructs" used by them are neglected. On the other hand, if motivation is brought back into the theoretical picture, then it may be possible to integrate interactionist accounts with the Marxist concept of ideology (1985, 200). This linkage defines grounded labelling theory. This theory is grounded in economy and ideology.

In formulating his grounded labelling theory, Melossi acknowledges the influence of Sutherland's (1939) "differential association theory." Two specific contributions are identified. First, not all interactions are equally important in terms of their emotional value. Second, Sutherland's concept of "differential social organization" suggested the idea of a number of significant audiences. Differential association theory, then, does play a part in the development of interactionist theory. But is it, itself, an interactionist account?[16]

Differential Association Theory

As originally formulated by Sutherland (1939) and later revised by Sutherland and Cressey (1966), differential association theory is an interactionist account of both conformity and deviation. However, because of its inclusion of motives, its emphasis on the original or random causes of deviance and its acceptance of the traditional notion that social control is caused by deviance instead of vice versa, differential association theory differs from the interactionist accounts of Becker and Lemert. At the same time, the differential association and labelling accounts are similar to each other in the centrality given by each to "symbolic interaction" (Mead 1934) and the way in which individuals define situations.

Also central to both accounts is their opposition to a conception of deviation as an expression of individual biological (e.g., body-types) or psychological (e.g., psychopath) pathology. Instead, Sutherland and Cressey (1966) define both conformity and deviation as forms of learned behaviour. Both are outcomes of ordinary, everyday, normal processes of learning that occur when individuals interact with each other.

The societal context for learning in complex, industrialized, capitalist societies such as the United States and Canada is characterized by "differential social organization" (1960, chapter 5). This means that Canadians and Americans grow up and live in communities composed of groups holding conflicting values, norms, and attitudes towards obeying and disobeying the law. Because individuals are usually members of different groups holding conflicting values, they are routinely subjected to a variety of cross-pressures regarding conformity and deviance in general and law-abiding and law-violating behaviour in particular.

According to Sutherland and Cressey, differential association theory represents an attempt to explain both conformity and deviation. More specifically it "purports to explain the criminal and non-criminal behaviour of individual persons" who are members of a number of groups supporting conflicting definitions of law-abiding and law-violating behaviour. Their theory is also a process theory, a theory of "the processes by which persons become criminals" and conformists (1966, 80).

The major source of the differentiation between conformists and criminals are their respective patterns of association. In any community, three major kinds of groups co-exist. The first holds definitions favourable to law violations, (e.g., street gangs); the second holds definitions favourable to law-abiding behaviour (e.g., boy scouts), and the third supports definitions that are neutral with respect to both law-abiding and law-violative behaviour (e.g., hobby clubs). Individuals whose associations with members of the first group exceed the number of associations with the second and third groups, are most likely to become criminals. In the words of Sutherland and Cressey: "A person becomes delinquent because of an excess of definitions favourable to violation of the law over definitions unfavourable to law violation" (1960, 78).

As defined by Sutherland and Cressey, definitions refer to the *content* of what is learned via differential association. Specifically, definitions refer to techniques of committing crime, opportunities for putting these techniques to profitable use as well as motives for engaging in criminal conduct and justifications for law-violative behaviour. Insofar as different, co-existing groups hold different definitions, they teach members a different content.

These groups can be differentiated according to the priority, intensity, frequency and duration of their associations. Priority refers to group associations experienced earliest in life. Thus family and adolescent peer groups have priority over occupational groups. Intensity refers to both the prestige of the group holding either conformist or criminal definitions and the strength of the emotions that characterize group associations. Frequency refers to the number of associations and duration to how long these were maintained.

With these differences in mind, we may now conclude that the individual who is most likely to become a criminal is one whose family and long-time (boyhood), close neighbourhood friends hold definitions favourable to the violation of laws.

Interactionist Theory: Critical Evaluation

The outstanding contribution of the interactionist theoretical perspective is the "anomalous inversion" of the deviance-social control relation. Strain theorists saw social control being caused by deviance. Interactionists viewed social control as a major cause of deviance. Control theorists associated social control with a decrease in deviance. Interactionists associated the control process with career deviance. In reversing the traditional view of the deviance-control relation, interactionists opened the way for a sustained examination of a neglected partner in the production of crime and deviance, those who make and enforce rules.

The interactionist theoretical perspective requires an observational methodology known as ethnography. Ethnographic accounts of deviant politicians, plumbers, prostitutes and so on have provided the sociological community with a wealth of interesting and important information about deviant conduct and about how such conduct is a product of both freedom and constraint.

Next, interactionists have provided recent generations of graduate students with an outstanding and largely successful example of how the development of sociological theory can be furthered by challenging the ideas of the sociologically established. In Canada, such well respected students of deviance as Spector (1977) and West (1979) became part of this challenge.

Among the major weaknesses of interactionism is, first and foremost, that it develops only half of that which is needed for an adequate theory of crime and deviance. As Gibbs (1972), among others, has pointed out, in addition to the interactionist account of reactions of deviance, we need an account of why, in the first place, people regularly behave in ways that elicit social control reactions.[17]

Another weakness of this perspective is its failure to relate the wider economic and political system to social control actions and reactions in small-scale social settings. Melossi's reformulation is a step in this direction.

Finally, interactionists bequeath a contradictory intellectual legacy to future generations of students when they insist on an approach that simultaneously requires that serious notice be taken of the deviants' definitions, meanings, and so on *and* also involves the imposition of the observer's own definitions on them. Thus, the interactionist sociologist applies the concept of "role deviance" to deviants-in-interaction who do not use the concept of role in describing how they get through their conformist-deviant day (Cicourel 1973). Again, deviants may refer to each other as "deviants," or they may use some other term. Rarely do they use the term "outsider." Yet, this term has been imposed on all of them by Becker.[18]

Turning now to the interactionist-differential association perspective, we discover its most evident strength to be present in Sutherland's early contribution (1939) to the *sociological* study of deviance. Group memberships and associations and not individual biological or psychological factors were responsible for the learning of conformist and criminally deviant behaviour.

Equally valuable was the formulation of a perspective designed to explain both conformity and deviance. This effort is as worthy as it is rare. Also of some importance is the fact that the differential association perspective is based on valid and useful cultural-conflict assumptions regarding the nature of contemporary, capitalist societies such as Canada and the United States.

Positivist sociologists such as Hirschi (1969) and Jensen (1973) may well agree that the differential association perspective possesses all these strengths, but they are more than offset by what they regard as a major flaw. Their research does not support hypotheses derived from the perspective. Other research, also conducted by a positivist sociologist, does, however, support such predictions (Matsudea 1981).

The differential association perspective has also been criticized for its neglect of a very important source of definitions, the mass media (Glaser 1956). Sutherland and Cressey focus on associations and communication in various community groups. However, it is also possible for individuals who identify with criminals portrayed in the mass media to engage in law violative behaviour independently of definitions provided by intimate local groups.

Finally, theorists such as Vold have criticized the differential association thesis because it diverted attention away from a problem of great significance for sociologists interested in the study of deviance. This problem has to do with why, in the first place, some normal learned behaviours are defined as crimes (e.g., many working-class activities related to street gambling) while others (e.g., various forms of fraudulent business practices) are not (Vold 1979, 246).

CLASS CONFLICT PERSPECTIVE: THE INFLUENCE OF KARL MARX

According to his friend and colleague, Friedrich Engels, Karl Marx was above all a fighter, a revolutionist.[19] He was also a great preacher and scholar. For Marx, these roles were inseparable. As a warrior-scholar-preacher, his achievements are great. Not included among these achievements is a systematic theory of crime and deviance. In view of this generally accepted conclusion, it may be surprising to discover a number of contemporary sociologists whose sole claim to immortality is a Marxist-conflict theory of these very phenomena. Our surprise decreases, however, when we learn that their theories were influenced not by Marx's sparse and scattered references to crime, but by his general class conflict theory of social change.[20] Specifically, Marx's general theory helps them understand the relation between the economy, class conflict and three problems of major interest to sociologists of deviance. These are the causes of crime and deviance, the origins of and function of laws.

Marx's General Theory

One important goal of Marx's general sociological theory is to provide a scholarly account of and to help bring into being, the economic and political conditions necessary for individuals to rediscover and actualize their essential selves. Capitalism, with its major class division and antagonistic class relations, its inequality, its exploitation of both human labour and nature in the interests of capital accumulation, dehumanizes, alienates and "denatures" human beings. Socialism, characterized by the abolition of private property, of the inequality based upon its differential possession and by the replacement of a highly developed division of labour with a system in which each individual performs a variety of occupational and other social roles, will return to individuals the feeling of being free, of joy in labour, of being integrated with nature and with their fellows (Marx 1963). Socialism would actualize Marx's image of man. Capitalism negated this image. Marx's general theory is an attempt to replace the latter social formation by the former one by showing how history made such a transformation inevitable.

The starting point of Marx's general materialist-conflict theory is the premise that "man must be in a position to live (obtain food, clothing, shelter) in order to be able to make history" (1939, 7). This premise is the basis for Marx's *materialist* account of class formation, class conflict and revolutionary change under a historically specific set of circumstances. A materialist account is one that explains human nature, the origins and functions of ideologies, class formations and class conflict by pointing to the economy, to real people at work, earning a living under historically specific economic arrangements.[21]

Marx's general conflict theory is an historical materialist one.[22] This theory may be stated as follows: scarcity motivates human labour. For much of man's early history, human labour did not produce goals and services beyond the essential requirements of consumption. An improvement in human skills, knowledge, materials and social organization helped human labour produce a surplus beyond the needs of immediate consumption. In pre-capitalist or "tributary societies," rulers (the state) used force or its threat to take the surplus away from those who helped produce it. With the political fragmentation of European societies and the rise of a mercantile class, an autonomous economic realm emerged, alongside the state. State laws guaranteeing the right to private property helped merchants appropriate the surplus legally. They return some of it in the form of taxes to the state. Gradually, mercantilism was replaced by capitalism.

Capitalists were those who owned the instruments of production. They now legally appropriated most of the surplus and used much of it to achieve even greater surpluses in the future (capital accumulation). The state benefited from this by obtaining increased revenues. In return, it co-ordinated capitalist activities and interests and created and enforced laws (e.g., law of contract) supportive of capitalism. What the workers and capitalists thought about their respective situations in life and their relation to each other was determined by where each group stood in relation to the means of production. In addition, capitalists rely on the state and on their control over both communications and the instruments of production to conceal from the proletariat (those who do not own the instruments of production) the real material reasons for their situation in life, their alienated and oppressed situation. Ideological forms of consciousness (false consciousness) are disseminated by capitalists. Capitalist ideologies justify capitalism to capitalists and workers alike.

Ownership and non-ownership of the instruments of production divides society into two major social groupings, capitalists and workers. As a result of contradictions endemic to capitalism, capitalists become their own grave-diggers.[23] For example, by massing workers in factories, they facilitated worker communication and consciousness of class. With the development of class consciousness, conflicts between workers and individual capitalists were transformed into class conflicts between workers and capitalists generally.

Capitalists, Marx predicts, would not voluntarily relinquish control of an economic system that generated massive inequality in wealth and standard of living. They would be willing to use force to prevent social change. For their part, the workers would come to see revolutionary violence as being the only way of creating a radically transformed, more egalitarian socialist society. The result would be a revolution. The workers would win. In winning, they would also liberate the capitalists.

CONFLICT THEORY: CONTEMPORARY FORMULATIONS

Causes of Crime/Deviance: Taylor, Walton and Young, Spitzer

In their first and most influential book, *The New Criminolgy*, 1973, Taylor, Walton and Young see crime as, "a product of inequitable economic relationships in a context of general poverty" (p., 218).

Inequality, in short, is a major cause of crime. As capitalist exploitation is a major cause of inequality, capitalism is the major cause of crime in capitalist societies (1973, 219). Capitalism should be labelled criminally deviant, not only because it causes crime but principally because of what it does to people. It oppresses, exploits, degrades and enslaves their minds and bodies. Socialism is the key to a "liberating consciousness" among individuals.

The New Criminology, promises a "full blown Marxist" and a "fully social theory" of crime and deviance. It delivers neither. A rather general statement of things to be taken into account in formulating an explanation of crime and deviance is not a theory, much less a full blown, fully social Marxist one. On the other hand, their critical analysis of existing non-Marxist theories is very good.

In their second book, *Critical Criminology,* 1975, Taylor, Walton and Young focus more explicitly on the process of rule making and rule breaking. They go on to state that these "processes are fully social in nature (and) . . . are paramountly conditioned by the facts of material reality . . . the political economy is the primary determinant of the social framework . . . the process involved in crime-creations are bound up, in the final analysis, with the material basis of contemporary capitalism and its structures of law" (1975, 20).

Unique to their Marxist position is the belief that crime is not normal, is not a fact of life in all societies. As the principal cause of crime is inequality, removing inequality will abolish crime. A socialist social formation will be crime free because it is egalitarian. It will also be crime free for another reason: the state will not have the power to define "radical diversity" as deviant.[24]

This 1975 version is presented at almost the same level of generality as the original Marxist version from which it was derived. Believing perhaps that greater progress would attend efforts to lower the level of generality, scholars such as Balbus (1973), Bierne (1979), Greenberg (1977; 1980) and Spitzer (1975) have formulated equally materialistic but less general Marxist theories of the causes of crime.

According to Spitzer, "Marxian conflict theory must illustrate the relationship between specific contradictions, the problems of capitalist development and the production of a deviant class" (1975, 639). To illustrate the interrelations among these three elements, Spitzer uses the following example: capitalist development depends, in part, on well-educated, skilled, disciplined workers and on the inculcation among them of capitalistic, bourgeois values. Educational institutions help meet these requirements. At the same time, universities may expose students to the real exploitative nature of capitalism. The combination of learning to think critically and of being critical of capitalism may produce students who are regarded as troublemakers. They are labelled "radicals" or members of a deviant class, i.e, "social dynamite."

Somewhat more generally, Spitzer goes on to theorize about the relation between capitalism, contradictions and the production of deviants. In order to prosper, capitalism needs to constantly increase its level of productivity. One way of doing this is to replace people with machines. One consequence of this is to increase the number of the unemployed, the relative surplus population. There are two kinds of surplus population, floating and stagnant. The former move into and out of employment with increases and decreases in productivity. Floaters remain attached to the economy, albeit intermittently, and are, to this extent, controlled by it. They have a stake in its performance.

In time, as more machines replace persons, floaters come to represent a smaller proportion of the total surplus population. The relative size of the stagnant element increases. Those who make up the stagnant surplus population are almost permanently unemployed. Not being attached to the economy, they are not disciplined by it. The "invisible hand" of the market is now replaced by the "visible fist" of the state. The state intervenes to ensure that the process of capital accumulation is not hindered by these potential troublemakers. State intervention produces criminals, dependents and deviants.

Spitzer's structural account suggests that the state plays handmaiden to the economy. The state, in other words, works on behalf of those who control the instruments of production, the capitalists. Marx did say this. However, Marx also described a specific historical situation in which the state in a capitalistic society played a relatively independent role with respect to the economy. Miliband develops the first or instrumental conception, Hall et al. and Poulantzas the second, or structural conception.

The Captured State: Instrumental Conceptions — Miliband

Although he did not offer a systematic study of the state, Marx did provide more than a single conception of it.[25] One of the most influential of these was his instrumental conception. This conception of the state is most forcefully expressed in the *Communist Manifesto*. Here, he states that "the executive of the modern state is but a committee for managing the common affairs of the whole bourgeoisie." Later, in the same work, he refers to political power as "merely the organized power of one class for oppressing another" (1959, 74). This instrumental conception is nourished and elaborated upon by political scientist Ralph Miliband (1969).

Miliband's starting point is his opposition to a bourgeoise or liberal "pluralist model" of the state. In this model, the state is conceived of as a neutral referee mediating the competition between a number of interest groups. No single group exerts a predominant influence on the state, because the state itself ensures that power is diffused across various interest groups or power blocs and not concentrated in any one (1969, 2–3).

In contrast to this pluralist thesis, Miliband maintains that there is a class grouping in which most power is concentrated and that the state actively promotes the interests of this group.

For Miliband, the state consists of the following institutions: "the government, the administration, the military, the police, the judicial branch, the subcentral government and parliamentary assemblies" (1969, 54).[26] The interrelations among these institutions form "the state system." The state or state system is subordinate to the ruling class.

The ruling class is "a fact of life in advanced capitalist societies." The "fact" Miliband is referring to is this: "the vast majority of men and women (are) governed, represented, administered, judged and commanded in war by people drawn from other, economically and socially superior and relatively distant classes" (1969, 67). Although few in number, the ruling class owns most of the property, wealth and income in the society. Capitalistic societies characterized by a ruling class are also characterized by vast economic, political and social inequality.

On the basis of this description, we may define the ruling class as consisting of the dominant few (elites) who successfully govern, represent, administer, judge and command in war, the subordinate many.[27]

Having defined the state and the ruling class, the next step in the development of Miliband's thesis involves the establishment of an empirical or factual basis supporting the hypothesis that the state works *at the behest of* the ruling class. The major line of evidence furnished by Miliband takes the form of pointing to the similar social origins of business and state elites.[28] The individuals who run large businesses and state bureaucracies are the same people. They came from the same privileged backgrounds, went to the same schools, share the same ideologies and have the same material interests.[29] In short, they belong to the same class, the ruling class. Naturally, state elites are going to make sure that the state intervenes in business in ways that promote the interests of business. This remains so, even when the state passes laws (e.g., worker safety legislation) which, on the surface, may appear to be against business interests.

From an instrumental perspective, then, laws, their origin and functioning, represent ways of protecting and furthering the long-term interests of the ruling class. If the state does not actually act *at the behest of* the capitalist ruling class, it "does act autonomously *on its behalf*" (Miliband 1983, 64).[30]

The Relatively Autonomous State: Structural Conceptions

According to Hall et al. (1978), instrumentalists such as Miliband and Panitch (1977) make an important contribution to theorizing about the state by emphasizing "the essential class nature" of the capitalist state. At the same time, an instrumental conception does not provide the basis for an adequate theory of the capitalist state because "it obscures what is specific to the state under capitalism – the basis of its independence" (Hall et al. 1978, 204–205). The capitalist state is, for Hall et al., a relatively autonomous state. Developmental forces and contradictions within capitalism make an autonomous state performing certain organizing functions necessary for the maintenance of the capitalist mode of production as a whole, a mode of production that favours the dominant class and especially the ruling fraction within that class. If the state can also generate the necessary consensus among members of the subordinate class, then the state has generalized or universalized class rule.

Generalized class rule means that the dominant class rules through a class fraction that represents it politically, i.e., in both the government and in state agencies. It also means that the state ultimately serves not just the economic needs of the productive system or the specific class interests of just one fraction within the ruling class. Rather, it serves the interests of capitalism by regulating competition among various fractions within the dominant class (industrial, financial, agricultural, commercial, etc.) and also by helping reproduce the social capital — workers and consumers — of capitalism.

A capitalist economy does not have the political resources to solve the problem of conflicts among various capitalist fractions (intra-class conflict), or to generate consensus among subordinate populations that will lead them to accept existing degrees and patterns of inequality as legitimate. Herein lies the basis of the independence of polities from economies, of the state's independence from a dominant class whose power base is the ownership and/or control of the means of production.

As a relatively autonomous organizer, the state organizes things economically, ideologically, legally, and politically. This means that the state helps create and maintain markets, and investment climates and opportunities; the state makes and enforces such laws as the law of contract, laws that form a structure or framework for economic exchanges; it uses schools and the mass media to instil ideas favourable to capitalism; and, most importantly, the state organizes through politics, that is, through the use of political parties and democratically elected political representatives to maintain order in a society characterized by class conflict.

In this specific connection, Hall et al. make the following observation: "This . . . organization of hegemonic domination at the level of politics and the law is, indeed, what, above all, is specific in the functions of the capitalist state. Through the political and juridical sides of its activity, the state secures a certain kind of political order, enforces a certain type of legal order, maintains a certain kind of social order, in the service of capital" (1978, 206).

Poulantzas' Structural Thesis

As a Marxist, Poulantzas shares with Hall et al. and Miliband an opposition to the "pluralist-state-as-neutral-referee" thesis of liberal democrats. However, where Miliband seems to continue "a long Marxist tradition," in which the state is regarded as "only a simple tool or instrument manipulated at will by the ruling class" (Poulantzas 1969, 74), Poulantzas explicitly rejects this tradition.[31] Instead, he wishes to start a new Marxist tradition, one that embraces the thesis of the "relative autonomy of the state."[32] This thesis is a "structural" one. This means that the relation between the capitalist economy and the capitalist state is established, not by the similar motivations of economic and state elites, as Miliband suggests, but by the objective relational position of the state within the structure of capitalism.

The quintessential structural feature of capitalism is the *political* dominance of those (ruling class) who own/control the instruments of production over other social classes that do not. Within the politically dominant power bloc, power is unequally distributed across various capitalist fractions. The "hegemonic fraction" is the one with the greatest amount of political power. In different historical periods and more transient "conjunctures," the composition of the hegemonic fraction changes. Sometimes it consists of "financial capital," at other times, "monopoly capital" and so on. These societal class relations of dominance and subordination are condensed, reproduced and embodied in the state.

According to Poulantzas, "the state is composed of several apparatuses: broadly, the repressive apparatus and ideological apparatus, the principal role of the former being repression, that of the latter being the elaboration and incubation of ideology. The ideological apparatuses include the churches, the educational system, the bourgeois and petit-bourgeoise parties, the press, radio, television, publishing, etc. These apparatuses belong to the state system because of their objective function of elaborating and inculcating ideology irrespective of their formal juridical status as nationalized (public) or private" (1973, 47).

The relation between the state and the dominant capitalist class is characterized by relative autonomy or independence because state activity is governed by its own internal logic and unity.[33] This remains true precisely because relative autonomy is necessary, is required, if the state is to carry out its objective function of maintaining the dominant political position of the capitalist class and especially of the hegemonic fraction within it. In this connection, Poulantzas makes the following statement: "When Marx designated Bonapartism as . . . characteristic of all forms of the capitalist state, he showed that this state can only truly serve the interests of the ruling class insofar as it is relatively autonomous from the diverse fractions of this class, precisely in order to organize the hegemony of the whole of this class" (1969, 74).

In attempting to understand the complex nature of the relation between the state and the ruling capitalist class, it is important to remember that although Miliband and Poulantzas agree on the role of the state in furthering the long-run interests of this class, Miliband emphasizes the direct participation of the members of this class in running the state, while Poulantzas focusses on the *objective relation* between the state and the dominant class.[34] In carrying out its objective functions of maintaining social order and helping reproduce the conditions of economic production, the state ensures the domination of one class over the others. Class differences in power, in turn, are reflected in the state.

From Poulantzas' structural theoretical perspective, then, the origin and functions of laws are outcomes of class struggles occurring within the state apparatus. Overall, the content and bias of law do not adversely affect the long-run interests of the hegemonic fraction of the capitalist ruling class. The degree to which law primarily serves the interests of other fractions within the ruling class or other social classes depends on their relative political power within state apparatuses and the coincidental association between class interests and a capitalist state carrying out its objective functions.[35]

Turk's Group Conflict Theory

Austin Turk's theory attempts to explain the causes of criminalization. Criminalization refers to a process whereby the state changes the status of individuals from "person" to "criminal" in an attempt to regulate their conduct. Members of some social groupings are more often criminalized than others. Turk's (1969) group conflict theory tells us why this happens.

Important clues concerning the answer to this question are, for Turk, *not* furnished by Karl Marx. Turk is not a Marxist conflict theorist, even though conflict is central to his theory. Instead, Max Weber, the "ghost of Marx" and conflict theorist Ralph Dahrendorf, provided important building blocks for Turk. From Weber, Turk learned that there are three and not just one (social class) basis of power and inequality in society. In addition to the ownership of property *and* the possession of valued marketable skills, group members were ranked in terms of their status in the community and their possession of political power. Class, status and party represent, then, three significant bases of group formation and conflict. Dahrendorf, for his part, impressed Turk with the idea that the differential possession of authority, regardless of its source, was a more socially significant source of conflict than the possession or non-possession of property (Dahrendorf 1957, 165–173).

Society, for Turk, consists of a number of social groups possessing different attributes (e.g., skin colour) and/or who behave in different ways. These groups are not only differentiated from each other, they also stand in an hierarchic relation to each other. That is to say, some groups have more authority than others. A regular and recurring feature of social life is the exercise of authority by superordinates and varying mixtures of obedience and resistance to this exercise by subordinates.

Social groups vary in the rate at which their members are labelled criminal by agents of the criminal justice system. The highest rates of criminality characterize members of certain age, sex, income and racial/ethnic groupings. Why does this happen?

According to Turk, the fact that some groups are more criminalized than others means that they are more likely to achieve the social and legal status of criminal. A status of this kind is achieved when an individual is convicted of a criminal offence in a court of law. Differences in criminalization refer to differences in the rate at which members of different social groupings (poor blacks, the young, middle-class persons, women) are arrested and/or convicted of criminal offences. Criminalization occurs during the process of social conflict. The source of conflict is the resistance to authority by those over whom it is exercised. Groups vary in the amount or kind of resistance they express. For Turk, conflict is more likely to occur and to be more serious when it does occur, among groups who meet the following conditions.

First of all, conflict is more likely to occur and to be more serious among groups whose deviant attributes and/or behaviour are defined as illegal. For example, the possession of an extra Y gene allegedly responsible for violent behaviour may become grounds for detaining or otherwise legally processing men with deviant, XYY genes. Similarly, while gambling by the state (lotteries) or churches (bingo) is legal, gambling on horses or football games or on street corners by working or lower-class individuals is illegal.

Second, conflict is more likely to occur and to be more serious when, for both authorities and subjects, there exists a high congruence between *cultural norms* and *social norms*. Cultural norms are written or spoken statements of values (e.g., free enterprise, human life, monogamy, democracy). Social norms are the rules that are actually enforced by others. The distinction here is between "law in books" and "law as actually enforced." Conflict is most likely where the authorities actively enforce conformity with rules supporting their conceptions of the desirable (i.e., values) *and* the subordinate group places a high value on the attribute and/or act in question (e.g., abortion) and actively enforces compliance with rules supportive of its own value. Conflict, in other words, is more likely where there exists high congruence between cultural and social norms for *both* authorities and subordinate groups.

Third, the members of the subordinate group and the authorities are *unsophisticated*. Sophistication means "knowledge of patterns in behaviour of others that is used to manipulate them" (Turk 1969, 59). Subordinate group members who are unsophisticated will not be able to accurately perceive the consequences of their behaviour and, lacking the requisite basis (knowledge) for relying on more subtle forms of manipulation and persuasion, unsophisticated authorities fall back on overt forms of coercion.

Fourth, because they have the support of the group, subordinate group members who are *organized* are more likely to resist the persuasion or coercion of authorities than are members of unorganized groups.

Given inter-group conflict, authorities are more or less likely to successfully criminalize members of groups with whom they are in conflict, depending upon a number of factors. First of all, the authorities must pass (legislate) laws forbidding or requiring certain kinds of behaviour. Then the law must actually be enforced by citizens who report offences, by police officers who arrest and summon suspects, by juries who help determine guilt and by judges who sentence offenders. Here, the greater the degree to which legal norms are also supported by or congruent with social norms held by citizens, police officers and judges, the more likely citizens are to report violations, police officers to arrest, juries convict and judges to deliver prison terms. However, if those whose behaviour is made illegal are as powerful as or more powerful than the authorities who make it so, then the criminalization process will be far less successful. Thus, corporate executives are, because of their relatively great power, less likely to have their corporate behaviour defined as criminal in the first place, and even if it is, enforcement is quite likely to be very weak. Finally, group members who are properly brought up in their families, schools and churches are less likely to do things that bring them into conflict with authorities. Hence, they are less likely to be criminalized, because criminalization is one way in which authorities attempt to win social conflicts.

Applied to the case of, say, car thieves, Turk's group conflict theory predicts that the highest rates of criminalization will occur in communities in which (a) the police, prosecutors and judges regard the law as safeguarding their groups' moral values and/or economic interests, and car thieves regard the law as a means whereby business people are allowed to rip off people while poor people are not allowed to make a living by ripping off richer people whose cars are insured anyway; (b) the police and other criminal-justice system agents place a high value on honesty (cultural norm), a value that they feel should be strongly supported by society, that is made into a law (legal norm); (c) the authorities in these communities are more wealthy, have greater access to control over the mass media and local politicians than do members of the subordinate groups whose members engage in shoplifting and (d) various informal agents of socialization (parents, teachers, television) in these communities have not done a very good job of inculcating in individuals "norms of deference" to authority. The greater the number of such poorly conditioned individuals there are in a community, the higher will be the criminality rate.

For Turk, then, the criminality rate is simultaneously an indicator of success and of failure. By labelling a group member as a criminal, the authorities have (at least in the short-run) won. Specifically, they have triumphed over "a certain population of the intolerably different." However, the fact that members of this group had the nerve to become norm-resisters in the first place is "a measure of failure in the mechanisms by which individuals are conditioned to accept subordination" (1969, 73).

Conflict Theory: Critical Evaluation

Because of important differences between them, Marxist and group conflict theories will be evaluated separately. What these theories share is an opposition to consensus theories of crime and deviance. The opposition is well founded because social conflicts between classes, racial groups, age groups and so on, are as characteristic a feature of contemporary societies as is consensus on values and interests.

The major strength of Turk's group conflict theory is that it avoids committing itself to "total inter-connectedness" between *one* form of conflict, class conflict, crime, crime control and capitalism. Rather, class conflict is viewed as just one of a number of different kinds of conflict, some more closely related to the economy than others.

Second, by following Weber, Turk is being influenced by a theorist whose work places bureaucracy in the forefront of political analysis of society. Turk's work brings us closer to appreciating the relation between crime, crime control and the increasing bureaucratization of society.

The third major strength of the group conflict theory is that its author successfully conveys the idea that it was arrived at after research into and a careful consideration of alternative theories. Unlike some of his Marxist critics, he did not select his theory solely on the grounds of its ability to realize his vision of man, his version of an alternative socialist society.

Capitalist society, its earlier and contemporary versions, is perhaps more criminogenic than Turk supposes. His ahistorical approach keeps history and its important lessons a secret, secrets that are so well revealed by historian E.P. Thompson (1975). Turk's reluctance to consider more carefully the wider economic sources of crime and crime control unduly restrict his theoretical contribution. If non-Marxist Heilbronner (1985) has been read correctly, the logic of capitalism makes crime a surprise-free outcome.

Turning next to Marxist theory, one of its major strengths is the attention directed to the interrelations among wider social, economic and political influences and crime and crime control. One of the major problems with strain, control and especially interactionist theories is their failure to take these into account.

Another major strength of this theory is the stimulus given to historical studies of crime and crime control. This represents an important corrective to traditional, largely ahistorical approaches to these phenomena. In this connection, the work of the Marxist social historian, E.P. Thompson (1975), has been outstanding.

A further major strength of recent versions of Marxist conflict theory is that they have advanced our understanding of who makes legal rules and why, well beyond the point to which it was taken by interactionist theorists. As a result, the economy and the state have become much more firmly implicated in contemporary research on crime causation and crime control. In this specific connection, a good example is Hall et al., *Policing the Crisis* (1978).

Alongside its strengths, Marxist conflict theory also has a number of weaknesses, albeit not as many perhaps as Downes and Rock (1982), Hirst (1975), Sparks (1980) and Sumner (1976) collectively indicate. One glaring and rather obvious weakness stems from the failure of those who assert that capitalism is criminogenic and socialism is not, to demonstrate this by pointing to research that compares both types of society or the same society after it changed from the one to the other social formation.

Another weakness stems from the fact that in their polemic against "bourgeois sociology" and "bourgeois legalism," some Marxist theorists have formulated visions of future socialist societies that, according to Thompson, "throw away a whole inheritance of struggle about law and within the forms of law, whose continuity can never be fractured without bringing men and women into immediate danger" (1975, 261–267). In addition, their theories can never be falsified because the conditions they specify have not, as yet, been truly met. Thus, any existing socialist society characterized by crime and the power to criminalize diversity is not a "true" socialist society but an inauthentic, bogus one.

Finally, the Marxist conflict theories reviewed here tend to overlook the possibility that "superstructural" items, such as the law, have a life of their own, a life that cannot be reduced to either economy or politics. One of the major contributions of E.P. Thompson was to demonstrate the independence of the rule of law in eighteenth century England. One aspect of the law's independence was its ability to constrain the power of political rulers, the Whig oligarchy.[36]

SUMMARY

A theoretical perspective on deviance is a way of looking at deviance. Four theoretical perspectives were identified. These were strain, control, interactionist and conflict. The idea central to *strain* theory is that the failure to satisfy psychological and material wants or to make satisfactory progress towards realizing important values represents an important motive for deviance. *Control* theorists attempt to explain variations in conformity by emphasizing variations in the effectiveness of social control processes. In both the strain and control perspectives, deviance is believed to cause social control reactions. *Interactionist* theorists reverse this relation. They believe reactions to deviance cause deviance. More specifically, interactionists define deviance in terms of reactions and view reactions to deviance as a major cause of career deviance. *Conflict* theorists view deviance and reactions to it as manifestations of either class conflict or inter-group conflict. The state is central to both class and group-conflict perspectives. Two major class conflict conceptions of the state were identified. One was instrumental, the other structural. In the former, the state was dependent on the dominant economic class and more or less did what this class wanted done. In the structural conception, the state was relatively independent of the dominant class and used its basis of power and authority to regulate the dominant class in the interests of capitalism itself. The idea central to the group-conflict perspective is that criminalization is a manifestation of conflicts between groups including social class but also including other groups (e.g., gender, ethnic, etc.).

SUGGESTED READINGS

Stuart Hall, C. Critcher et al., *Policing the Crisis* (London: Macmillan, 1982), chapter 6, "Explanations and Ideologies of Crime" and chapter 7, "Crime, Law and the State."

A. Liska, *Perspectives on Deviance* (Englewood Cliffs, N.J.: Prentice-Hall, 1981).

E.P. Thompson, *Whigs and Hunters: The Origin of The Black Act* (New York: Pantheon, 1975).

NOTES

1. For example, Erikson (1962) formulates a functional-interactionist perspective, Griesman (1977) an interactionist-conflict one. In this connection, see also T. Hirschi (1969, 3–4).
2. The term "frustrated strivers" is Hirschi's (1971, 3). Gouldner is responsible for the "hollow man" characterization of interactionist deviants (1968). In more recent versions of the "new" criminology, deviants are characterized as being "different." See Taylor, Walton and Young (1975).
3. For a contemporary, Durkheimian functionalist analysis of political witch-hunting, see Bergesen (1984).
4. This functional conception of pornography as being of benefit to women represents a minority view among feminists who have

written on the topic. For a non-functional, anti-censorship, feminist approach to pornography, see Vance, *Pleasure and Danger* 1984.

5. Cohen's theory focusses on working/lower-class male adolescents. Although he is unaware of Cohen's theory, V. Malarek, a *Globe and Mail* reporter, has written an account of his own school experiences in Montreal, confirming much of what Cohen has to say. See Malarek (1983).

6. According to Matza, the commitment to delinquency is "a system of shared misunderstandings, based on miscues, which leads delinquents to believe that all others situated in their company are committed to their misdeeds" (1964, 62).

7. For more detailed discussions, see Hirschi (1971), Greenberg (1977) and Hirschi and Gottfredson (1985).

8. Following Durkheim, not Hobbes, Hirschi seems to equate attachments to others and the internalization of moral norms regulating deviant behaviour (1969, 16–19).

9. In sociology, positivism refers to attempts to describe and explain social phenomena by applying to them the objective, quantitative methods of the physical sciences. The term was first used (I believe) by one of sociology's founding fathers, French sociologist Auguste Comte. Durkheim, too, is a positivist. The best known contemporary positivists in the sociology of deviance include Travis Hirschi in the United States and John Hagan in Canada. For a good discussion of positivism, see Percy Cohen (1980).

10. It is important to note that societal reactions may restrict some opportunities while opening up others, and/or create villains who become heroes to members of their own groups. A good example of such an outcome is provided by Reginald Hill, a native Indian who regards himself as "not your average savage." Because Mr. Hill insisted on doing what the state and churches regularly do, run lotteries and bingo games without legal penalty, Mr. Hill faces two warrants for his arrest on six charges of running bingo games on the Six Nations Reserve in Ontario. At present, he is on the run from the police, but his own people consider him a hero. One elderly Cayuga Indian appears to speak for many when he observed that "he was filled with such hatred of the Canadian government" that he would "feel 20 years younger" if Reginald Hill "could screw them" (Platiel, 1986).

11. By contrast, achieved deviants are persons who are responsible in some way for their behaviour. A good example of an achieved deviant is the wife of a Cheyenne chief called Tall White Man. According to Jack Gibbs (1972, 6) "this brawny woman (250 lbs.) made an art of assault, using excrement as one of her more effective weapons. She forced one of her co-wives to end her marriage, drove

another co-wife to suicide, disgraced her children, destroyed her mother's tent and continually badgered her husband."

12. Erikson's functionalism derives in part from Mead's *Psychology of Punitive Justice* (1918). His interactionism derives from Mead's *Mind, Self and Society* (1934). By contrast, Becker was influenced only by the latter work.

13. Further support for this functional finding is furnished by W.D. O'Connor's study of Stalin's purge of political deviants during the 1930's. See O'Connor (1972).

14. In general, the more serious the offence, the less influential are non-legal (e.g., class-power) factors. Thus, class-power imputations are quite likely to influence police definitions of vandalism and less likely to influence their definition of homicide. Most delinquent acts are in fact quite minor.

15. A "vocabulary of motives" is an ideology. It describes, explains, justifies or discredits. As ideologies, vocabularies are used as weapons in social struggles. "Troublemaking," "danger" and "parasites" enter into vocabularies used by social-control agents against criminals and deviants. "The profit motive" is a vocabulary of motives used by capitalists "for delimited economic situations and behaviours." Mills (1963, 445).

16. In a number of texts (e.g., Akers 1977), differential association theory is classified under the heading of social learning theory.

17. Some sociologists offer definitions of deviance which refer to both deviant conduct and reactions to deviance. For an example, see Sagarin and Kelly (1982).

18. During the course of fourteen years of research in Canadian and U.S. prisons, I have yet to hear an inmate or guard refer to deviants in their respective groups as 'outsiders.'

19. See F. Engels' eulogy delivered at Marx's funeral (Engels 1963).

20. In this connection, see Taylor, Walton and Young (1973: 209 and 219), Hirst (1975), Taylor, Walton and Young (1975) and Sparks (1980).

21. In this connection, Marx writes, "In direct contrast to German (Hegelian) philosophy which descends from heaven to earth, here we ascend from earth to heaven. That is to say, we do not set out from what men imagine, conceive, nor from men as narrated, thought of, or imagined, conceived, in order to arrive at men in the flesh. We set out from real, active men and on the basis of their real life (labour) process, we demonstrate the development of the ideological reflexes and echoes of this life process" (Marx 1963, 181).

22. For a succinct statement of Marx's own account, see K. Marx, *Preface to a Contribution to a Critique of Political Economy*, K. Marx and F.

Engels, *Selected Works*, Vol. 1 (Moscow: Foreign Languages Publishing House, 1955), 362–364.

23. On page 53 of *The Communist Manifesto* (1959/1872), Marx notes: "But not only has the bourgeoisie forged the weapons that bring death to itself; it has also called into existence the men who are to wield those weapons, the working class."

24. In addition to Taylor, Walton and Young, other contributors to Marxist explanation of crime, deviance and social control in Canada include Hinch (1985), McMullan and Ratner (1982) and Maclean (1986).

25. For example, on page 73 of the *Communist Manifesto* (1959/1872), he says: "The proletariat will (after the revolution) use its political supremacy to . . . centralize all instruments of production in the hands of the state, i.e., of the proletariat organized as the ruling class." Here the state is superordinate. Elsewhere, the conception of an autonomous or independent state is provided. (See Marx 1968).

26. Panitch's definition of the Canadian state builds upon and extends Miliband's definition. Panitch (1977).

27. Among the elites that collectively make up the ruling or dominant class, economic elites appear to constitute a dominant faction. Why? "By virtue of (their) ownership or control (of property and capital), (they) command many of the most important sectors of economic life." (Miliband 1969, 15).

28. Other lines of evidence are that the members of elites which make up the ruling class have participated *directly* in the state system, i.e., they have helped regulate, govern, administer and so on. In addition, there are strong personal and friendly relations or ties between members of the ruling class and those who run state bureaucracies. (Miliband 1969, 48–68 and 119–145).

29. For Canadian evidence pointing to a different conclusion, see Clement (1975) and Resnick (1978). For a radical alternative to both the pluralist and Marxist conceptions of the state, see Harrison's (1983) anarchist conception.

30. This represents a reformulation of Miliband's earlier (1969) "crude view of the state as a mere 'instrument' of the ruling class obediently acting at its dictation." R. Miliband, *Class Power and State Power* (London: Verso Press, 1983), 64.

31. The tradition within which Miliband appears to work was called "vulgar Marxism" by F. Engels in his letter to Joseph Block. Vulgar Marxism suggests that the state, as part of capitalistic society's "superstructure" reflects, in a relatively straightforward way, its real basis, the economy.

32. The theoretical justification of this thesis is derived from Marx (1968).

33. For a good discussion of the nature and logic of capitalism and the state and of the relations between them, see Heilbronner (1985).
34. According to Poulantzas, "The relation between the bourgeois class and the state is an objective relation. This means that if the function of the state . . . and the interests of the dominant class . . . *coincide*, it is by reason of the system itself: the direct participation of members of the ruling class in the state apparatus is not the *cause* but the *effect* . . . of this objective coincidence." (Poulantzas 1969, 73).
35. For an explicit attempt to bridge the instrumental and structural conceptions, see Clement (1983).
36. In this connection, Thompson notes that the political ruling group employed the law "very much as a modern structural Marxist should expect it to do. But this is not the same thing as to say that the rulers had need of law, in order to oppress the ruled, while those who were ruled had need of none. Most men have a strong sense of justice, at least with regard to their own interests. If the law is evidently partial and unjust, then it will conceal nothing, legitimate nothing, contribute nothing to any class' hegemony . . . We reach then, not a simple conclusion (law-class power), but a complex and contradictory one. On the one hand, it is true that the law did mediate existent class relations to the advantage of the rulers. On the other hand, the law mediated these class relations through legal forms, which imposed, again and again, inhibitions upon the actions of the ruler" (1975, 260–261).

CHAPTER *THREE*

CORPORATE CRIME:
CRIME IN THE SUITES

WHAT IS CORPORATE CRIME?

SOCIOLOGISTS OF DEVIANCE have attempted to answer this question
in a number of ways. A review of these indicates that their definitions are influenced by three major considerations. First, should
they use the word "crime" or "deviance" to refer to corporate
misconduct? Second, is corporate crime the same thing as white-
collar crime? Third, is corporate crime a quality of the act or a label
successfully applied to corporate misconduct?

Corporate Crime and Corporate Deviance

Criminal and non-criminal forms of deviance may be differentiated from each other on the basis of the *source* of the rules being
violated, the *agents* who apply sanctions or punishments for rule
violations and the *nature and gravity* of the consequences for rule
violators subjected to these sanctions. The application of these
criteria yields three groupings, crime/criminals, offences/offend-
ers and deviance/deviants. Into which of these three groupings do
corporate rule violators fall?

According to agents of the state, i.e., those responsible for making and enforcing criminal, civil and administrative law, the answer is clear: they fall into the second group.[1] Legally speaking,

even such serious matters as killing, injuring and stealing are "offences" and not crimes when they are committed by corporations (Glassbeek 1984; Law Reform Commission of Canada 1976). If found guilty, corporations are labelled offenders and not criminals. Corporations share the state's legal-technical definition of corporate misconduct. Sociologists tend not to.

According to sociologist Laureen Snider, corporations should be labelled and treated as criminals whenever they engage in conduct that is "socially injurious and people are victimized, directly or indirectly" (1980, 349). Schrager and Short (1977) offer a definition that is quite similar to Snider's. For them, "organizational crimes are illegal acts of omission or commission of an individual or group of individuals in a legitimate formal organization in accordance with the operative goals of the organization which have a serious physical or economic impact on employees, consumers or the general public" (1977, 408).[2]

British sociologist Stephen Box (1983) likes the Schrager and Short definition, but he feels it could be improved in two ways. First, as illegal corporate conduct also harms other, often smaller corporations (e.g., via mergers and price fixing), the list of potential victims should be expanded to include them. Second, what needs to be more strongly emphasized is that "corporate crimes are crimes regardless of the source of law proscribing them, i.e., civil, criminal or administrative law" (1983, 200). Both of these amendments are included in the definition formulated by two American sociologists, Marshall Clinard and Peter Yeager. For them, all forms of corporate conduct punishable by the state are crimes (1980, 17).

The preceding discussion leads to the conclusion that corporate misconduct should be labelled corporate crime where such conduct seriously harms others and also violates criminal, civil and/or administrative law. This definition is useful in two ways. First, it refers to corporate conduct that merits the label "criminal" because it has serious social consequences and is engaged in by corporate actors who know or should know what they are doing. Second, by excluding capitalism itself and also serious social harms not proscribed by law, it stimulates theory and research on these topics. Thus, as we shall see in the theory segment of this chapter, conflict theorists want to know why relatively few socially injurious corporate acts are proscribed by law and, where they are proscribed and processd by law, why by civil or administrative and not criminal law.

Corporate Crime and White-collar Crime

One of the first sociologists to study white-collar crime was Edwin Sutherland. According to him, white-collar crime referred to crime in the upper- or white-collar class composed of respectable business and professional men (1940, 1). In a later publication, Sutherland defined white-collar crime as "crime committed by a person of respectability and high status in the course of his occupation" (1949, 9). In the same book, Sutherland defines white-collar crime as "organized crime" (1949, 217). By organized crime, Sutherland means crimes committed by individuals who work for business corporations.

Taken together, these definitions suggest that there is no major difference between white-collar and corporate crime. Both kinds of crime occur in the context of occupational roles and are committed by individuals who "wear good clothes" at work. Examples of white-collar criminals thus include such "robber barons" as J.P. Morgan and Cornelius Vanderbilt, shoe salesmen, clerks in stores and used-car salesmen. Embezzlement, fraud as well as illegal trade restraint, merger and price-fixing practices are all examples of the same kind of crime, white-collar crime.

In evaluating the usefulness of Sutherland's definition of white-collar/corporate crime, it is important to remember that his primary interest lay in demonstrating that this kind of crime was as serious and as "real" as the crimes (e.g., robbery, burglary) committed by members of lower socio-economic groups. For this reason, he did not really concern himself with the problems of making conceptual distinctions *within* the class of crimes he called "crimes of the respectable." Other sociologists, however, felt that this would be a very useful thing to do.

One major attempt to separate what Sutherland had joined together was undertaken by Clinard and Quinney (1973). They stick with Sutherland's conception of white-collar crime as business crime, but they then divide business crime into two major groupings, *occupational crime* and *corporate crime*. They defined occupational crime as "offences committed by individuals for themselves in the course of their occupations" and "offences by employers against their employees." Corporate crime they defined as "offences committed by corporate officials for their corporation and the offences of the corporation itself" (1973, 188). Thus, sexual harassment of a female secretary by her male department head is an occupational crime. When the same executive attempts to bribe a foreign buyer in order to induce him to purchase his company's airplanes, he is engaging in corporate crime.

The distinction made by Clinard and Quinney is preserved by Lawrence Sherman. According to Sherman, corporate crime is "crime committed by an organization and is collective rule-breaking . . . that helps achieve organizational goals." By contrast, occupational crime is crime committed *in* an organization. Occupational crime, then, "is individual or collective rule-breaking that does not help achieve organizational goals or is harmful to those goals" (Sherman 1982, 64). Price fixing is an example of corporate crime; embezzlement of corporate funds by an employee is an example of occupational crime.

The organizational goals referred to by Sherman are "the currently operative (actual) goals . . . imposed by those who run the organization" (1982), 65). Who are these people? The source cited by Sherman (J.D. Thompson's Organizations in Action, 1967) suggests that they are members of the corporation's *dominant coalition.* Although he acknowledges the strategic significance of this group, Sherman does not actually use them in formulating his definition of corporate crime as crimes by corporations. If this could be done, then, according to sociologists Clinard (1983) and Taft (1966), it would be a major step towards providing a very useful definition of *corporate* crime.

Business corporations are actually run by a relatively small group of executives who constitute or participate in a "dominant coalition."[3] A dominant coalition is composed of those executives who combine in themselves two types of authority. The first is the *authority of position.* The second is the *authority of leadership.* Authority is defined as "a character in a communication." The character referred to here is the willingness of the individual to whom the communication is addressed to obey the order, request, or instruction. Authority of position refers to the character of communications associated with different positions in the organization's hierarchy of positions. Usually, the higher the organizational position, the greater the number of subordinates willing to obey the instruction or request. Unlike authority of position, authority of leadership is associated with the possession of superior *personal* skills, abilities or talents.

The directors of a corporation usually occupy its highest positions of authority. Next in line of authority are the president and vice-presidents. Among the relatively small group of executives, a smaller number of directors and vice-presidents may possess superior, organizationally relevant talents and abilities. This small group-within-a-group forms the corporation's dominant coalition. When members of this group engage in acts punishable by the state and intended to benefit the corporation or help create and maintain an atmosphere conducive to the commission of such acts by subordinates, then we are dealing with corporate crime.

Objective vs Subjective Definitions: the Minamata

Minamata is the name of a small fishing village in Japan. Chisso is the name of the corporation that built a carbide and fertilizer factory in Minamata. This factory used mercury to produce carbide and fertilizer. The waste, contaminated with mercury, a deadly poison, was dumped in Minamata Bay. It was in this bay that local fishermen caught the fish they sold and consumed. In 1956, a young girl who ate the fish was brought in "suffering severe symptoms of brain damage" (Smith and Smith, 1975, 28). She was suffering from mercury poisoning. By the end of 1975, over 100 000 residents of Minamata were afflicted with mercury poisoning to a greater or lesser degree. After members of Chisso's dominant coalition learned of the socially harmful effects of dumping mercury into Minamata Bay, they continued to do so, "covered their actions, intimidated those who had fallen ill and failed to go public with evidence of hazard" (Ermann and Lundman 1982, 13). Does what Chisso did to the residents of Minamata constitute corporate criminality?

According to Ermann and Lundman (1982), the answer is that it all depends on whether the Japanese state called the behaviour criminal and punished those responsible. As this did not happen, the answer is no. In their subjective conception of corporate misconduct, "no action, not even Chisso's dumping of poisonous mercury waste into Minamata Bay, is intrinsically deviant" (1982, 13).[4] Corporate deviance, in other words, is not a quality of the act. It is, rather, "a social creation, the result of social processes and judgements" (1982, 13). The outcome of these processes and judgements is influenced in important ways by the distribution of power among accusers and accused. For Ermann and Lundman the Chisso corporation's actions were not defined as criminal or deviant because the power and resources of a large corporation were greater than the power and resources of its accusers, the residents of Minamata.

In contrast to this subjective definition are objective ones that focus on the quality of the conduct itself. Thus, Clinard and Yeager (1980) define corporate crime as "acts punishable by the state" whether or not such acts are actually discovered and punished by regulatory agencies. Moreover, these two scholars call all such acts crimes, even if the state does not. The criterion they use is the fact that the behaviour in question is proscribed or required by law.

Whether the law is criminal, civil or administrative is irrelevant to their definition of corporate crime.

The definitions of corporate crime offered by Schrager and Short (1977), Snider (1980) and Box (1983) are also objective. However, they differ from the Clinard and Yeager definition in this important respect: whereas for Clinard and Yeager, only the quality of the state's reaction to corporate misconduct was relevant; for Schrager and Short, *the quality of corporate misconduct* itself is also relevant to the definition of corporate crime. More radically inclined sociologists such as Quinney (1980) and Young (1981) also offer objective, quality-of-the-act definitions. However, unlike all of the other definitions included here, theirs is not based upon legal criteria. For them, the defining criterion of corporate crime is the quality of corporate misconduct. Thus, for Young, seriously harmful corporate conduct is criminal whether or not the behaviour is proscribed by law (1981, 327).

When applied to the Minamata incident, all of the objective definitions discussed here would make the Chisso corporation's conduct criminal. For Quinney and Young, it is criminal because of its intrinsically harmful nature. For them, corporate crime is a quality of the act. Schrager and Short, Snider and Box would also define the corporation's conduct as criminal partly because of its seriously harmful consequences and partly because it was prohibited by civil and administrative law. As acts contravening these laws are punishable by the state, the definition offered by Clinard and Yeager also defines Chisso's conduct as criminal.

Nothing that has been stated here should lead one to conclude that objective definitions of corporate crime are true and subjective ones false, or vice versa. Definitions, as indicated in Chapter 1, should be evaluated, not according to their truth or falsity, but according to their usefulness for the problems being investigated and their political implications.[5] Thus, for Snider (1980), Goff and Reasons (1978) and Clinard and Yeager (1980), an objective definition is preferable because they are interested in explaining the amount and distribution of corporate crime. For this purpose, they must rely on official statistics, i.e., "objective data." By contrast, Ermann and Lundman are interested in describing how the process of interaction between corporations and their accusers is associated with the ability of corporations to have such labels as "normal business activity" or "deviance" rather than "crime" attached to their rule violations. In dealing with this problem, a problem in which the label "crime" is regarded as an outcome of interaction, subjective definitions are more useful.

CORPORATE CRIME IN CANADA: HOW MUCH?

The amount of corporate crime known to official agencies and to scholars who have investigated the phenomenon represents only a fraction of the total amount that really exists. The phrase most commonly used to refer to what investigators discover is "only the tip of the iceberg" (Dubin 1981; Snider 1980; Reasons et al. 1981). There are a number of reasons for this state of affairs. Many of these are described by Clinard and Yeager in the following terms: "Government inquiries have shown that corporate violations are exceedingly difficult to discover, to investigate, or to develop successfully as legal cases because of their extreme complexity and intricacy" (1980, 6).

With respect to the first or how much question, then, the most general and valid answer seems to be, much more than most Canadians, governmental agencies, and professional scholars are aware of. A second conclusion is that, compared with the United States, governments in Canada, federal, provincial and municipal, are not willing to devote resources to collecting systematic information on corporate crime. This means we in Canada have information on only a small fraction of various "tips" of the total corporate crime iceberg. For example, in one of the richest provinces in the country, Ontario, no government agency collects information of the dollar cost of criminal practices with respect to the selling and repair of motor cars. This information is not available from any federal agency either. Another example: the National Centre for Criminal Justice Statistics collects a wide variety of criminal statistics, excluding corporate crime statistics.[6]

Finally, the relatively small amount of information on corporate crime that is collected by government departments is not published in a way that enables the reader to compute rates, estimate dollar costs or determine the proportion of all Canadian firms that are crooked or that are crooked in various industries. A third conclusion, then, is that the official statistics on corporate crime in Canada that are available for research purposes do not permit one to answer a number of interesting questions about the amount and distribution of corporate crime in Canada. Scholars use them because they are the only regularly published statistics available.

With these *caveats* in mind, we can now get on with an examination of two broad categories of corporate crime, economic crimes and violent crimes. Most of the information on economic corporate crime and crime control is published by the federal Ministry of Consumer and Corporate Affairs. Statistics on violent corporate crime are published by the Workmen's Compensation Board, also a federal agency. To a greater or lesser degree, these sources of information are supplemented by the findings of commissions of inquiry and U.S. data.

Economic Corporate Crimes

There are a number of giant corporations in Canada. Because of the vast economic resources they control and the wide range of goods and services they provide (everything from birth control products to mortuary practices) they vitally influence the lives of most Canadians from the cradle to the grave. When very large corporations steal, then, many people are victimized, and the amounts involved can be staggering, just by virtue of the giant scale of their operations.

In this connection, consider the Amway Corporation. Between 1963 and 1978, this corporation engaged in deceitful business practices that cost the Canadian taxpayer over $26 million dollars. This comes to an average yearly figure of about $1.7 million dollars (*The Globe and Mail*, Nov. 8, 1982, p. 3).[7]

Another large corporation, CCM, agreed to contribute to an employees' pension fund. At the time they were hired, a pension at the end of their working lives was, perhaps, one factor influencing the employees' decision to work for CCM. Yet, CCM did not put any money into the employees' pension fund for an 18-month period prior to declaring bankruptcy. As a result, Crawford (1984, A8) notes that "workers at CCM Inc. . . . have lost more than $2 million in pensions." Many employees who expected to retire on pensions of $15 000 a year will have to make do with $9 000. This figure pales in comparison to the over $4 million stolen from the public by two well-established businessmen who rigged bids on Hamilton harbour dredging contracts (*The Hamilton Spectator*, July 19, 1975, p. 1). These men were subsequently convicted. Another major site for crooked business activities is stock exchanges (Allen 1979). One in particular, the Calgary Stock Exchange, seems to have been associated with illegal activity for some time (Graham 1986). The economic and social costs of these illegal activities may run into hundreds of thousands of dollars. An accurate estimate of the amounts involved has yet to be calculated.

Turning from individual corporations and institutions to the groups of corporations that make up an industry, we discover that some industries appear to be especially criminogenic. The automobile industry is one of these. Metropolitan Toronto (Ontario) had a "ghost-car" program devoted to controlling crime by businesses that sell and/or repair cars. Between 1979 and 1984, 2 200 criminal charges were laid for "abuses in the car selling and repair business." If one can assume that New York State and Ontario devoted roughly the same resources towards detecting these offences and if Ontario garages were only half as crooked as their counterparts in New York State, then 37 cents of every dollar was paid by Ontario car owners for unnecessary or shoddy work.[8]

The same conclusion applies equally well to statistics on corporate crime published by the Ministry of Consumer and Corporate Affairs (Table 3-1). In this table, Restraints to Competition cover illegal mergers and monopolies. Most of the offences listed under Marketing Practices cover false and deceptive advertising. The 38 270 offences represent not all the offences that actually occurred, but only those that resulted in the filing of a complaint. Relatively few complaints result in convictions. Thus, for the year 1982–1983, the latest year for which complete data are available, the ratio of complaints to convictions was 63:1 for restraints to competition and 98:1 for marketing practices.

TABLE 3-1 *Complaints of Economic Crimes by Business Corporations, 1982–1985*

	#	%
Restraints to Competition	2 242	5.8
Marketing Practices	36 028	94.2
Total	38 270	100.0

Sources: Tables 16 and 18, Consumer and Corporate Affairs,1984–1985, Estimates, Part III, Expenditure Plan, (Ottawa: 1986)

More detailed information on the process of attrition (loss of cases) is provided in Figure 3-1. During the year 1982–1983, the total number of complaints was 12 049. Figure 3-1 describes what happened to these complaints as they were processed by investigators, prosecutors and judges. For a start, 74 percent of the complaints were found not to warrant further action. In other words, these complaints either did not constitute law violations or, if they did, the offence could not be successfully prosecuted. Twenty-six percent of the complaints were deemed worthy of at least a preliminary investigation, because there was some substance to them. This investigation reduced the 26 percent complaints of substance to 18 percent. These were formally investigated. Only 5 percent survived, and less than half of these were referred to court. At the end, 190 or 1.6 percent of the original 12 049 complaints resulted in a conviction.

FIGURE **3.1** *Referrals and Results: The Process of Attrition, 1982-1983**

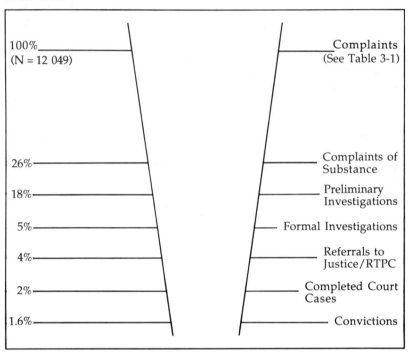

Note: 1982–1983 is the last year for which complete figures are available. The data used to describe the process of attrition were taken from Table 16 and 18, Consumer and Corporate Affairs, 1984–1985, Estimates, Part III, Expenditure Plan (Ottawa: 1986).

If the probability of being convicted for a corporate economic crime is low, so too is the severity of the punishment applied to firms that are convicted. Between 1980 and 1983, the median fine levied against a corporate criminal was $1 200 (Consumer and Corporate Affairs, 1984–1985, Estimates, Part III Expenditure Plan). By comparison, the maximum fine for spitting on Oakville, Ontario's fine sidewalks is $2 000. Between 1889, when the Combines Investigation Act was passed, and 1972, there have been many serious violations of its provisions. Yet, according to Reasons, "no one was put in jail during this 83 year period" (1982, 156).

Shoddy business practices are one thing, potentially lethal practices are quite another. Table 3-2 shows that the Canadian aviation industry was cited for an average of 960 hazardous violations per year during the period 1977–1979. Most (60.6 percent) of the violations cited in deterrent actions by government officials (Transport Canada) involved hazardous practices. Like other officially reported corporate crime statistics, these, according to an experienced aviation industry investigator, "are only scratching the surface" (Dubin 1981, 339).

TABLE 3-2 *Violations Most Frequently Cited in Deterrent Actions, 1977–1979*

	#	%
Hazardous[a]	960	60.6
Non-hazardous	627	39.4
Total	1 593	100.0

Sources: Dubin (1981), Vol. 1.
Note: a. Hazardous violations include low flying, reckless flying, altering or falsifying documents, certificate of airworthiness not in force.

Finally, in assessing the contribution made to illegal economic forms of victimization by Canadian corporations, it is important to consider not only direct, but also indirect effects. Clearly, a car repair business that bills a customer for services it did not perform is engaging in a direct form of victimization. Less obvious are the effects of such conduct on the moral climate of the country. Scholars who have made a significant contribution to the study of corporate crime believe that corporate economic crimes also contribute to the victimization of the public via their effects on street crimes. This occurs because the belief that corporate crime is wide spread lowers the moral climate of society. If the well off make a living by ripping off the public, why should the less well off not do the same thing? (Simon and Eitzen 1986, 1).

The findings of Clinard and Yeager (1980) suggest that a majority of U.S. business corporations have played a part in lowering the moral climate of their society. Specifically, they found that between 1975 and 1979, 60 percent of the corporations they studied had legal action taken against them by one or more of 25 regulatory agencies (1980, xi). They also found large corporations engaged in more serious and frequent illegal activities than smaller ones. Since Canada is as capitalist a society as the United States, and has also a much higher ratio of very large to small business corporations, there are good reasons for believing that economic corporate crime is as widespread in Canada as it is in the United States.

Violent Corporate Crimes

According to Monahan, Novaco and Geis (1979, 118), corporate violence is "behaviour producing an unreasonable risk of physical harm to consumers, employees, or other persons as a result of deliberate decision-making by corporate executives or culpable negligence on their part." Among a number of sociologists who have studied corporate crime, the area of occupational health and safety is one in which corporate violence is most clearly evident. Just as taverns in the poorer segments of cities represent a significant site for assaults, woundings, manslaughters and murders, occupational health and safety responsibilities are a major site for corporate violence.

The Ontario Federation of Labour (1982, 2) cites statistics that support this conclusion. Thus, we learn that "every 16 seconds, one Canadian worker suffers a disabling injury on the job." Even more alarming is their contention that these "represent only the tip of the iceberg" because these victim statistics cover only those claims for compensation that the Workmen's Compensation Board has accepted. This means that work-related injuries that are not validated by the board are not counted.[9] Official statistics on work-related injuries seriously underestimate their actual number. Official statistics on criminal code assaults also seriously underestimate their actual number. When these two sets of statistics are compared, the corporate assault rate is 25 times greater than the criminal code or street assault rate (Table 3-3). If a minimal correction is made, that is, if injuries to workers not even covered by Workmen's Compensation are added to the figure of 1 210 000 injuries, then the corporate assault rate is more than 30 times greater than the street assault rate.[10]

TABLE **3-3** *Officially Reported Corporate and Criminal Code Assaults, 1981*

	#	Rate*
Corporate assaults	1 210 000	12 872
Criminal code assaults	112 911	465

Sources: For corporate assaults, Labour Canada, Employment Injuries and Occupational Illnesses (Ottawa: Minister of Supply and Services Canada, 1982) and Canada Yearbook. (Ottawa: Minister of Supply and Services Canada 1985), Table 20.3 for population and assaults.

Note: * Rates are for 100 000 workers and Canadian residents respectively. The worker population in 1981 was 9.4 million. The population of Canada in the same year was 24.3 million.

Compared with assaults, the most serious kinds of violent crime, those resulting in deaths, are less likely to be seriously under-reported. Official statistics on these offences provide more reliable estimates of their actual amount. When lethal street crimes, murder and manslaughter are compared with work-related deaths, we discover that the rate for work-related deaths is almost four times greater than the combined rate for murders and man-slaughters (Table 3-4). When the 25 percent adjustment is made (for workers who were killed at work but not covered by Work-men's Compensation), the corporate death rate is more than six times greater than the street death rate.

If deaths and injuries are added to each other, the result is a measure of total violent crime. Table 3-5 indicates that the corpo-rate rate of violence is 28 times greater than the street violent crime rate. When the correction factor for workers not covered by Work-men's Compensation Board statistics is applied, this figure in-creases to over 30.

TABLE 3-4 *Officially Reported Corporate and Criminal Code Deaths, 1981*

	#	Rate
Corporate deaths	960	10.1
Criminal Code deaths	648	2.7

Sources: Labour Canada *Occupational Injuries and Occupational Illnesses* (Ottawa: Minister of Supply and Services Canada, 1982) and *Canada Yearbook, 1985* (Ottawa: Minister of Supply and Services Canada, 1986), Table 20.5.

TABLE 3-5 *Officially Reported Violent Crime, Corporate and Criminal Code, 1981*

	#	Rate
Corporate violent crime	1 210 960	12 883
Criminal code violent crime	113 559	467

Sources: Labour Canada, *Occupational Injuries and Occupational Illnesses* (Ottawa: Minister of Supply and Services Canada, 1982) and *Canada Year Book, 1985* (Ottawa: Minister of Supply and Services Canada, 1986), Tables 20.3, 20.5.
Note: Corporate violent crime includes deaths and injuries. Criminal code violent crime includes murder, manslaughter, infanticide and assaults.

The statistics on corporate violence reported here and in earlier publications by Reasons et al. (1981) and Glassbeek and Rowland (1979) are not unique to Canada. Similar estimates of incidence have been provided for England and Wales by Box (1983) and by Reiman (1979) for the United States. Taken together, these cross-national statistics on corporate violence suggest to Reasons et al. that "injury and illness from the work place has reached epidemic proportions" (1981, 26). In addition to deaths, injuries and illnesses to hundreds of Canadian workers, the total economic cost of these forms of corporate violence during the year 1981 has been estimated at "ranging between $5.7 billion to $20.9 billion to 1.7 to 6.3 percent of the gross national product" (Labour Canada, 1982, 4).

Finally, it is relevant to note that hundreds of Canadian businesses made a contribution, albeit an unequal one, to these costs, human and economic (Labour Canada, 1979). These contributions range from a staggering rate of roughly 91 injuries per 100 workers employed by the Freshwater Fish Marketing Corporation to a relatively low 13 injuries per 100 workers employed by the Canadian Penitentiary Service.[11]

PERSPECTIVES ON CORPORATE CRIME

In Chapter 3, four major theoretical perspectives were identified. Each of these will now be applied to a specific substantive topic, corporate crime. This procedure has the advantage of clarifying the relationship between each theory and research on corporate crime. This is important because the problems investigated and the research methods used are not the same for all of the four major theories. This separate treatment procedure also has one disadvantage. It gives the impression that each theory was applied independently of the others. This is not so. Actually, most attempts to explain corporate crime contain parts or elements taken from other theories. Most theories, then, are eclectic, that is, they are characterized by elements borrowed from other theories. In reading this section, the eclectic nature of most theories of corporate crime should be kept in mind.

Strain Theory

Strain theoretic explanations of corporate crime take two general forms. One is derived from the anomie theory of Merton (1957). The roots of the other can be traced back to the differential-association/subcultural theory of Sutherland. A contemporary exponent of anomie explanations of corporate crime is Stephen Box (1983). Clinard and Yeager offer a strain-subculture explanation of the same phenomenon (1980).

Anomie Merton's anomie explanation is based on the assumption that criminal behaviour is motivated by the strain experienced by individuals who have learned to value making money but who are denied access to legitimate opportunities (jobs) for achieving this cultural goal. According to Box, this assumption is more likely to be valid for corporate executives in capitalist societies than for lower-class individuals.[12] For this reason, Box believes that Merton's formulation does a good job of explaining corporate crime but a poor job of explaining lower-class crime. In other words, Merton provides a better explanation of such corporate crimes as price fixing and maintaining hazardous work environments than he does of such street crimes as burglary, robbery and mugging.

Central to Box's Mertonian analysis is the idea that corporate crime is a response to corporate anomie. Business corporations are also formal organizations. One defining attribute of such organizations is the collective, planned pursuit of such organizational goals as profit, growth and larger market share. The achievement of these goals is made difficult by the existence of a number of factors. Some, such as employee unions, are internal to the organization. Others are external to it. These fall into two groups. Consumers with their complaints and governments with their laws represent one group. The organization's competitors, that is, other organizations producing the same or similar goods and services, form the second group.

Taken together, the presence of unions, consumer groups, governments and competitors induces uncertainty in the business environment. Corporations are not always certain about the reaction of one or more of these groups to their business decisions. In Box's strain hypothesis, an actual or perceived "increase in these environmental uncertainties will increase the strain towards corporate criminal activity . . . ." (1983, 37).

The strain referred to by Box is caused by a *disjunction* between an emphasis on corporate goal achievement and uncertainty regarding the actual achievement of these objectives. Corporate executives are highly motivated towards the achievement of corporate objectives. The existence of unpredictable hindrances to the achievement of these objectives posed by the "problem groups" noted above induces a strain towards evading, avoiding and transgressing laws designed to protect consumers, the environment, the health and safety of workers, and so on. The result is corporate crime.

Strain-subcultural Theory The socially induced strain that helps cause corporate crime is actually experienced by individuals in business corporations. However, as individual corporate executives talk about and share their work-related experiences, corporate strain comes to be experienced collectively. It is also responded to collectively. Unlike Merton's individualistic anomie thesis, strain subcultural theory emphasizes the *collective*, problem-solving nature of corporate crime.

One of the earliest theories of corporate crime, differential association, was formulated by Edwin Sutherland in 1939. According to Sutherland (1939, 5), corporate crime, like any other crime:

> is learned in direct or indirect association with those who already practice the behaviour and those who learn the behaviour are segregated from frequent and intimate contacts with law-abiding behaviour. Whether a person becomes a criminal or not is determined largely by the comparative frequency and intimacy of his contacts with the two types of behaviour. This process may be called the process of differential association.

This theory is also a subcultural one because differential association takes place within subcultures.[13] Business corporations are characterized by corporate subcultures. A corporate subculture consists of definitions of corporate situations, the nature of corporate problems and ways of solving them. The primary carriers of corporate subcultures are corporate executives. The manner in which the content of these subcultures is transmitted and maintained is word-of-mouth. Nothing is written down. In other words, communication and control by members of a corporate subculture are informally organized.

As collective, problem-solving, informally organized entities, corporate subcultures owe their origin to the presence of problems requiring solutions not available or permitted by either the official rules and regulations, civil and criminal laws or by general societal norms such as fairness. Where subcultural solutions involve the selection of means punishable by the state, the corporate subculture is criminogenic. Not all business corporations have criminogenic corporate subcultures. Those that do tend to produce more corporate crooks because, as they rise in the corporate hierarchy, corporate executives tend to come into more frequent and intimate contact with other executives holding authoritative definitions favourable to law violation, that is, with members of the criminogenic corporation subculture (Clinard, 1983, 77).

Almost 40 years after its original formulation, Sutherland's corporate subculture/differential association theory was reproduced by Clinard and Yeager in their study of corporate crime in America. According to these authors, corporate violations "stem from the corporate way of life" (1980, 298).[14]

The subculture or corporate way of life of a business corporation consists of norms (rules) and values (conceptions of the desirable). Put another way, the subculture of a corporation refers to its "living code," its "business norms," or its "way of life." A corporation's way of life is influenced by a variety of internal and external factors.[15] Among the most important of the internal influences is the ethical/moral atmosphere created or maintained by the corporation's dominant coalition (Clinard and Yeager 1980; Clinard 1983). The degree to which top management creates or sustains a corporate culture supportive of or opposed to illegal conduct depends in turn on (a) the primacy given to the goal of profit, (b) the degree of competition, (c) the stability of the economic and political environment, and (d) how widespread illegal conduct is among firms that constitute an industry.

The more widespread the diffusion of illegal conduct, the greater the pressure for profits, the more uncertain and competitive the market or the consequences of governmental action, the more likely is top management to create or maintain an atmosphere or way of life conducive to corporate crime.

The culture or way of life of a corporation or industry is learned via the processes of socialization and social control. Where the corporation's way of life is criminogenic, the individual executive or manager learns to become a crook as part of his occupational role. Socialization refers to this kind of occupational role learning. Should a manager attempt to question some of the more crime-conducive outlooks that are being taught (e.g., the achievement of short-run corporate objectives is more important than the means used to achieve them), then prospects for promotion, if not continued employment, may be jeopardized. Social control refers to the corporation's use of sanctions designed to inhibit deviation from the norms of its culture.

Having described the process in terms of which individuals learn to become corporate crooks, Clinard and Yeager (1980, 68–73) conclude their theoretical account of corporate crime by identifying the *content* of socialization. Among the things that executives learn is how to deal with the problem of breaking rules one may have once believed in or may still believe in outside of the job. Specifically, they learn a number of rules that help neutralize any guilt they may feel. Included among these rules are the following: all legal measures constitute government interference with the free enterprise system; there is little deliberate intent in corporate violations, many of them are errors of omission rather than commission, and many are mistakes; if there is no increase in corporate profits a violation is not wrong.

Social Control Theory

Contemporary social control explanations of corporate crime fall into three major groups. These are control-anomie theorists influenced by Durkheim's anomie-at-the-top thesis, bond theorists influenced by Durkheim's social attachments equal social control equation and deterrence theorists influenced by Beccaria and his followers.

ANOMIE-CONTROL THEORY As we discovered in Chapter 2, Emile Durkheim had a strong and abiding interest in the sources of social order, in the process of social control and in the vulnerability of humans. All three concerns are reflected in his anomie theory. Durkheim's anomie formulation differs from Merton's in two important respects. First, whereas Merton drew attention to lower-class crime or "anomie-at-the-bottom," Durkheim emphasizes "anomie-at-the-top," that is, among members of society's most successful and powerful class groupings. Second, for Merton the major instigator of the strain that led to crime was the *disjunction* between goals and the availability of legitimate means. By contrast, Durkheim locates the major cause of anomie in the *too successful* achievement of cultural goals.

The anomie that is induced in individuals who achieve great wealth and power facilitates deviant and criminal behaviour in two ways. First, their past success leads them to believe that they can achieve any goal. Thus they set higher and higher goals for themselves. At the same time, anything less than complete success in achieving these goals is viewed as failure. To such individuals, failure is intolerable. Intolerable strain facilitates such strain-reducing activities as crime or deviance. Second, great success inculcates in individuals the belief that their success is due to their own individual efforts. They do not have to rely on others. They become individuated. Individuated individuals tend not to have strong group attachments. They are loners. To be a loner is to be vulnerable, that is, to weaken the restraining effects of the opinions, praise and blame conferred on one by others. A weakening of such group-based restraints facilitates crime and deviance (Durkheim 1951, 254).

Durkheim himself did not apply his anomie-at-the-top thesis to the topic of corporate deviance. Box does this. The "competitive ambition and moral flexibility" displayed by corporate executives who make their way to the very top of the corporate hierarchy "prepares them to engage in crime should they perceive it as being necessary for the good of the company" (1983, 39). The higher they go, the less accountable and constrained they feel. As a result, the most wealthy and powerful corporate executives tend to be the biggest crooks. This, according to Box, explains why the largest corporations, multinationals, are more criminogenic than large ones and why large ones are more criminogenic than small ones.[16]

BOND THEORY In applying Durkheim's anomie thesis to corporate crime, Box emphasizes the moral deregulation or normlessness caused by great success. By way of contrast, Hirschi's social control or bond theory builds upon Durkheim's individuation route to crime. Durkheim believed that moral behaviour and being at-tached to others went together (1951, 209). This occurs because those who are motivated to violate social norms (e.g., selflessness, fairness, honesty) are inhibited from doing so by the negative reactions or sanctions they expect from the others to whom they are attached. Loners, however, are not attached to others. There-fore they tend to be indifferent to their reactions.

Corporate executives who become members of the dominant coalition in a very large business corporation acquire great wealth, power, and prestige. Their achievements tend to individuate them, to make them loners. Following Hirschi (1969, 16–18), corporate loners would tend not to use the anticipated reactions of others as a guide to conduct. The norms of others are not their norms. The norms that help bind others together do not apply to them. Be-cause their bond to others, to society, is weak, successful corporate loners feel "free to deviate," free to do what is effective rather than what is right, legal or appropriate.

Hirschi's bond theory can also be integrated with organizational theories of corporate crime. According to Cressey, "the phe-nomenon to worry about" when studying corporate crime is "or-ganization" (1972, 26). Mary McIntosh contends that "the study of organizational crime requires organizational concepts" (1975, 8). Which concepts? According to Clinard and Yeager, hierarchy and differentiation were among the most criminogenic attributes of bureaucratically organized business corporations (1980, 44–46). Hierarchy of authority and differentiation of occupational roles facilitate corporate crime because they enable executives to "pass the buck." Specifically, hierarchy permits executives to say that they were ordered to do what they did by their bosses. It's not their fault. Differentiation means making one of many corporate deci-sions that together result in criminal conduct. This tends to attenu-ate the sense of responsibility each executive feels for the final outcome. Thus, Clinard and Yeager found that large business corporations were more criminogenic partly because they contained many more levels of authority and specialized work roles and divisions.

This finding does not surprise sociologist Stuart Henry, for he maintains that "the structure of a system of relations which divides responsibility for human lives into authority and hierarchy relations is the most lethal devised by man. It simultaneously commands action and limits responsibility" (1985, 73). This means that corporate executives are "free to deviate" because the structure of their corporate bureaucracy frees them from reponsibility for their decisions. Their stake in conformity, they believe, will not be jeopardized by the job-related decisions they make. After all, they are not fully responsible for making them.

Stake in conformity is, according to Hirschi (1969), one element of the individual's bond to society. The possibility that criminal or deviant conduct will jeopardize the investments in conformity built up by an individual acts as a major inhibitor of such conduct. Corporate business organizations characterized by hierarchy and differentiation tend to sever or attenuate the association between corporate conduct and stake in conformity. Therefore, they are criminogenic.

DETERRENCE THEORY Cesare Bonesana, Marchese de Beccaria, was an economist and mathematician. He was also one of the founding fathers of deterrence theory. In 1767, he published his ideas on deterrence in a book entitled *Essay on Crimes and Punishment*. In this book, he outlined his plan for a more effective system of justice. Deterrence was one of the basic principles of this system.

The idea of deterrence as a crime control strategy rests on two assumptions. First, human beings are motivated primarily by pain and pleasure. Second, in their efforts to obtain a balance of pleasure over pain in satisfying their wants, they act in a rational or calculating manner. The best or most effective law in the criminal justice system is one that ensures that the costs of criminal conduct outweigh the gains. In such a system, punishment controls criminal conduct by creating realistic fears concerning the consequences of engaging in such conduct.

Contemporary formulations of deterrence theory improve upon original formulations by specifying more precisely the conditions under which and the extent to which the objective of deterrence is achieved. Thus, present-day contributors such as Andenaes (1974), van den Haag (1975) and Wilson (1975) share the view that legal punishments that are swift, certain and severe are most likely to deter under the following two conditions. First, they are applied to offences that are most evidently rational or calculative in nature. Corporate crimes constitute this kind of offence. Second, they are backed up by extra-legal sanctions such as public opinion.[17]

In considering deterrence itself as an objective, contemporary deterrence theorists make an important distinction between "general" and "specific" deterrence. Specific deterrence has to do with the effects of punishments on the individual to whom they are applied. General deterrence refers to the effects of the punishment of specifc individuals on a wider audience. Thus, in 1961, when General Electric pleaded guilty and was fined for breaking the law by fixing prices (Geis 1982, 126), a concern with specific deterrence would lead one to focus on the effects of these punishments on GE, while a concern with general deterrence would divert attention to their effects on other corporations in the same industry and/or other business corporations generally (Geis 1967).

Deterrence theory has been used by Goff and Reasons (1976) to explain corporate crime in Canada. Their overall conclusion is that corporate crime occurs because it pays. For example, restraint of trade agreements are prohibited by law (Combines Investigation Act). Yet, these agreements are not uncommon because "Penalties . . . have been insufficient as a deterrent, with the possible financial rewards . . . far outweighing the possible loss as a result of fines imposed by the government" (1967, 489).

Governments in Canada and the United States do not appear to accord corporate crime control a very high place on either their crime control or human health and safety priorities. For example, the U.S. Congressional Office of Technology Assessment reviewed the work done by the Occupational Health and Safety Administration during the first 13 years of its operation. Their main conclusion was that this Administration "had shown little measurable results in protecting workers" (Noble 1985). In fact, during the most recent year for which statistics were available, 1984, work-related injuries and illnesses increased most. This 12 percent increase represented "5.4 million illnesses and injuries . . . and 3,740 work-related deaths" (Noble 1985, 11).

Closer to home, the Ontario New Democrat caucus reviewed the effects of the Ministry of Labour's new "get tough" policy regarding the enforcement of the province's Occupational Health and Safety Act. They discovered not only that "in 1985, 426 800 workers were injured and 168 died in work-related accidents" but also that "the Ministry, instead of prosecuting the violators, is collaborating with employers to hide the true extent of the problem from public scrutiny" (Ont. New Dem. 1986, 1). The Ministry of Labour's lack of interest in enforcing the provisions of the Act are viewed by the authors of the report as encouraging violations by making penalties for such conduct highly unlikely.

More generally, deterrence theorists contend that a deterrent effect is not achieved because each and every one of the factors or variables that make deterrence effective is undermined. Thus, the legislation (Combines Investigation Act) that is intended to regulate corporate crime has so many loopholes that it is very difficult to enforce. Secondly, most corporate crimes remain undiscovered, that is, they are also corporate secrets. The state cannot punish conduct it is not aware of. If agents of the state do become aware of a corporate crime, corporate lawyers specializing in corporate law can often get the better of government lawyers whose training is not as specialized. The result is delay and/or a failure to convict. If convicted, the penalties are rarely severe. Where fines are imposed, they amount to little more than a "licensing fee" and tend to be regarded as such by corporate executives (Braithwaite and Geis 1981, 61). Finally, these executives work in a society characterized by a relatively tolerant attitude towards the criminal activities of corporations. As a result, they tend not to anticipate severely punishing community or societal reactions to the crimes of their corporations. In sum, neither certainty, nor swiftness, nor severity nor extra-legal sanctions characterize the policing of corporate crime in Canada. This is why it is endemic in our society.

In concluding this discussion, one *caveat* is necessary. Like most other deterrence theoretic explanations of corporate crime, Goff and Reasons conclude that deterrence does not work. This may well be a valid conclusion. However, because they relied exclusively on official statistics on discovered corporate criminals to test their theory, they have no way of knowing how many corporations who might have engaged in criminal conduct did not do so, either because of their respect for the law and/or because they wished to avoid experiencing legal punishments of any kind. In other words, Goff and Reasons' conclusions may apply to specific but not to general deterrence.

Interactionist Theory

Earl Rubington and Martin Weinberg are interactionist theorists. One problem of central interest to them is how individuals and groups come to be defined as deviant. This is how they describe the definitional or labelling process:

For deviance to become a social fact, somebody must *perceive* an act or event as a departure from social norms, must *categorize* that perception, must *report* that perception to others, must get them to *accept* this definition. Unless all these requirements are met, deviance as a social fact does not come into being (1981, 9).

Ermann and Lundman (1982, 228) believe that, "A similar view of the defining process should be taken for organizational deviance". From their interactionist perspective, business corporations who pollute, lie, kill, injure and steal are deviant "only to the extent that they are perceived, reported, accepted and treated as deviant" (1982, 228). A business corporation that gets away with committing such offences is not deviant. Why and how this happens are questions of considerable importance to interactionist theorists.

A good illustration of an interactionist account of successful corporate crime is provided by Dowie and Marshall (1982). Following Becker, the sequence of events described by them constitutes a moral drama in which accusers and the accused attempt to impose one of four labels on a drug: "not recommended," "possibly effective," "probably effective" and "effective." The kind of label that emerges out of the interaction among accusers, accused and government regulative agencies has major consequences for consumers as well as the pharmaceutical corporation marketing the drug. Thus, if the Federal Drug Agency labels the drug "not recommended," it must be taken off the market. The label "effective" means it can be sold anywhere, including the armed forces. The in-between labels mean that the firm must conduct more and more vigorous testing. These labels then, directly affect profits by allowing, prohibiting or restricting sales. Also, when further tests are stipulated, it increases the costs of producing the drug. This may also decrease profits.

Bendectin is a drug made by a subsidiary of the large pharmaceutical company, Richardson-Merrell. It is prescribed for pregnant women who suffer from nausea and vomiting. Bendectin helps relieve both. Like thalidomide, it also causes serious birth defects. Bendectin was first marketed in 1957. In 1963, after the thalidomide scandal, Bendectin was tested for the presence of a chemical (teratogens) that is known to cause birth defects. Dr. Robert Staples, who conducted this research, discovered the same kinds of birth defects in rabbits who were given Bendectin as in those to whom thalidomide was administered. According to Dowie and Marshall (1982, 262), Richardson-Merrell executives were aware of these results.

In the United States, the Federal Drug Agency must by law approve all drugs prior to their sales. Bendectin was submitted for approval. What Richardson-Merrell wanted was the FDA's "effective" label. What it did not want, what they wished to avoid, was the label "harmful" (Dowie and Marshall 1982, 273). In the latter endeavour, they were successful. Between 1957 when it was first marketed and 1980, Bendectin caused birth defects in 140 000 children (Dowie and Marshall 1982, 262).

Federal law requires manufacturers of drugs to report all adverse side effects to the FDA. Failure to do so is an offence liable to criminal prosecution. "Staples' original report was never shown to the FDA, nor was the experiment repeated" (Dowie and Marshall 1982, 265). In addition, as time went by, increasing evidence of Bendectin's deadly side-effects were presented to both the FDA and Richardson-Merrell executives. In 1966, especially good evidence of the drug's harmful effects was provided by a Canadian doctor, Dr. Donald Patterson. Other doctors, all over the world, read Patterson's study and confirmed his conclusions. Yet, as time went by, the label applied by the FDA got better. It went from "possibly effective" to "probably effective" to "effective" (Dowie and Marshall 1980, 273).

From Richardson-Merrell's point of view, the labelling process was quite successful. No executive was prosecuted. The corporation was not fined or punished. Bendectin continued to be sold and profits accrued.

A number of factors were responsible for the outcome of the moral drama described here.

First of all, Richardson-Merrell used their great resources to bribe and otherwise manipulate doctors who were asked to perform additional tests (Dowie and Marshall 1982, 269). Second, the company lied and actually hid files containing information harmful to its case (Dowie and Marshall 1982, 272). Third, Dr. Marion Finkel, a former employee of a pharmaceutical company, seemed to believe that she was still responsible for the welfare of the pharmaceutical industry, while acting as associate director of the FDA's New Drug Evaluation section. She was ultimately responsible for labelling Bendectin. FDA researchers working under her would routinely be transferred to other jobs, or have their reports altered, if they found that Bendectin could have harmful side effects (Dowie and Marshall 1982, 274–277).

In sum, the combination of the resources of a large company, the willingness of company executives to use these resources in almost any way that reduces losses and increases profits and a sympathetic, strategically placed FDA official, successfully overcame efforts to label Bendectin harmful by a number of doctor-re-searchers, some of whom worked for the FDA, while others were employed by such prestigious groups as the American Medical Association and the National Academy of Sciences.

Conflict Theory

In Chapter 2, we learned that Karl Marx formulated two conceptions of the state. As each was elaborated upon and developed by later generations of Marxist scholars, one became known as the instrumental thesis, the other the structural thesis. Instrumental and structural conceptions of the state figure prominently in contemporary Marxist conflict accounts of corporate crime. In these accounts, the general theoretical debate between instrumentalist Miliband (1969) and structuralist Poulantzas (1973; 1975) is reproduced.

INSTRUMENTAL ACCOUNTS Instrumental Marxists have been challenged by a number of questions directed at them by their critics. Some of the most challenging of these are: If the state serves as handmaiden to the corporate community, why do we have laws to regulate corporate conduct? Why are business corporations prosecuted and punished by such agents of the state as regulatory agencies? Why do these policing agencies exist in the first place?

In his *Crimes of the Powerful*, 1978, Pearce attempts to explain the development of laws regulating U.S. business activity, specifically anti-trust laws. According to Pearce, these laws were created because they were useful to the business community and because they helped the state perform its "objective function" of guaranteeing "the reproduction of the economic system" (1978, 61).

The state can best ensure the maintenance of capitalism by inculcating in citizens generally a belief in its legitimacy. By passing laws that give the impression that the law is fair, i.e., that it applies to the powerful as well as to the powerless, it helps buttress its claim to legitimacy. Occasional punishment of individual corporations works towards the same end. Individual corporations are punished or sacrificed so that capitalists, as a class, can preserve their dominant position. Additionally, laws regulating corporate conduct are written in such a way as to be virtually unenforceable. This means that corporations, or at least the major ones, will not be unduly interfered with by charges, prosecutions, convictions and punishments.

For their part, business corporations actually co-operated with the state in creating anti-combines legislation because it "provided a means by which monopoly capital could be achieved against dangerous competitors . . . without danger of popular reactions" (Pearce 1978, 87). Pearce contends that the attitude of big business towards the law is essentially pragmatic. They will support laws that help increase the ratio of profits to losses and oppose those that increase the ratio of losses to profits. From this, it follows that all extant laws intended to regulate business conduct exist because they serve the interests of business, especially big business.

But, why are citizens generally not aware of what is going on so they can do something about more effective legislation and enforcement? The answer is "mystification." The state and big business by virtue of their control of educational, religious and the mass media help create and maintain an "imaginary social order" (Pearce 1978, 94). We are all led to believe that this imaginary social order is real. Believing in this order, we also tend to accept the claims for legitimacy made by the state, the sanctity of the market as a regulator of business activity, that bigness is due to efficiency, that democracy prevails in business because numerous small shareholders really control things, that a free-enterprise system exists and so on.

For Pearce, then, theorizing about corporate crime means "demystifying" it (1978, 104). This is done by contrasting an imaginary social order with the real social order. Important clues to the nature of the real social order in capitalist society are provided for Pearce by Karl Marx.

Instrumental accounts of corporate crime in Canada have been formulated by Glassbeek (1984) and sociologists Snider (1980) and Goff and Reasons (1978). Glassbeek, a lawyer, has focussed his attention on the corporate contribution to deaths and injuries in the work place. [18] According to Glassbeek, society is divided into major social classes, a ruling class and a subordinate class (1984). Those who own or manage large business corporations constitute an important fraction of the ruling class. The capitalist mode of production generates these classes and the struggle between them. Criminal behaviour is rooted in the class struggle. Since two social classes are involved in the class struggle, one might expect members of both classes to be subject to the same kind of law. This does not happen. Instead, civil and/or administrative law is applied to corporate killing, maiming and injury, while criminal law is applied to the same behaviour when it is engaged in by citizens generally. Why the difference?

Influenced by the Marxist scholars he cites, Glassbeek provides the following answer to this question. Those who own or manage large business corporations constitute an important fraction within

Canada's ruling class. Members of this class have more power than members in the subordinate class. This power differential is reflected in the ability of business interests to "capture" the state. In order to help the business community, the state passes criminal laws that help "reduce the strains inherent in the capitalist mode of production" (Glassbeek 1984, 42). More generally, the ruling class authorizes the state to "repress the class struggle in favour of the ruling class" (1984, 42).

According to Glassbeek then, the criminal law is not applied to Canadian business corporations because the social class that really runs society, the ruling class, never intended it to be used against a dominant fraction within that class. Beyond this, even the civil and administrative laws that are applied to business corporations are not effectively employed against them. The instrumental theses of Snider (1980) and Goff and Reasons (1978) represent an attempt to explain the co-presence of these laws and their ineffective enforcement.

In their studies of corporate crime in Canada, Snider and Goff and Reasons focus on the Combines Investigation Act. Their major finding was that this piece of legislation has many loopholes and is very poorly enforced. Where convictions do occur, punishments are relatively minor. This state of affairs is due partly to the fact that the state is dependent on healthy business corporations to provide taxes and jobs. Well-written legislation and effective enforcement might deter corporate crime, but it would also inhibit corporate growth and success. For the Canadian state, this is too high a price to pay.[19] At the same time, the presence of these laws helps maintain the legitimacy of the state because they symbolize society's opposition to such things as false advertising, price fixing, pollution and so on.

STRUCTURAL ACCOUNTS Structural accounts of corporate crime or its regulation in Canada can be divided roughly into weaker and stronger versions. In the development of corporate crime theory, weak versions played an important part. They were among the first to provide an alternative to instrumental accounts of the same phenomenon. Their starting point is a state that has not just one function, capital accumulation, but three: capital accumulation, legitimation and coercion. These three functions stand in a contradictory relation to each other. Devoting too many resources to one may jeopardize the others. Thus, catering to capital accumulation by completely ignoring corporate crime may jeopardize the legitimacy of the state itself. The state is vitally interested in creating or maintaining its legitimacy. The central ideas here are that the state has relative autonomy to pursue its own objectives and that the pursuit of these means not only catering to but also regulating corporate conduct.[20].

These ideas are developed by Snider and West (1980). A relatively autonomous state actively engaged in performing three major contradictory functions is central to their theory. One problem with the theory is that their structural conception of the state is not linked in any systematic way to corporate crime. Yet, it is offered as an explanation of corporate crime.

A recent attempt to overcome the linkage problem was undertaken by Smandych (1984). According to Smandych, Canadian combines legislation originated during a period of labour-capitalist conflict and represented an attempt by the state to secure industrial peace. Industrial peace would, in turn facilitate capital accumulation, an outcome dear to the hearts of both the state and the business community. Smandych believes that this structural explanation does a better job of accounting for the emergence of anti-combines legislation in Canada than does the instrumental account of Goff and Reasons. However, all he appears to succeed in doing is providing another instrumental version. Thus, whereas Goff and Reasons (1978) contend that this legislation was created to reduce conflict between small and large businesses and so help the capitalist class as a whole, Smandych maintains that it helped this class accumulate capital by reducing labour-business conflict.

Weaker structural accounts of corporate crime are intended by their authors to capture the complexity of the relation between the state and the corporate community, complexity that appeared not to have been fully appreciated in instrumental accounts. The notions of the relative autonomy of the state and of multiple, contradictory state functions constitute an attempt to provide a more complex and therefore better theoretical conception of the state. The linkage problem, that is, the problem of identifying the relation between the structural characteristics of specific state apparatuses with specific kinds of corporate crime or crime control in given historical circumstances is not well attended to.[21] Stronger versions go beyond weaker ones by furnishing more complex conceptions of the state and by dealing more adequately with the linkage problem. Evidence of both contributions is present in Poulantzas-influenced structural accounts of regulatory agencies.

Regulatory agencies are as strategic for understanding corporate crime as police forces are for understanding street crimes. They are central to both non-Marxist, i.e., liberal, and Marxist instrumental and structural explanations of corporate crime. In most of these accounts, the problem to be explained is not merely the *dual* role of such agencies as protectors and regulators of business activity, but also variations in the relative emphasis they place upon protection and regulation in different historical periods and in dealing with businesses of different kinds. Because these variations influence the corporate crime rate, an adequate explanation of them constitutes an important step towards formulating an adequate explanation of corporate crime.

Following Poulantzas, there are four key concepts for understanding the behaviour of regulative agencies: unequal structure of representation, unequal equilibrium of compromises, hegemonic fraction and class conflict. Viewed historically, one outcome of the political class struggle was the establishment of a state that represented the power of the two classes involved (proletariat and bourgeoisie), the power of the various fractions within these classes and the "national interest." The logic of these frequently contradictory and unequal representations requires a relatively autonomous state.

Regulative agencies are part of the state apparatus.[22] Variations in their activity reflect the unequal equilibrium of compromises they are forced to make. Inside the state, there are many organs and agencies. These represent various power blocs within and across the two major social classes. Power differentials among these power blocs are reflected in the power possessed by various state agencies. Those agencies that represent the "hegemonic fraction," that is the most powerful group within the dominant class, tend to dominate other state agencies. In Canada, agencies (e.g., Finance) that represent merchant-financiers represent the hegemonic fraction (Clement 1975). The long-term political interests of this fraction (and class) help explain the bias shown by the capitalist state and its agencies.

Inside the state, then, various branches representing different intra and inter class interests are in constant competition with each other. Policies supported by one branch (e.g., Labour) may contradict policies advocated by others (e.g., Health). Thus, whether the economic interests of particular industries or businesses are catered to or their harmful conduct regulated more effectively depends upon the relative power of various state organs and also upon the relation between protection-regulation and the political interests of the hegemonic fraction.

As a structure of class and professional technical (i.e., civil servant) relations, the state helps reproduce the rule of the dominant class and the position of the hegemonic fraction within it. This is done in various ways. The unequal equilibrium of compromises is one of these. Regulatory agencies actively participate in this process. Such participation involves emphasizing protection in some periods and regulation in others, greater protection for some industries and greater regulation for others. In part, these variations occur because the relative power positions of various organs and agencies inside the state do change. In addition, the national interest as well as the long-term political interests of the hegemonic fraction may sometimes be better served by protection and at other times by regulation. The same thing is true for some industries and not others. The end result of the unequal equilibrium of compromises is the pattern of business law enforcement routinely discovered by corporate crime researchers.[23]

SUMMARY

Corporate crime refers to acts punishable by the state that are engaged in by corporate executives for the benefit of the corporation. Objective definitions emphasize the law violative conduct of executives. Subjective definitions focus on societal reactions to corporate conduct. It is difficult to estimate accurately the actual amount of corporate crime in Canada or the United States. There seems to be quite a lot of it around because researchers frequently conclude that corporate crime is endemic to corporate business activity in capitalist societies. Statistics support the view that corporate violence and economic crimes probably do far more social damage than street crimes.

Strain theorists attempt to explain crime by pointing to corporate anomie. This condition is caused by a disjunction between the corporation's emphasis on achieving organizational objectives and a business environment that introduces uncertainty into the picture. Subcultural versions of strain theory emphasize learning to conform with a criminogenic corporate way of life. Here, corporate crime is a solution to problems facing corporate executives. Social control explanations of corporate crime fall into three sub-groups: anomie, bond theory and deterrence theory. In the anomie formulation, the lack of regulation experienced by highly successful executives is emphasized. The bond formulation also focusses on these individuals, but attributes their criminal conduct to their individuation, i.e., their lack of attachments to others. For deterrence theorists, corporate crime is endemic to business corporations because the profits to be made from violating the law far exceed the penalties imposed for such conduct. Interactionist theorists attempt to explain corporate crime by pointing to societal reactions that tend to define harmful and technically illegal conduct as harmless, legitimate business activity. Finally, conflict theorists make the state central to their explanation of corporate crime. In the instrumental conception of the state, the state does what is necessary to help corporate enterprises increase their profits. Ineffective corporate laws and poor law enforcement facilitate the achievement of this objective. In the structural conception, the state is relatively independent of business corporations and does in fact regulate individual corporations and industries in the overall interest of capitalists and capitalism. As a result, class rule is generalized.

SUGGESTED READINGS

M. Clinard and P. Yeager. *Corporate Crime* (New York: Macmillan, 1980).

Don Mitchell, *The Politics of Food* (Toronto: James Lorimer, 1975).

Upton Sinclair, *The Jungle* (Toronto: Penguin, 1982).

L. Snider, White Collar Crime in *The Canadian Encyclopedia* (Edmonton: Hurtig Publishers, 1985), Vol. 3, p. 1937.

Still Not Healthy, Still Not Safe. A report of the Ontario New Democrat Caucus, Second Task Force on Occupational Health and Safety, July 1986.

NOTES

1. *Criminal laws* refer to conduct defined by the state as intentional harms directed against itself. Agents of the state, e.g., police officers, enforce these laws. Conduct prohibited by the criminal code includes murder, rape, robbery, burglary. *Civil law* regulates harms experienced by one individual(s) as a result of the conduct of one or more persons. Agents of the state, e.g., judges, hear civil cases, not to fine or imprison convicted criminals, but to ensure that the party that is harmed is adequately compensated. Restitution is the usual penalty for civil offences. Civil laws permit a person to sue a neighbour who builds a fence on his property, a dog fancier to sue a breeder who sold her a deaf dog advertised as being "sound in mind and body" and an ex-fiance to sue the girl he intended to marry but who jilted him, for the return of the ring he gave her. *Administrative laws* are laws made by federal agencies and cover the conduct of business corporations as well as enterprises that the government itself runs, e.g., parks, hunting and fishing and so on. Individuals and corporations violating administrative laws are not called criminals but offenders.
2. A similar definition is offered by Simon and Eitzen (1986).

3. This concept was originally referred to but left undefined by J.D. Thompson in his book, *Organizations in Action,* (New York: McGraw-Hill, 1967). A clearer understanding of what is meant by a dominant coalition may be gained by reading Chester Barnard's book, *The Functions of the Executive,* (Cambridge, Mass.: Harvard University Press, 1968). The source of the definition of a dominant coalition presented here is Barnard's *Theory of Authority* (1968, ch. 12).
4. See also Farrell and Swigert (1985).
5. For example, a definition of terrorism that excludes U.S. state-sponsored terrorism and includes Libyan state-sponsored terrorism would be negatively evaluated on both grounds. See Griesman (1977) and Herman (1982).
6. Personal conversation with a senior analyst in the National Centre for Criminal Justice Statistics, Statistics Canada, Ottawa, January, 1986.
7. According to Clinard and Yeager, the oil, car and pharmaceutical industries are the most criminogenic industries in the United States (1980, ch. 11).
8. In the "ghost-car" program, government officials first thoroughly inspect a car and then take it to an unsuspecting garage for repairs. Metro Toronto operates such a program as part of the crime-control activities of its Auto Watchdog Committee. A report issued by this committee refers to the results of the New York State and California ghost-car program.
9. According to Ontario Federation of Labour estimates, approximately 25 percent of the work force is not covered by the Workmen's Compensation Act.
10. In evaluating the statistics presented in these tables, it is relevant to note that some unknown proportion of workplace assaults and deaths may occur for reasons other than corporate negligence or wrongdoing. Also relevant is the fact that the assault statistics presented in this Table may well represent only about one-third of all actual assaults. See Solicitor General of Canada (1983).
11. Cited by Reasons et al. (1981, 27). Safest groups of federal employees are those in Justice where about 0.33 percent are injured and the severity rate is 0.
12. This is because lower class individuals are not as exclusively committed to the cultural goal of success as Merton assumes. They have a variety of goals, and, so far as occupational achievement goes, their goals are realistic and limited. Hence, the disjunction is not as great as Merton supposes. See Box (1983, 35).
13. Another possibility, one mentioned by Clinard (1983), is that business corporations with criminogenic corporate subcultures tend to

attract and recruit top management executives who have not developed strong inhibitions against engaging in unethical or criminal conduct so long as organizational objectives are achieved in the process.

14. Seemingly unaware of the work of Sutherland, Christopher Stone also emphasizes the relevance to corporate crime and corporate crime control, of the "culture of the corporation." Stone, a law professor, describes and evaluates the significance of corporate culture in his influential book, *Where the Law Ends: The Social Control of Corporate Behaviour* (New York: Harper and Row, 1975).

15. Where primary emphasis is placed not upon profit but on the pursuit of other kinds of organizational objectives, other kinds of corporate crimes are likely to occur more frequently. Thus, where the goal of a corporation is to create a stable market environment, corporations attempt to influence the government in a number of legal and illegal ways.

16. One of Clinard and Yeager's major findings was that large business corporations were more criminogenic than small ones.

17. For an extended discussion of the rational nature of corporate crime and the significance of extra-legal sanctions, see Andenaes (1972) and Sutherland (1949, 217–233). Andenaes (1974), Palmer (1977), Pepinsky (1980, ch. 6) and Zimring and Hawkins (1973) offer more detailed explanations of deterrence theory. For a good review, see Cook (1980).

18. Reasons has also studied occupational health and safety in Canada. The book he co-authored with Ross and Patterson, however, is theory-free. This tends to make it difficult to describe his theoretical contribution to the topic.

19. Thus, until the whole affair became public, saving 400 jobs in New Brunswick's Star Kist plant seemed to be more important to federal politicans than enforcing Fisheries Act regulations that might jeopardize them. See *The Globe and Mail*, November 22, (1985), page A6.

20. For some scholars, the growth of the state is criminogenic because it tries to run everything, including business corporations, by creating and applying hundreds of rules or laws. The end result is that most businesses, in the normal course of business, violate one rule or another. Corporate crime becomes normal not only because of the presence of so many rules but also because conformity with one rule means breaking another (Young, 1981). In sum, the state helps cause corporate crime in the process of achieving an objective — growth of state bureaucracies — made possible by taxes generated by the very corporations whose conduct becomes increasingly subject to state regulation.

21. One recent attempt to do this was undertaken by Livy Visano (1985). For an attempt to bridge instrumental and structural approaches, see Clement (1983).
22. For a good attempt to apply Poulantzas (1973 and 1975) to the origin and functioning of regulatory boards in Canada, see Mahon (1977) and (1980).
23. This thesis can also be applied to a pattern in which regulation gradually becomes more effective over time, but not without a struggle. An examination of Ontario's attempt to regulate pollution demonstrates this pattern and supports the thesis. See Reschenthaler (1972) and Doren (1978).

CHAPTER FOUR

POLICE DEVIANCE —
THE DARK SIDE OF THE FORCE

WHAT IS POLICE DEVIANCE?

THE CONDUCT OF POLICE officers is more or less well regulated by at least five different sets of rules. Some of these are written, others are unwritten; they exist in the culture. Included among the written rules are the Criminal Code, Police Regulations and the decisions of judges (Judge's Rules).[1] The social norms of other police officers, their peers and of the general public are unwritten rules. Objectively defined, police deviance refers to behaviour that violates any of these norms. To the extent that the norms themselves prescribe (or proscribe) different and conflicting ways of behaving, conforming with one set may mean deviating from another. For example, perjury is a crime. Telling lies violates social norms. Yet, police officers do tell lies in court and also when they appear before police commissions of inquiry and citizen complaints tribunals. They do this in order to protect their fellow officers. Telling the truth would involve deviating from peer group norms prescribing secrecy and loyalty (Sherman 1974).

Another relevant thing to note about these rules is that they differ in the range of behaviour they cover. Thus, the Police Act in Metropolitan Toronto not only prescribes such legally relevant behaviour as the conditions under which an officer may kill someone, but also a whole range of behaviour varying from showing deference to superiors, to wearing the appropriate uniform, to being clean shaven. By contrast, the Criminal Code contains no rules governing the dress, demeanour or appearance of police officers. In addition, Criminal Code rules (laws) relating to the use of deadly force may be less restrictive than police act regulations.[2] What this means is that it is easier for police officers to be defined as deviant under the Police Act than it is under the Criminal Code. This is because the latter contains more rules governing a much wider range of behaviour. In addition, there are fewer legal safeguards for officers accused of violating Police Act regulations than for those accused of committing crimes.[3]

To more radically inclined sociologists, police officers in a capitalist society are deviant even when they conform with the Criminal Code and police regulations. To them, police officers are deviant because they help enforce rules supporting a system, capitalism, that is deviant. Their deviance is *in* their law enforcement behaviour.[4]

Police officers themselves may agree that policing is sometimes a dirty job. However, they also add that "somebody's got to do it." "What would society be like," they ask, "if there were no police officers?" Beyond this rather general stance, police officers go on to formulate what can best be described as a strategic definition of police deviance. Thus, a police officer who snitches on his peers (e.g., Serpico) is deviant because of what he actually does. Snitching violates police subcultural rules. This is an objective definition. However, when the same police officer violates someone else's rules — Criminal Code for example — this does not automatically make him a criminal. Actually committing a crime is not enough. For his behaviour to be labelled criminal, he has to be found *guilty* of the alleged crime. This criminal label is an indeterminate outcome of the interaction among accusers, the accused police officer, a judge or members of a civilian complaints board.[5] Here, the police offer a subjective definition of police deviance, one that focusses attention on the *processing* of deviance.

Equally strategic but articulating a different ideological position are the Janus-faced (two-faced) definitions of a number of interactionist sociologists. When they study the behaviour of members of relatively powerless "bottom dog" social groups, they offer subjective definitions. Objective definitions they reserve for studying the police, other state agents of control and members of powerful, "top dog" groupings.[6]

Subjective and objective definitions have obvious implications for questions relating to the amount, type and distribution of police deviance.

POLICE DEVIANCE: HOW MUCH?

As the evidence will indicate, there is a "dark side" of policing in Canada. The dark side includes various forms of deviant and illegal behaviour, a side that is associated with images of a tarnished badge.[7]

The image of Canadian police forces has in fact been tarnished on a number of occasions and in a variety of settings. These range from towns, cities, and entire provinces, to Canada as a whole. From this list, two places have been selected for more detailed study. These, it should be emphasized, are neither the only places in Canada where badges have been tarnished, nor are they necessarily the places where the most serious forms of tarnishing have occurred. The first place is the small town of Kentville, Nova Scotia, and the second is the large municipality of Metropolitan Toronto.

Police Misconduct: Kentville, Nova Scotia

Between July 25, 1983 and February 9, 1984, members of the Nova Scotia Police Commission (NSPC) met on twenty-one occasions to inquire into the Kentville Police Department. The initial reason for the inquiry was a request by Kentville's chief of police for an investigation into the "work and conduct" of his second-in-command, Sergeant Fred Young. As a result of the testimony of witnesses, the inquiry was broadened to include the whole police department.[8]

Kentville is a small town with a small police force. In addition to the chief of police, it averaged between 10 and 11 police officers during the period covered by the inquiry, 1978–1983. Kentville's police officers reported an average of 618 civilian offences per year for this five-year period. Only three percent of these were violent offences. Liquor and property offences accounted for almost 83 percent of the offences reported by the police. The offence caseload per police officer varied between 57 and 77 offences.

In the course of dealing with suspects, most of Kentville's police officers engaged in conduct prohibited by law or by departmental rules and regulations. One of the chief culprits was the chief himself, Allan McCrae. In addition to making "deliberately misleading" statements, the Commission found the chief had "showed extremely poor and unprofessional judgement" in verbally attacking a local town councillor (NSPC 1984, 139–140). Moreover, the Commission found that between August 1, 1978, when he became Kentville's police chief and July 25, 1983, when the inquiry began, over 30 complaints were made against one or more members of Kentville's police force. Included among these were complaints of racist remarks, assaults, and entrapment. Yet, Chief McCrae "had not disciplined any of his men for disciplinary defaults under the Code of Discipline in the regulations made under the Police Act" (NSPC 1984, 86–87, 139). Because they found "his conduct is such as not to satisfy the requirements of his position as Chief of Police," the Commission recommended that Chief Allan McCrae be fired or retired (NSPC 1984, 175).

Sergeant Fred Young, the chief's second-in-command, was not fired or retired. He was, however, reduced in rank from sergeant to corporal (NSPC 1984, 176). His conduct, the Commission found, "did not satisfy the requirements of his position as second-in-command" (NSPC 1984, 176). Although he had the authority to lay charges, Sgt. Young failed to discipline officers known to have engaged in prohibited conduct. Indeed, Sgt. Young appeared to be a "phantom sergeant." He had the rank of second-in–command but seemed unable or unwilling to discipline and lead the men under him. To members of the Commission, he gave the impression of being "an overweight, sloppily dressed individual who lacked leadership and supervisory capabilities" (NSPC 1984, 145).

If Sergeant Young was not a leader of men, the same thing cannot be said for Constable Murphy, a police officer "who has been the subject of much controversy in Kentville" (NSPC 1984, 147). Constable Murphy was a leader. His leadership was based partly on personal qualities and partly on his relationship with the chief of police. Chief McCrae had in fact undermined the authority of his official second-in-command and had replaced him with an unofficial second-in-command, Constable Murphy. There were more complaints about Murphy's conduct than for any other officer on Kentville's police force. He was, according to members of the Commission, "his own boss," a "law unto himself." The Commission recommended that Murphy be fired or retired (NSPC 1984, 176).

In addition to Sgt. Young and Constable Murphy, the town of Kentville employed an additional eight or nine police officers. Members of the Board of Inquiry found that five of these men had engaged in the conduct complained about by citizens to the Commission. Included among these complaints were assaults, entrapment, and the unauthorized use of Mace. In addition, most of the policemen on Kentville's police force appeared reluctant to tell the truth. At one point or another, most police officers testified before the Commission of Inquiry. A review of their testimony led to this conclusion: "With few exceptions, the Commission was disappointed in the quality of the evidence given by the police officers before the inquiry." Members of the Commission "expected that the evidence given by a police officer should always be frank, forthright, and factual" (NSPC 1984, 177). This expectation was not always met.

The misleading statements made by Kentville's police officers were associated with matters pertaining to the conduct of the inquiry itself and one or more of the 30 complaints received by the Commission. Nineteen of these complaints were reviewed, and eleven were found to be justified. These were made by twelve different citizens against seven of Kentville's eleven-member police force.

In sum, a review of the evidence presented in the *Report of the Inquiry into the Kentville Police Department* yields the following conclusions. First, a "rotten apple" explanation of police misconduct is not consistent with the Commission's findings. Instead of a "rotten apple" or two, most members of Kentville's police force made a contribution towards the darker side of the policing of Kentville.

Second, if we want to understand how an entire barrel can become rotten, we must investigate the behaviour of those who manage or supervise the work done by the "barrel." In the present case, the management of the Kentville police department by Chief McCrae and Sgt. Young helped produce police officers who felt that any means, rather than only legally authorized or proper means, could be used in carrying out their work.

Finally, chiefs of police and other officers in supervisory positions appear to be reluctant to find their subordinates guilty of misconduct because this would reflect poorly on them. In addition, various interest groups, including police associations, tend to get quite upset when supervisory officers accept the evidence of a civilian complainant over the word of police officers.[9]

One fairly recent solution to the problem of adequately regulating the behaviour of police officers is the creation of community control agencies such as police review commissions and public complaints commissioners. Creators of such agencies believe that citizen complaints would be more fully recorded and more frequently and fairly investigated if a civilian, a public complaints commissioner, was also given responsibility for hearing and processing them.

Police Deviance: Metropolitan Toronto

In Canada, Metropolitan Toronto was the first major city to create the office of Public Complaints Commissioner (PCC).[10] This office was created by provincial legislation.[11] The work to be done by the Commissioner and his staff was defined as a pilot project that was to last three years, from December 21, 1981 to December 1984. The project itself was established in order "to improve methods of processing complaints by members of the public against police officers on the Metropolitan Toronto Police Force."[12]

Prior to the establishment of the Complaints Project in 1981, citizens who wished to complain about the conduct of police officers in the Metro Toronto police force could do so only to a police officer. There was no civilian authorized to process their complaints. Following the creation of the Public Complaints Commissioner (PCC), citizens could also complain to a civilian empowered to review police investigations of citizen complaints, to conduct independent investigations, and to present the citizen's case to the Police Complaints Board. It is this Board that administers sanctions to police officers found guilty of the conduct complained about by the citizens whose cases are being heard.

The Commissioner's office also keeps fairly detailed statistics on citizen allegations of police misconduct and on the disposition of citizen complaints. What follows is not a record of the actual amount of various kinds of police misconduct among Metro Toronto's police officers, but a record of police deviance processed by the Public Complaints Commissioner's office.

During the first four years of its operation (1981–1985), the office of the PCC received 3 041 separate complaints or cases.[13] Any given complaint may contain one or more allegations of wrongdoing. The average number of allegations per complaint was two. Table 4-1 shows that almost two-thirds (63.0%) of these allegations involved physical or verbal aggression, or coercive threats. By contrast, corruption is rarely complained about. One reason for this may be that corruption is a "collusive crime," that is, one in which the citizen and the police officer both gain and for that reason agree to keep quiet about it. An example of a collusive crime would be the case of a police officer's accepting money or gratuity in return for not giving out a speeding ticket that would lead to an increase in the motorist's insurance premiums.

The total number of police officers whose behaviour was complained of between 1982 and 1985 was 3 650.[14] It should be noted that these statistics refer to neither the actual number of deviant police officers nor to the actual amount of police misconduct. They refer only to citizen complaints about officers alleged to have engaged in such misconduct.

On the average, the allegations described in each complaint referred to roughly two (1.9) officers.[15] Most complaints involved

TABLE **4-1** *Number of Allegations by Type*

Type of Complaint[a]	1982	1983	1984	1985	Total%[b]	
Assault	290	385	302	385	1 362	25.9
Verbal abuse/						
rudeness	291	356	291	289	1 277	23.3
Harassment/threats	184	222	158	161	725	13.8
Corruption	5	12	9	8	34	0.6
Other[c]	347	532	497	537	1 913	36.4
Total	1 117	1 507	1 257	1 380	5 261	100.0

Sources: Public Complaints Commissoner, Second Annual Report, Table 9; *Third Annual Report,* page 11; *Fourth Annual Report* (Toronto: Office of the Public Complaints Commissioner, 1983, 1984, 1985).

Notes: a. Any given complaint may contain one or more allegations. Therefore, one cannot assume that only 2 624 allegations were contained in 2 624 separate complaints.

b. These are percentages of allegations made in complaints.

c. Other includes unlawful arrest, unlawful search, deceit, intoxication, sexual harassment, irregularity in procedure, damage to property and traffic irregularity.

only one police officer. Specifically, 49.8 percent of the complaints fell into this category. This does not mean that only one officer was involved in the incident that generated the civilian complaint. One or more officers may have been present, but only one officer's behaviour was complained of in almost 55 percent of the recorded complaints.

As one might expect, Metro Toronto police officers vary in the number of years they have served as police officers.[16] Does experience as a police officer, as measured by years of service, have anything to do with the number of civilian complaints? Common sense suggests that experienced officers would receive proportionately fewer complaints because age and experience have taught them how to enforce the law without contravening departmental rules or the criminal law. This hypothesis is supported by the following finding: officers with less than five years of service constitute approximately seven percent of the uniformed police force and are mentioned in 28.4 percent of the civilian complaints. Officers with five or more years of police service constitute about 93 percent of the uniformed force and receive approximately 72 percent of civilian complaints.[17] The finding that less experienced officers receive a disproportionate number of complaints suggests that experience and civilian complaints stand in an inverse relation to each other. As experience increases, complaints decrease.[18]

In addition to years of service as a police officer, the kind of police work being done by the officer also appears to be associated with complaints. Table 4-2 indicates that the enforcement of laws and by-laws relating to traffic and criminal investigation account for almost two-thirds of all complaints. One fairly obvious reason for the relatively high proportion of complaints in the first category is the fact that police officers have many, many more contacts with highway code, parking and other traffic violators than they do with other kinds of offenders. Thus, the complaints are proportionate to the number of police-citizen/suspect contacts. The number of complaints lodged by civilian/suspects being investigated by the police may well be disproportionate to the number of police-suspect contacts, but the data needed to test this hypothesis was not available.

TABLE **4-2** *Number of complaints by Precipitating Situations*

Precipitating Situations	Complaints			
	1981	1982	Total	%
Traffic[a]	241	231	472	34.6
Criminal Investigation	159	260	419	30.7
Arrest	94	127	221	16.2
Interrogation	23	21	44	3.2
Request I.D.	16	12	28	2.0
Domestic	13	8	21	1.5
Other[b]	63	98	161	11.8
Total	609	757	1 366	100.0

Source: Public Complaints Commissioner, *Second Annual Report* (Toronto: Office of the Public Complaints Commissioner, 1983), Table 10, p. 58.
Notes: a. Includes violation and parking.
b. Includes by-law investigation, during court proceedings, landlord-tenant disputes, and "no apparent precipitating factor."

Although it accounts for only 3.2 percent of all complaints in Table 4-2, interrogation has, in the recent past, accounted for some of the most serious and persistent allegations of misconduct among Metro Toronto's police officers (PCC 1984b). The victims here were suspects looked upon by the police as hardened criminals. The same tactics may not be so readily used against nonprofessional criminals. In any case, the police do not usually have to rely on illegal methods of obtaining information requisite to obtaining a conviction in court. This is because The Canadian Charter of Rights and Freedoms and the courts have provided a legal context that does not appear to be all that great a hindrance to police investigations.[19] For example, the Charter would seem to guarantee the individual the legal right not to answer questions put to him or her by a police officer. However, the courts restrict this right to preliminary hearings and trials and to arrested persons. It does not apply to a suspect who has not been arrested but is simply being questioned by the police. Since the right not to answer is a common law right, a police officer need not inform the individual being questioned of this right (Haliechuk 1986). Again, Section 10(b) of the Charter gives the courts power to override even such fundamental freedoms as the right to talk to a lawyer (Sect. 1), when matters of demonstrable urgency are involved. For this reason and also because of the minor or technical nature of police violations against Charter provisions, Greenspon finds that "there has not been a single case involving a serious charge where the accused has walked out of the courtroom door during the first three years of the Charter's existence" (Greenspon 1986). Thus, law in the books (the Charter) as well as law in action (court decisions) continue to give the police fairly wide discretion in investigating crime. There really is no pressing need for the police to violate the law because the law in Canada is so accommodating to the reality of policing crime.

Going beyond neglect of legal rights, police officers assigned to the Metro Toronto hold-up squad were accused by a number of suspects of using violence and torture to obtain confessions from them. The torture referred to by some suspects was "dry submarining" (Henshel 1983, 43). Here, the suspect is handcuffed and his head is enclosed by a plastic bag. The opening of the bag is gradually tightened, suffocating the panic-stricken individual. This procedure is repeated until a confession is produced. The office of the Public Complaints Commissioner investigated 23 separate incidents of coercion, assaults and torture that hold-up squad officers were alleged to have engaged in between 1979 and 1981.[20]

Police Deviance: Canadian Provinces

The Public Complaints Commissioner is responsible only for processing complaints against members of Toronto's police force. Complaint data on police forces operating elsewhere in the province must come from other sources. These sources do not publish the relevant statistics. One of the very few published accounts of police misconduct in other jurisdictions in Ontario was provided by the Canadian Civil Liberties Association (CCLA) in 1971 (CCLA 1971). One of the Ontario communities policed by the Ontario Provincial Police and singled out for an inquiry was Kenora. The investigation by CCLA staff was carried out at the request of the Lake-of-the-Woods Pow Wow Club. During the one week CCLA staff were in Kenora, they received "more than 20 affidavits . . . in which native people related stories of alleged improprieties committed by certain members of both the Ontario Provincial Police and local police" (CCLA 1971). The improprieties referred to included "entering homes without knocking," "the application of physical force," "feeling a woman's chest to determine whether liquor was hidden there" and "lifting a woman's dress up over her head . . . in front of other people."

Allegations of police misconduct are not confined to municipal and provincial police forces. Recurring complaints have also been made about the conduct of members of Canada's federal police force, the Royal Canadian Mounted Police. Major sources of information on Mountie deviance are the *Commission d'enquête sur des operations policiers en territoire Québécoise* (Keable Commission 1975) and the *Royal Commission of Inquiry into Certain Activities of the Royal Canadian Mounted Police* (McDonald Commission 1977).

MOUNTIE MISCONDUCT   The word misconduct, as it has been used to this point in the chapter, is a euphemistic way of referring to various forms of police deviance, including criminal deviance. According to testimony presented to the Keable and McDonald commissions (and reported in Dion 1982), Mountie crimes include arson, kidnapping, obstructing justice, perjury, blackmail, burglary, theft, bombing, disseminating information known to be false, entering premises without a search warrant and intimidation. In addition, the Mounties have illegally intercepted and opened mail and have obtained confidential unemployment, health insurance, and income tax information. If we focus only on crimes committed by officers in Quebec between 1971 and 1978 and reported in the Keable Commission Report, then we discover that over 25 different RCMP officers, varying in rank from superintendent to corporal, engaged in the commission of offences that could have resulted in an average penitentiary sentence of about five years per officer.[21]

When the RCMP were responsible for national security, any Canadian resident could become a victim of Mountie crimes. But not all Canadian residents or groups of them seem to merit the same degree of Mountie attention. Early in their history the RCMP singled out native people and striking workers for special attention (Brown and Brown 1973). Since the 1960s, a fair proportion of RCMP resources has been devoted to reducing drug-related offences. During the 1970s, a great deal of attention was devoted to dealing with radical or separatist francophone groups in Quebec. In 1971, a special section, G-section, was established in Quebec, with its headquarters in Montreal. The primary objective of this section was "counter-terrorism." G-section remained in existence only from 1971 to 1977, but in that time it established such a reputation for illegal conduct that some students of the Mounties wondered whether RCMP terrorism was any better than the alleged terrorism the Mounties were attempting to combat (Sawadsky 1980; Mann and Lee 1979).

For example, the Keable Commission heard testimony concerning the writing of a false communique by two RCMP officers (Dion 1982, 123). This communique, made to appear as if it had been written by the FLQ,[22] urged the people of Quebec to engage in acts of sedition and terrorism. On another occasion, plans were made for the arrest of innocent people who just happened to be in the vicinity of the premises of the Agence de Presse Libre du Québec while it was being broken into and burglarized by members of the RCMP, the Quebec Provincial Police, and the Montreal Urban Community Police Department. On still another occasion, an RCMP corporal burned down a barn when the RCMP discovered that they could not bug a planned meeting there between Quebec activists and the Black Panthers. Burning the barn was one way of preventing the meeting (Dion 1982, 76).

The illegal activities of members of Montreal's G-section were not isolated events. Rather, they were routinely engaged in by Mounties who saw themselves as loyal officers who "operated by fear, coercion, and blackmail" because their superior officers whose job was to protect national security had authorized them to do whatever was necessary to combat terrorism in Quebec (Dion 1982, 113). In relying on illegal means of conducting war on groups alleged to be terrorists, the RCMP were joined by members of two other police forces, the Montreal Urban Community Police Department and the Quebec Provincial Police.

In 1984, responsibility for surveillance on Canadian residents was shifted from the RCMP to a civilian agency, the Canadian Security Intelligence Service (CSIS). This civilian agency is supervised by the Security Intelligence Review Committee. In June 1985, the Chairperson of this committee reported that civilian intelligence agents were still tapping phones, opening mail, and bugging the homes of Canadian citizens, just as their RCMP predecessors had done. The major difference is that these activities are now done "only when they are absolutely necessary, and then always in accordance with the law." This means only after obtaining a warrant from a federal judge. Unlike their RCMP predecessors, agents employed by the CSIS appear to be much more law abiding (Harris 1985, 8).

Prior to 1983, G-section was part of the Security Service Branch of the RCMP. Approximately twenty percent of the force's police officers worked in one or other of the ten or eleven sections that made up this branch. The remainder worked in the Criminal Investigation Branch. Among these "regular" Mounties, those on the Drug Squad have achieved a certain degree of notoriety for their unwillingness to be constrained by the law in obtaining convictions. According to ex-Mountie James Hunt, the beating of suspects happened fairly frequently.[23] The major reason for Mountie violence against drug addicts and dealers was "to speed up investigations." Mountie reliance on force and fraud was, for both the Drug Squad and Montreal's G-section, an effective way of obtaining informers. The use of informers was a fairly reliable way of obtaining convictions and, more generally, of disrupting the work of those attacking the "moral fibre" of Canada, or its national security.

In sum, the evidence on police deviance presented here indicates at least four things. First, it is a recurring pattern of activity and not an isolated phenomenon. Second, police officers who are in administrative or supervisory positions condone illegal conduct by the officers in their charge by not doing more to investigate and regulate such conduct. Third, police officers often justify their illegal behaviour by referring to their "good intentions." Finally, illegal behaviour by police officers is widely distributed across Canada.[24]

Regulation of Police Deviance: Metropolitan Toronto

In 1983, civilian complaints against 1 062 Metro Toronto police officers were brought to the attention of the Chief of Police. Five percent (54) were disciplined.[25] More specifically, 26 were "counselled and/or cautioned"; ten were "advised/spoken to"; 14 were charged under the Police Act, and four were charged under the Criminal Code.[26] Put another way, we discover that no action was taken against 1 008 or 94 percent of the officers complained about by civilians.[27]

Of the 1 062 officers whose cases were disposed of by the Chief of Police, 69 or roughly six percent were also reviewed by the Public Complaints Commissioner (PCC).[28] In 44 (64 percent) of these cases the Commissioner decided that no further action was warranted. Another eight officers had their cases closed because the complainants withdrew their complaints.[29] Seven cases were informally resolved. Here the officers and complainant(s) were satisfied that the matter had been satisfactorily dealt with and had signed a form to this effect. In five more cases the Commissioner felt that it was not in the public interest to convene a hearing of the Police Complaints Board. No reasons for this decision were offered. Finally, hearings were convened in five cases. Thus, seven percent of the 69 cases resulted in a hearing by the Police Complaints Board. The outcomes of these hearings were not available because they had not yet been completed.[30]

To sum up: in 1983, the Chief of Police of Metropolitan Toronto disposed of complaints against 1062 officers. Five percent or 54 officers were subjected to some form of disciplinary action. In 69 cases, complainants requested a review by the PCC. Seven percent or five of these officers were to have appeared before the Police Complaints Board and were, therefore, subject to the possibility of disciplinary action.

During the same year, the Public Complaints Commissioner began an investigation into 23 separate complaints against police officers assigned to the hold-up squad. In March 1984, the Commissioner published the results of his investigation (PCC 1984b). In 12 cases, the investigation did not get very far because the complainants did not wish it to. Some of them felt this way because they were already doing time in a penal institution and "feared that lodging a complaint would jeopardize their prospects for parole." One complainant had left the country. Another was advised by his lawyer not to pursue the matter. Of the remaining 11 cases that were fully investigated, the Commissioner found five cases in which "there is insufficient evidence to substantiate the allegations made." In the remaining six cases, the Commissioner found "significant discrepancies in officers' testimonies at trial and . . . an inability to account for their whereabouts at relevant times." These cases were referred to the senior Crown counsel. This individual came to the conclusion that "there was insufficient evidence of a trustworthy nature on which to base a criminal charge" (PCC 1984b, 13). The end result of all this investigative activity was that none of the police officers mentioned in the 23 original complaints was proceeded against to the point of appearing before a judge or members of the Public Complaints Board.[31]

Reactions to the very low rate of conviction indicated by these statistics come from three major groups. For the first group, the police and their supporters, they accurately reflect the reality of policing. Most police officers do behave in legally authorized ways most of the time. In and of themselves, civilian complaints are not an accurate measure of police misconduct, because the kinds of people whom police arrest use such allegations either to get back at officers or to set up a bargaining situation in which a complaint will be withdrawn in return for a reduction in the number or seriousness of the charges laid against the complainant. Section 24 of the Charter of Rights and Freedoms will, according to police officers and Crown attorneys, only increase the number of false or frivolous civilian complaints (see Mackintosh, n.19 above). When it does occur, police misconduct, for this group, is largely caused by inexperience.

Into the second group fall the office of the Public Complaints Commissioner and its supporters. The reactions of this group emphasize the legal status of the police officer and Chief of Police, the legal criteria upon which conviction and punishment must be based and the practical considerations that must be taken into account by any regulative agency, including theirs.

Treating each of these points in the order in which they are mentioned, it is relevant to note first that policing in Canada has been markedly influenced by case law in both Britain and Canada. One very significant case-law contribution has to do with the definition of a police officer's job in Canada. The definition that seems to be taught in police colleges all over Canada was offered by Viscount Simonds:

> "There is a fundamental difference between the domestic relation of servant and master and that of the holder of a public office and the state which he is said to serve. The constable falls within the latter category. His authority is original, not delegated, and is exercised at his own discretion by virtue of his office: he is a ministerial officer exercising statutory rights independently of contract.[32]

This widely accepted definition of the police officer's legal status limits the ability of his superiors, including the Chief of Police, to regulate the exercise of discretion by the officer on the beat. In turn, the legal status of the Chief of Police is such that "No Minister of the Crown can tell him that he must, or must not, keep observation on this place or that; or that he must, or must not, prosecute this man or that one. . . . The responsibility for law enforcement lies on him. He is answerable to the law and to the law alone."[33] This means that neither politicians nor members of various interest groups have a legal basis for attempting to regulate the exercise of discretion by police chiefs. Only the courts can do this.

Second, the sanctions or punishments that are meted out by the police chief or Public Complaints Board are those that may be legally administered by a labour relations tribunal. These sanctions are usually job-related. Sometimes the sanctions involve a loss of wages. In other cases, reprimands are given. These may be included in the officer's personal file. However the burden of proof required before these sanctions can be applied is not a tribunal criterion, "weight of his evidence," but a much more stringent *criminal* burden of proof. A criminal burden of proof is proof "beyond a reasonable doubt."[34] Much of the work of police officers is "low visibility" work. That is, only the officers and suspects are present. In the absence of independent witnesses who can corroborate complainant testimony, this level of proof is very difficult to achieve. Also relevant here is the fact that complaints are lodged after a fairly lengthy time lag. This makes it even more difficult to secure the requisite proof.[35]

Third, with respect to practical considerations to be taken into account, the Public Complaints Commissioner is well aware of the criticisms made against a community control agency that has to rely on police officers to investigate civilian complaints against other police officers. A principle of natural justice — no person shall be a judge in a case in which he or his group has an interest — would appear to be breached. Yet, Commissioner Linden points out that police co-operation could only be effectively secured if they were permitted to play a part in investigating complaints made against them. Without real police co-operation, the work of the Complaints Commission would be greatly hindered. Practical considerations then, made it necessary for the police to be allowed to investigate civilian complaints. The police are experienced investigators and complainant who did not like the results of their work, could ask for a review.

The third group reacting to the 1984 report of the Public Complaints Commissioner includes the Canadian Civil Liberties Association, the Toronto-based Citizen's Independent Review of Police Activities (CIRPA) and their supporters. Members of CIRPA tend to draw attention to the lawlessness of the police and the contribution made to this outcome by the fact that police officers themselves investigate and adjudicate each other (Henshel 1983). In this arrangement, they discern a built-in bias towards poorly-conducted investigations of civilian complaints and a reluctance to take the appropriate disciplinary action even in those few cases in which police officers are found guilty of misconduct.

One way in which CIRPA attempted to substantiate its allegations was to point to the result of an investigation undertaken by a well-respected, independent observer, Donald Morand. Morand is an Ontario Supreme Court Justice who chaired a royal commission that inquired into a number of allegations of brutality by Metro Toronto police officers that were reported in the *The Globe and Mail* and the *The Toronto Star* during the early months of 1975. In 1976, Morand published a report in which he reached the following conclusion:

> The allegations were of the most serious nature. They demand swift, complete and impartial investigation. . . . The (police) investigation which was done was totally and hopelessly inadequate . . . an effort was made to dissuade (the complaining civilian) from pursuing the complaint (Morand 1976, 174 and 176).

Also cited by CIRPA are the comments made by County Court Judge Ted Matlow. Before him were three people charged with conspiracy to commit burglary. They had been charged by five police officers. Thirty-one fellow officers were called as witnesses. The three accused were acquitted because Judge Matlow "had strong doubts about the reliability of the evidence" provided by some of these men.[36] In this connection, Justice Morand had noted that one of the most disturbing things that had come out in the hearings held before him was "the extent to which I found the evidence of police officers mistaken, shaded, deliberately misleading, changed to suit the circumstances and sometimes entirely and deliberately false" (1976, 177).

Finally, CIRPA members cite the Murdock Case. A complaint was made by one Robert Smith against Constable Murdock. Smith alleged that Murdock had punched and kicked him a number of times after he had refused to provide a breath sample at a police station on January 26, 1984. The complaint was being heard by the Police Complaints Board. Brian Grosman, chairperson of the Board, wanted to know: (a) why it took five months after the incident occurred for the complaint to reach him; (b) why police officers did not question a civilian who may have witnessed the incident; (c) why the complainant was deported two months after he lodged a complaint of police brutality against Murdock and (d) why the police had assigned Constable Murdock to investigate the charge against himself (Henton, 1985, 13). The Complaints Board found Murdock guilty of police misconduct. He is (1986) appealing this verdict.[37]

On the basis of the evidence presented here, we may conclude that police deviance is not effectively controlled by either the police bureaucracy itself or by more-or-less independent regulative agencies such as civilian-run complaints boards.[38] Perhaps it would be more accurate to say that police deviance *is* as effectively regulated as politicians, property owners and most of the Canadian public want it to be.

PERSPECTIVES ON POLICE DEVIANCE

Although the theories described in the pages that follow differ from each other in a number of ways, all of them share an opposition to the "rotten apple" theory of deviance usually offered by the police themselves. The police in Canada appear to be highly regarded by themselves, the media and the public. Behind the positive attributions and evaluations lies a "good apple" theory. Central to this theory is the idea that policing in Canada is done well because the individuals who become police officers are high-quality people. In addition to being taller and larger, they are more honest, brave, law-abiding and loyal to their country than most of us. Quality police officers or "good apples" make a good police force. In every large basket of applies one must expect to find a few bad ones. These few "bad apples" are responsible for most of the illegal behaviour that tarnishes the image of Canadian police forces as a whole.

This psychological theory of conformity and deviance stands in sharp contrast to the sociological theories of police deviance presented in this chapter. Central to these theories is the emphasis on the *social* determinants of police deviance. Sociologists usually refer to police deviance as being socially structured by such factors as the presence of laws and departmental rules, the presence of groups in society that want the police to perform opposing tasks and the influence of police peer groups. The difference between "structured" and "bad apple" deviance is clearly revealed in the following statement:

> When sociologists find that a set of social conditions are so arranged that the people involved are virtually pushed into frequent deviant behaviour, they speak of "structured deviance." Such deviant acts are apparently less the product of conscious choice by the actors involved, than of the structure of their work and social lives. A parallel may be found in the example of a street corner that is the scene of repeated auto accidents. Eventually someone realizes that the problem is not just a series of careless drivers but a badly designed intersection (Mann 1981, 3).

Sociologists, generally, tend to focus on the intersection or the interaction between intersection and drivers, not on drivers as individuals. In the same way, sociologists who study police deviance emphasize its *social* inducements and not the deviant psychological states of a very small number of officers. The conditions under which police officers work invite all police officers to engage in various deviant acts. Very few accept this invitation because they are sadists or psychopaths; most are normal men and women whose occupational behaviour is structured or shaped by conditions existing within the organization, the specific community of which it is a part, and in society as a whole.

Strain-subcultural Theories

Central to strain-subcultural explanations of police deviance is the image of police officers as insufficiently appreciated, frustrated law enforcers. Their job is to enforce the law of the land. Yet, the Charter of Rights and Freedoms, civil and criminal law, Judge's Rules, police rules, the courts and civil libertarians make it difficult to enforce the law effectively, that is, in such a way as to reduce crime. At the same time, the public does not understand police work, cannot always be relied upon to help police officers, and does not really award them the status their dangerous and important job warrants. The police subculture emerges as a reaction to these varied sources of frustration or strain. Its primary function is to reduce strain by providing alternative, peer-supported ways of achieving personal and organizational objectives.[39] Strain-induced, peer-supported practices include perjury, corruption, and violence.

McGill University sociologist Willam Westley was primarily interested in explaining the illegal or unauthorized use of violence by the police (1970).[40] During their official or formal training, police officers learn that the legal use of physical force is restricted to self-defence, making an arrest, and protecting innocent citizens. They are told that the penalties for the unauthorized use of force include dismissal from the force, and criminal and civil sanctions. Yet, Westley learned that almost 70 percent of the 73 incidents of police violence he discovered were justified on unauthorized or illegal grounds.

Why would police officers so frequently engage in conduct that could have them fired, jailed, or that could entail the payment of substantial sums of money to their victims? The answer, according to Westley, is that in the perceptions of police officers, the rewards for using violence in an instrumental, calculated manner are more immediate, certain, and greater than are the rewards for obeying the law or the penalties for breaking it.

These perceptions are nourished, first, by the occupational subculture of the police, and second, by the perceived connection between using violence and the realization of objectives approved of by the public and central to a definition of a valued police role.

A subculture is a collective solution to a problem. The problems of the police stem from the nature of their job. Employed in a service occupation, the police must discipline and punish the citizens they serve. This leads to resentment on the part of the public and the isolation of the police from civilians. Police officers regard their job as dangerous. They see themselves defined as outcasts by civilians. Reacting to and building upon their social isolation, they form occupational sub-communities characterized by an extreme emphasis on secrecy and loyalty. With the suppport of secret and loyal colleagues, it becomes easier to coerce respect from those who are unwilling to give police the respect their calling deserves. The occupational subculture of the police, then, solves the problems of social isolation, lack of respect and legal restrictions in fighting crime effectively (Sherman 1974, 196–205).

One way of fighting crime effectively is by making "good pinches." A good pinch involves making an arrest in such a way as to secure the conviction of an individual who is suspected of having committed a major offence or series of major offences. Good pinches, according to Westley (1970, 36), represent one major way of simultaneously obtaining respect for the occupation, promotion for the officer and prestige from colleagues. Obtaining confessions from suspects is a reliable way of making certain kinds of good pinches. Police officers find that violence can be usefully employed in the service of eliciting confessions from suspects and information from informers.[41]

Under certain more-or-less clearly-defined conditions, the police are legally authorized to use force. The strain-subcultural explanations offered by Westley (1970) and Reiss (1968) describe how and why violence is expanded from its legitimate to its illegitimate use. In the process, they also convey the idea that police subcultural norms condoning illegal and/or unethical ways of policing are accepted and acted upon by all police officers, or most of them. Clifford Shearing's work is important because it points to *variations within* the police subculture.

As is true of people in other occupations, the behaviour of police officers is rule guided. According to Shearing, police officers are placed in a difficult or stressful situation because the two major sets of rules used as guides for their behaviour sometimes stand in a contradictory relation to each other. In other words, official police departmental rules say one thing (illegal actions must be reported to supervisory officers) while unofficial police subcultural rules say another (keep secrets, be loyal to your peers). Based upon their interpretations of and reactions to both sets of rules, Shearing constructed a typology of roles, "real officers," "good officers" and "cautious officers" (Shearing 1981a).

Good officers tend to be influenced least by police subcultural norms that conflict with official ones. At the other end of the continuum stand "real" officers. These are described as "hard-nosed." Police officers who deviate from legal and departmental rules are most likely to be found in this group. Real officers are also likely to be most influenced by police subcultural norms.

If work-related problems or occupationally-induced strain helps explain the origin and functioning of police subcultures, we learn from Shearing that these subcultures are not homogeneous. Instead, there are important variations within them. Also contributing to variations in police conformity and deviance is the kind of work in which officers are engaged. Some kinds of police work are more criminogenic, are more likely to be guided by deviance-inducing peer-group norms. In this connection, the distinction between "reactive" and "proactive" policing is relevant.

When citizens provide information to police officers about an alleged crime and the police investigate or react in some other way to this informaton, they are engaged in reactive policing. By contrast, proactive policing occurs when the police themselves attempt to discover and solve crimes by going undercover, using informers, wire tapping and surveillance. According to estimates, only 20 percent of police work is proactive (Black 1968).

A major locus of proactive policing is drug law enforcement. Drug offences are sometimes referred to as "victimless" or collusive crimes because the dealer, runner and user all have an interest in keeping their crimes a secret. Moreover, the dealer — the primary target of the police — is insulated from detection by various intermediaries. Finally, importing drugs and dealing them are activities that are not ordinarily visible to police officers routinely patrolling their beats. Detective work is usually a prerequisite to a good drug pinch. Given these conditions, "good" detective work frequently involves drug dealing by detectives, supplying drugs or immunity from arrest to addicts, blackmailing addicts and so on.

In an article entitled "The Invitational Edges of Corruption," Peter Manning and Lawrence Redlinger (1976) describe in some detail the criminogenic environment of narcotic law enforcement. Organizational and community pressures, pressures to "do something about the drug problem," are associated with recurring patterns of police corruption. To be an effective police detective is to accept the invitation to tell lies, to frame, threaten, and beat-up lower-level drug offenders in order to get the major drug dealers.

Crimes involving drugs, as well as robberies, are usually investigated by detectives who are under considerable departmental and community pressure to solve them. Because neither police super-ordinates nor citizens are present during the conduct of most investigations, detective work is less visible than is the work of patrol officers. Also, the suspects they work upon are often experienced crooks. They may well be members of a criminal subculture that severely punishes "snitches." These facts, plus the influence of a "detective subculture" (Ericson 1981), help explain much of the deviance discovered in Toronto's hold-up squad.

Central to the strain-subcultural explanations of police deviance described here is the idea that fighting serious crime is the core of the police officer's job and that doing a good job sometimes means having to break the law. Doing a good job also means instilling in members of social groups regarded as "police property" (the young, the poor, members of certain ethnic minority groups, homosexuals) a certain respect for the police and the law from which they derive their authority.

In sum, the societal and organizational context responsible for the acceptance of this idea of policing includes the following:

- a definition of the role of the police in which crime fighting is central;
- legal and departmental rules inhibiting the effective realization of this objective;
- the ambiguous relation between legal rules and the behaviour they are supposed to regulate;[42]
- the absence of supervisory police officers or civilian witnesses when rank-and-file police officers exercise their discretionary authority, which makes it difficult to obtain corroborative evidence;
- the reluctance of senior administrative police officers to conduct investigations that might tarnish the image of the force for which they are responsible;
- the reliance by senior administrators on strictly legal criteria when processing citizen complaints about police conduct;
- peer (subcultural) group support for police decisions and actions that are illegal or that deviate from departmental rules, but that tend to achieve career, occupational, and law enforcement objectives more effectively.

The concurrence of these conditions helps to create and maintain a strain-reducing, criminogenic subculture for members of an occupational group that is legally responsible for enforcing the law and who define crime fighting as their primary objective. The presence of these contextual conditions in a number of societies partly explains why "almost everywhere the police tend to assume

powers not granted them by law, to overstep regulations"
(Radzinowicz and King 1977, 185).

Control Theories

Social control theories of police deviance are held by two major
groups of sociologists. Included in the first group are those primarily interested in explaining variations in *conformity* among
police officers; police deviance they take for granted. They would
make the same assumption if they were studying choirboys or
nuns. The second group includes those interested in the police as
deviants. Taking conformity for granted, they want to explain
variations in the amount and nature of police *deviance*. What
members of both groups share is the belief that the relative *absence*
of effective social control by conventional authorities, institutions
and publics is a factor or variable that must be included in an
adequate theory of police conformity and/or deviation. Specifically, this idea is evident in Hirschi's social control theory.[43]

As indicated earlier in the text (Chapter 2), Hirschi's bond theory
is highly regarded in some circles because its major hypotheses
have been confirmed by empirical research findings. Such a happy
outcome is not as likely to obtain when and if his theory is applied
to the topic of police deviance. Some important modifications may
be necessary if bond theory is to become adequate to the task of
explaining variations in police conformity.

This conclusion is based on the following considerations. In
bond theory, being alone and being deviant go together. In contrast to loners, gregarious people are more likely to be conformist.
However, among police officers, deviance and peer-group attachments seem to be associated. Put another way, police officers who
are most strongly attached to the police subculture are most influenced by it and are also least likely to conform with legal and
departmental rules.

Another example. For Hirschi, a high stake in conformity and
conforming behaviour go together. Police officers do have a high
stake in conformity. Their reputation as being more law abiding
and honest than the average citizen is necessary for them to obtain
and keep their jobs. Yet, a high stake in conformity and deviance
appear to go together. This is what one must conclude on the basis
of evidence that suggests that deviance is endemic to police work
(Box 1983). Presumably, this means that conformity is at least as
low among police officers as it is among those with a much lower
stake in conformity, i.e., the young, the uneducated and the poor.

To conclude that bond theory, as formulated by Hirschi, does not adequately explain police conformity, is not to say either that a modified version would not be adequate or that the process of social control is irrelevant to an understanding of police deviance. The inclusion of peer-group and situational pressures is clearly relevant to understanding the relation between social control and police deviance, because conformity with legal and departmental rules is punished by peers. In sum, the *presence* of effective peer-group control is associated with the relative absence of conformity with other people's rules.

Actually, when the consequences can be very serious for police officers, other people's rules do seem to be effective in regulating police behaviour, regardless of the strength of peer-group attachments. The "other people's rules" being referred to here are rules relating to the use of firearms. Thus, most U.S. states have a "fleeing felon" statute. This legally authorizes a police officer to use deadly force to capture unarmed suspects who are fleeing from non-violent but serious, i.e., felonious, crimes. Within these states, communities vary with respect to the firearms policy adopted by their police departments. Those with the tightest or strictest firearms policies have the lowest rates of police shootings. Moreover, when police shootings do occur in these communities, they are more likely to occur in an effort to defend lives than to prevent or terminate crimes (Fyfe 1982; Lundman 1985).

One of the two major variables included in deterrence theories of police deviance is a concern with the seriousness of the consequences for rule violations. The other is the probability of these consequences actually being applied to the deviant. Other things being equal, the more certain, swiftly applied, harsh, and public the punishments for police deviance, the lower the likelihood of its occurrence. Publicity ensures that the deterrent effect operates at both the individual and general levels. Having identified the ideal set of conditions under which punishments will effectively deter police deviance, most deterrence theorists then confine themselves to explaining why punishment does not effectively deter the specific kind of deviance they are investigating (Pepinsky 1980).

In the case of police deviance, this takes the form of pointing to the opportunities for deviance, the fact that police work often takes place under conditions of "low visibility," that supervisors are not really interested in catching and punishing police deviants because it reflects poorly on them and so on. Taken together, these occupational conditions deter official discovery. Therefore, the issue of swift and certain official punishment does not arise. Most importantly, punishment, far from being certain, is certainly rarely applied (see Box 1983; Ericson 1981; Sherman 1974).

Finally, among deterrence theorists, it is possible to identify two orientations. In one, attention is directed to the organizational matrix of rewards, punishments, their interactions and perceived probabilities. Viewing this matrix as a Skinner Box dispensing rewards and punishments, their concern is with why the Box does not work properly. They are not all that interested in why the Box was constructed the way it was in the first place. Why, in other words, does it rarely dispense punishments for police deviance? The second group of theorists is interested in this question.

Although he is not a deterrence theorist, a good example of this second orientation is provided by Reiner (1978). Reiner's major point is that the police hierarchy is not adequately controlled and therefore does not have to worry too much about its failure to control subordinates. This occurs because policing is relatively autonomous from the state. The state, the government and the political and economic interests towards which it is biased need to know that they can rely on the police to effectively control their domestic adversaries. The price of reliable police support was police autonomy from political/civilian control. In sum, we get the ineffective kind of policing we deserve, because we get the kind of government we deserve.[44]

Interactionist Theories

Interactionist accounts of police deviance cover a variety of topics.[45] Three of these are selected for closer examination. The first has to do with the *transition* from occasional to career deviant. The second, full of irony, shows how police efforts to control citizen deviance actually increase it. This happens, not because of labelling, but because of the dynamics of interaction itself. The third topic focusses on the intentional efforts of police detectives to produce crimes and criminals. By and large, detectives do what they intend to do by interpreting and using rules in legal ways. They also engage in illegal conduct because it helps them achieve personal and organizational objectives with less hassle.

SELF-LABELLING: THE GRASSEATER TO MEATEATER TRANSITION
According to Sherman (1974, 196–205), the best predictor of whether or not a rookie policeman will engage in corrupt practices (grafting) is the presence or absence of grafting, of corrupt peers in the division or precinct to which he is assigned. Within such a division, grafting police officers fall into two major groups. The first consists of "grasseaters." These are "reactive" police deviants. These officers react in deviant ways to opportunities that become

available. Thus, a bribe is offered, and they accept it. A stereo is left behind by robbers, and the investigating officer captures it for himself.

"Meateaters," the second group, do not confine their crooked ways to taking advantage of available opportunities. They actually create opportunities. Thus, not content with accepting bribes, they move on to extortion, to demanding money by threat of harm. Again, instead of waiting around for civilian robbers to do their work, meateaters plan and carry out robberies themselves.

Sherman conceives of meateaters as secondary deviants. Compared with grasseaters, they engage in more serious deviant practices more frequently. Moreover, they may also have gone beyond the limits of tolerable deviation set by their own peers. In other words, they are "double deviants," having violated both the law and peer subcultural norms. Of course, not all grasseaters become meateaters. In Lemert's (1951) interactionist account, differential social control reactions explain why some do and others don't. By contrast, Sherman (1974, 198) calls upon self-labelling "without the intervention of (another) agent of control" to explain the transition. For some reason, perhaps because of an unusually large bribe, some officers feel "there is no turning back now," label themselves as crooks and go on to be full-time police crooks. Although Sherman does not suggest it, the more obvious source of change in self-identity from police officer to crook is the gradual change in the frequency and nature of police grafting itself.

SOCIAL CONTROL: IRONICAL EFFECTS AND POLICE DEVIANCE
Ironical effects are effects or consequences that are directly opposite to those that a given action or process was intended to produce. The police deviants referred to here are secondary deviants, but they are secondary in a way that differs from Lemert's conception. Specifically, they are secondary deviants because their actions have the unintended effect of causing deviance or of increasing its frequency and seriousness.

One of the most novel accounts of how authorities create new forms of deviance while attempting to control others, we shall call "Heroin, Methadone and the Pee (urine) Market."[46] When he was President, Richard Nixon did a number of things designed to increase his job security. One of these involved taking the advice of conservative Harvard criminologist, James Q. Wilson (1975), on how to solve the drug problem by controlling heroin addiction. Methadone, a drug that gave roughly the same "high" as heroin but that did not possess its nasty addictive quality, would be dispensed to heroin addicts as part of a Methadone Maintenance

Program. Heroin addicts would come to the clinic, take a urine test (on a random basis) and, if *the urine contained no heroin*, methadone would be freely given. In time, heroin addicts would be weaned away from heroin to methadone and, as methadone was non-addictive, they could soon be taken off methadone.

What Wilson did not know was that methadone was, in fact, addictive and that its effects were as potentially lethal as those associated with heroin use. Also, when mixed with other, cheaper substances, it gave off a "good high." Soon, methadone was being distributed for sale on the streets. In order to obtain methadone for dealing, heroin addicts would buy "clean" i.e., heroin-free urine, place this in the little bottle at the clinic and obtain their supply of methadone. Conversely, those who were now addicted to methadone, but could not get enough to sell and/or use, would buy "dirty" i.e., heroin-contaminated urine. This they would take to different clinics, put it in the little pee bottle and show it to clinic personnel to prove they were heroin addicts. They would then start receiving a supply of methadone. The end result was a flourishing drug trade in both heroin and methadone. In addition, the excitement of "beating the man" and his random pee tests gave addict clinic-users an additional high (Silberman 1978).

In this account, the social control efforts of authorities escalated the drug problem. Escalation is one of the three "ironies of social control" identified by Gary Marx (1981). The other two are non-enforcement and covert facilitation. Marx focusses on "the behaviour of social control agents before or during rule breaking" (1981, 222). As an example of escalation, Marx points to "police riots." These occur when police actions intended to contain or regulate a peaceful crowd turn this crowd into a rioting mob. Another example he cites is high-speed chases: "In a Boston suburb, a car being chased by two police officers . . . killed a foot patrolman. The young driver was subsequently charged not only with speeding but with manslaughter" (1981, 224).

Covert facilitation refers to getting someone to violate the law, a practice facilitated by law and police department policy. Entrapment (placing police officers in public washrooms to encourage approaches by homosexuals) is one major form of covert facilitation. Another involves the use of decoys. For example, the police are interested in reducing the number of muggings in their community. They see a drunk sleeping in his car. They wake him and tell him to go home. He starts off. They follow waiting for him to be attacked, then they arrest his attacker.

In the case of non-enforcement, the contribution made by police officers to criminal deviance is, according to Marx, "more indirect" than either covert facilitation or escalation (1981, 226). A good example of non-enforcement is that of a vice squad detective who permits an informant to continue to use and distribute prohibited drugs in exchange for information concerning a major drug supplier. In time, the informant, permitted to use and distribute small quantities of drugs, may himself become a major supplier through supplying information to the police against his competitors.

DETECTING CRIME AS DIRTY WORK   In his study of the Dutch police, Maurice Punch defines the interactionist approach to policing in the following terms: "People working within this paradigm emphasize the extent to which social life is fragile, negotiated and in a constant process of construction in interaction with others" (Punch 1985, 2). Men act in situations "because they are busily assessing, evaluating, interpreting, defining, revising and, most basically, symbolizing the situation to themselves."[47] A good example of work within the interactionist paradigm is Richard Ericson's *Making Crime* (1981).

According to Ericson (1981), detectives are essentially bureaucrats. Highly rule-conscious, the interpretation and use of legal, organizational and subcultural rules is central of their bureaucratic role. Their orientation towards these rules is essentially pragmatic. That is to say, they interpret and use rules in such a way as to help them get through their working day with relative ease, while still making progress towards their publicly-defined objective of capturing criminals. Their personal goal is to use the rules in such a way as to be able to justify to their superiors that what they did did not violate rules for which they could be held legally and/ or organizationally accountable.

Detectives are bureaucrats, but they are bureaucrats with a will. They are not malleable, not hollow persons whose behaviour is completely determined by rules. Instead, Ericson sees them as choosy bureaucrats. In his words, "they have an interpretative capacity, able to take into account organizational influences in the formulation of action that reflects these influences" (1981, 209). The choices they do make are structured or influenced by the law, the police department, their peers and the wider community. In addition to the vagueness of many laws, vagueness that permits a great deal of interpretative leeway, their job confers on them a high degree of autonomy, of freedom to pursue organizational and personal objectives. On some occasions, they use their occupational autonomy to make choices that are criminally deviant. One good example of a deviant choice is the illegal practice of "left-handing" search warrants.[48]

Together with interrogations, searches are an important part of the process of producing or making crimes out of incidents and criminals out of persons in organizationally defensible ways. Under ordinary circumstances, a detective who wishes to search the home of an individual must obtain a search warrant signed by a justice of the peace. A JP's signature ensures its legality. Usually a JP signs a search warrant when the detective identifies the "reasonable and probable" grounds upon which his request is based. Specifically, detectives must convince the JP's that they have reasonable and probable grounds for believing that the evidence they are looking for is in the place they wish to search. Most JP's are quite co-operative, routinely signing warrants presented to them. However, some actually exercise their legal duty to inquire into the grounds stated by detectives. The difficulties caused by the latter kind of JP and the extra time it takes to hunt up the former, more numerous kind, can both be avoided if the detective simply signs the warrant himself. This is illegal. It is done because the legal, organizational and community context in which detectives work facilitates such conduct.

The general public seems indifferent as to how interrogations and searches take place, so long as felons are captured. The law is somewhat ambiguous with respect to what it permits detectives to do, and this ambiguity is exploited by them. Judges permit evidence to be used in their courts, even when it is obtained in ways that violate general social norms (e.g., lying, coercion, manipulation) so long as the evidence itself is trustworthy. Justices of the peace are also members of a criminal justice bureaucracy. Their careers are more likely to prosper when they co-operate with detectives than when they make things difficult by insisting upon legally correct search procedures. The end result of these occupational or work conditions is a detective force whose members choose to engage in deviant conduct because it enables them to do a better job detecting crimes and capturing criminals.[49]

Conflict Theories

Police accounts of their role in capitalist societies emphasize their political neutrality, their commitment to the rule of law, law that was enacted by the democratically elected legislators. The police, then, see themselves as impartial enforcers of laws they did not make. The laws they refer to, laws that authorize police officers to interfere with the lives and liberty of citizens and to use force where necessary, also hinder the achievement of the primary goal for which the laws were enacted in the first place, i.e., to control crime. They see the crime they are attempting to control as being "non-political." After all, all political parties in all democratically elected assemblies (e.g., Parliament) agree that crime harms everyone and want it controlled. This must mean that everyone in society regards crime as harmful, as morally wrong, as something that needs to be controlled. The police, in their own view, are the last line of controllers, the last line of defence between criminals and the vast majority of respectable citizens.[50]

Conflict theorists tend to regard this police account as primarily ideological; its function is to mystify citizens with respect to the real nature of policing. Policing in their view is a thoroughly biased enterprise. Many of the laws enforced by police represent not consensus, but the imposition of one class or group's values and interests over others. The police themselves are participants in the process of conflict because they help make laws that favour one group over others. Not infrequently, the favoured group are the police themselves. Laws amplify police power and help generate more policing. Even laws that do appear to be the result of consensus (e.g., sexual assault laws) are enforced by police in a biased manner. As part of the state's crime control apparatus, police bias is usually exercised in favour of members of those groups and classes who, because of their wealth, property, and power, are the "winners" in social conflicts. The state, for political and economic reasons, is biased towards winners.

In this demystified conflict account, the police are deviant because they do not even do what a politically biased rule of law requires, that is, impartial enforcement of the laws that do exist. Beyond this shared attribution, Marxist and group conflict theories vary in the emphasis they give to and the reasons they cite for the real nature of policing in a capitalist society.

Marxist conflict theories of police deviance may be classified as either instrumental or structural. In the former, police deviance is intimately associated with the fact that the police are part of a state crime-control apparatus that operates on behalf of the ruling and middle classes. Members of these groups have more wealth, power, status and property. The police help them keep what is theirs. In so doing, they help maintain inequality. In structural theories, the deviance of police officers is associated with both the fact of their relative autonomy within the state apparatus of control and their attempts to further increase their independence from political and civilian control over policing. Instrumental and structural theories may be separated from group conflict explanations of police deviance. In group conflict theories the groups in conflict include not just social classes but also nations, races, age groups, gender groups and so on. Police deviance is associated with police efforts to make and enforce the law in a groups-in-conflict societal and international context.

MARXIST INSTRUMENTAL THEORIES   One widely read and rather extreme instrumental account of police deviance has been provided by Richard Quinney (1974). In his *Critique of the Legal Order*, Quinney regards the police in capitalist societies as deviant because they help maintain a thoroughly iniquitous socio-economic system, capitalism.[51] Politically, Quinney is for socialism because it is an egalitarian, humane system. He is against capitalism because it creates and maintains an inhumane degree of inequality. As part of the capitalist state's crime-control apparatus, the police are necessarily involved in helping the ruling class protect its interests. This they do by legally repressing the working class as a whole, but especially the unemployed, unemployable segment of this class, the lumpen proletariat. Lumpens and workers who have not accepted the ideology foisted on them by capitalists, are legally and illegally repressed most fiercely because they represent the most overt threat to capitalist interests, i.e., they are a socially dangerous class. In sum, policing in capitalist societies is deviant because of the function it performs.

Compared with Quinney, historian Robert Storch offers a more sophisticated account of police deviance. In Storch's (1982) study, policing is deviant only if one believes that it is morally wrong for one social class to use law enforcers to impose its life style on another.[52]

The first organized police force was created in London in 1829. The forerunners of London's police officers were "watchmen" who used to patrol the streets with a view to maintaining the peace. This usually meant enforcing not legally enacted laws, but customs. These were rules for living made by the community itself over a long period of time. Gradually, politicians, organized as councils, passed laws legally authorizing and legitimating what watchmen did to preserve order. With major changes in the economic realm, a number of these laws became inconvenient to members of more powerful social groups (e.g., landowners, Whig politicians and, later, capitalists). As a result, *interpretations* of the law began to change. This gave rise to social conflicts. The forerunners of modern police officers were used to enforce interpretations favourable to the powerful. The courts also supported them. Initially then, the police were an "appendage" of the law, an appendage whose law-enforcement activities reflected the political and social interests of economic elites (Manning 1977, 101–102).

The laws being referred to here covered both "criminal" and "public order" offences. Robbery, rape, burglary are examples of the first; drunkeness, gambling, rowdy street games and rituals are examples of the second. During the period 1850–1880, Storch describes the police as performing the role of "domestic missionary" on behalf of middle-class, evangelical religious groups. During the 1840s, these groups had laws passed that required the police to regulate such unchristian working-class leisure pursuits as dog-and cock-fighting, bull-and badger-baiting, public drinking, gambling and other forms of "loose and lewd" conduct.

Helen Boritch, a University of Toronto sociologist, has extended this instrumental line in her historical analysis of policing in Toronto (1984). Boritch's extension takes the form of showing that the Metro Toronto police not only enforced laws supporting a middle-class life style and economic interests, but they also *wrote* laws biased in the same direction. Boritch focussed on by-law enactment during the years 1859 to 1955. Her focus is important, not only because by-laws cover a much wider area of behaviour than do criminal laws, but also because they represent a more stringent form of social control. Thus, where criminal laws tell us what we must not do, by-laws tell us what not to do *and* what we must do. Thus, you must clear your driveway of snow; you must get a licence to engage in a variety of business activities, hold parades, sell liquor, run a massage parlour and so on.

The primary targets of the by-laws enforced and enacted by the police were "working class morals, recreations, family life and economic activities" (Boritch 1984, 10). Thus, when working-class Chinese owned and operated laundries and were successfully competing with laundries run by whites, the middle-class-run Laundryman's Association had by-laws enacted that placed laundries under police supervision and authorized the police to use force, if necessary, to move Chinese laundries out of middle-class neighbourhoods. On the basis of her analysis, Boritch concludes that the police in Toronto were, during the period surveyed, instruments of middle-class control.[53] Furthermore, although the police themselves emphasized their role as law enforcers and not law makers, they routinely engaged in law making. In short, the police were not merely domestic missionaries, they were helping God create Toronto the Good.

In Toronto then, the police are implicated in the maintenance of class inequality. The same situation appears to obtain elsewhere. Box, for example, discovers it in the United States and Britain; Henshel discovers it in Toronto, and readers of this chapter have discovered police deviance in Canada generally.[54] According to

Box (1983), the unauthorized use of force by police officers, usually directed against members of lower- and working-class groups, can be explained by the fact of social inequality.[55] Growing inequality increases the fears of the middle and upper classes. As individuals or as groups (unions, riotous mobs, criminals), those who have least may take more active steps to reduce inequality by taking from those who have most. The police help calm their fears by using excessive and unauthorized force to enforce the law where this proves to be more effective than doing things legally. For their part, the middle classes are quite happy to ignore "police brutality" because it is used on their behalf. Because of the tendency of members of the middle class to delegate the "dirty work" involved in maintaining inequality to police officers, Silver (1966) has called unauthorized policing a form of "delegated vigilantism."[56]

MARXIST STRUCTURAL THEORIES   The concept of "relative autonomy" is central to structural theories of police deviance. In these theories, two matters are given prominence. The first has to do with the process of increasing relative autonomy from state (and civilian) control. The second concerns the ways in which police autonomy facilitates police deviance. Compared with instrumental accounts, structural theories are rare. A good or strong version of a structural theory is provided by Robert Reiner (1978 and 1980).

Reiner's starting point is the position of the police in the class structure of capitalist societies. The central thesis of his earlier article is that "the police occupy a contradictory place in the class structure" (1978, 168).[57] Ideologically and politically, the police are conservative. They favour the maintenance of the status quo and are suspicious of deviations from the normal which may threaten the status quo. On the other hand, during the specific historical period starting in the mid 1970s, the police experienced pressures in the direction of making them more politically radical and therefore deviant. The specific pressures identified by Reiner are those that foster the unionization of police officers. For Reiner, then, to the extent that unions are "the main vehicle of working-class consciousness" (Lockwood 1958, 13), the role of the police officer as a member of a unionized working-class grouping contradicts the role of political and ideological supporter of the ruling and middle classes.

Police officers come mainly from working-class backgrounds. Unionization rekindles and amplifies as well as expresses class experience and interests. Now, the state can no longer automatically rely on police support for the status quo. It must work harder to win and keep this support. The price paid by the state is both

political and economic. Politically, the state passes laws that pro-
hibit political interference with the decisions made by chiefs of
police. Economically, police wages are increased to levels com-
mensurate with their collective, unionized power.

For these reasons, the police, in Reiner's analysis, have relative
autonomy within the state apparatus of control. This means the
police are not only interdependent parts of a state system but they
are also *independent.* They use their independence to pursue their
own organizational and institutional interests and values. The
"proletarian aspects of their place" have helped bring this about
and may, in the future, make rank-and-file police officers even
more radical.

Turning now to the deviance-facilitating aspects of their relative
autonomy, a major area of "police deviance" has been the use of
political power to neutralize the effectiveness of such regulatory
agencies as civilian review boards. In the United States, the police
have managed to abolish police complaints agencies (Reiner 1980).
In Britain, they rarely make decisions that result in police officers
being found guilty and punished for allegedly using unauthorized
force against members of lower and working classes (Box 1983).
"Cones of silence" among their peers and relative immunity from
prosecution by outsiders constitute, for sociologists such as Box, a
licence to deviate so long as their intentions are good. Good
intentions turn out to be those that have to do with doing what the
state wants done as long as this does not threaten major police
values and interests.

GROUP CONFLICT THEORIES   Group conflict theories of police
deviance are based on the assumption that inter-group conflict is
endemic to capitalist societies. In such societies, the police are
implicated in the process of solving conflicts. Frequently, they
solve conflicts by acting on behalf of members of some groups and
against members of others. As a result, members of the latter
groups tend to regard the police as unfair, oppressive and unjust.
Because of the way in which they perform their role, then, deviance is endemic to policing. Routinely, the police favour powerful elites over less powerful social groups or they act on behalf of
these groups rather than on behalf of society as a whole (Manning
1977, 15–19; Bittner 1970, 14–16, 44–46).

When the groups in conflict are societies as a whole or society as
a whole and politically radical groups within it, policing becomes
"political", according to group-conflict theorist Turk. In the context of "political policing," police deviance is defined as "demonstrable violations of legal rules and blameworthy failures to ac-

complish organizational objectives" (Turk 1981, 111). The major operative goal of political policing is "preventing radical political changes." More specifically, their task has to do with "detecting and neutralizing any present or potential deviations from the ground rules of conventional politics" (Turk 1981, 114).

One major cause of deviance among police organizations (e.g., the pre-1983 RCMP) engaged in political policing is structurally induced contradictions. This simply means that political policing is regulated by contradictory pressures. On the one hand, the police are responsible for preventing radical political changes. On the other, they must carry out this responsibility in legally and ethically correct ways.

Police organizations solve the problem of contradictory pressures by taking a pragmatic tack. Given the great significance of their operative goal — prevent radical political changes — they simply weigh the relative costs and rewards of failure. They do whatever is necessary to prevent the collapse of the existing political system and then attempt to legitimate their behaviour on the grounds of "national security." If they are successful in using any means instead of legal and ethical means, their society wins the conflicts it is engaged in. Here, deviance becomes little more than "a political overhead cost of doing business" (Turk 1981, 118).

SUMMARY

Definitions of police deviance appear to be influenced to an important degree by ideological orientations. Thus, objective definitions tend to be offered by those who are opposed to the police role or to certain forms of police conduct. Subjective definitions appear to be formulated by those adopting a more sympathetic stance towards policing. Deviance, the evidence suggests, is common among police forces of different types, sizes and degrees of professionalism.

A bad-apple (psychological) theory of police deviance does not adequately explain the findings on police deviance. Sociological theories do a much better job. Strain-subcultural theories emphasize the problems endemic to policing and regard police deviance as an attempt to solve them. The bond version of control theory does not appear to be well suited to explaining police deviance. The deterrence version fares better. Deterrence theorists maintain that police deviance is common because neither the public, the government nor the police themselves are interested in discovering and punishing police deviants. The nature of policing also makes it difficult to effectively regulate police conduct. Interactionists focus on peer reactions to police deviance as well as self-labelling, to explain the transition from occasional to career deviant. Ironical versions of control theory point to the unintended and opposite effects of intended control actions and reactions. Finally, Marxist conflict theorists attempt to explain police deviance by formulating instrumental and structural conceptions of policing, the state or both. By way of contrast, group-conflict theorists see police deviance as being necessary if the police are to win conflicts they become involved in on behalf of the groups or society to which they owe political allegiance.

SUGGESTED READINGS

T. **Barker** (ed.), *Police Deviance* (Cincinnati, Ohio: Anderson Publishing, A Pilgrimage Book, 1986).

R. **Ericson,** *Reproducing Order: A Study of Police Patrol Work* (Toronto: University of Toronto Press, 1982).

J. **Skolnick,** *Justice Without Trial* (New York: John Wiley and Sons, 1966).

C. **Steedman,** *Policing the Victorian Community* (London: Routledge and Kegan Paul, 1984).

NOTES

1. For a more detailed description of these rules and their enforcement, see R. Ericson (1981, ch. 3).
2. These differences have very serious implications for citizens. Cities where the rules relating to police use of deadly force are not stringent and refer to vague criteria, such as "under specified conditions" that are never specified, have higher rates of police killings than do cities with clearly-defined, stringent rules (J. Fyfe 1982).
3. For example, police officers are not allowed to have lawyers present, innocence is not necessarily presumed and rules of evidence favour accusers.
4. Although he is not referring to police officers, Friedenberg's analysis of prison guards can be extended to police officers because both are part of Canada's "punishment industry." Within this industry, Friedenberg notes that, compared with prisoners, prison guards "occupy rather different relationships to the means of production — a difference which, in Marxist terms, would itself seem sufficient to account for . . . their abuse of prisoners" (1985, 174). See also Reiman (1979, 129–130). For an approach that conceives of police officers as "guard labour" helping to reproduce "the formal structure of capitalism," see O'Connor (1975, 304).
5. In this connection, see Doob (1985).

6. For examples, see Douglas (1984a), especially Ch. 26 and Douglas and Johnson (1977), especially their Introduction.
7. A fine example of bright-side or shiny-badge statistics on policing is provided by Toronto's former chief of police, Jack Ackroyd. "In an average day in Metropolitan Toronto, the police stop and summons 1 631 people for violations of the Highway Traffic Act; they make an average of 413 arrests, question 1 476 persons and investigate 175 traffic accidents. In addition to this, they respond to an average of 5 000 calls from the public, many of which involve crisis situations and dispute resolutions. So, with nearly 9 000 contacts a day, at the majority of which police and citizens have conflicting goals, we have less than one complaint each day handled by our Complaints Bureau." Chief J. Ackroyd, Comments, in W.S. Tarnopolsky (ed.) pp. 111-116 *Some Civil Liberties Issues of the Seventies*. (Toronto: Carswell, 1975). See also, *Task Force on Policing in Ontario*. Chairman, L.B. Hale. February, 1974, Queen's Park, Toronto.
8. Nova Scotia Police Commission. *Report of the Inquiry into the Kentville Police Department*, July 18, 1984.
9. For a more detailed presentation of the rationale underlying community control over policing, see Luna-Gardinier (1983).
10. As of July 1985, only one other Canadian city, Winnipeg, has a similar office. It was established in 1984. As I understand it, the Winnipeg office deals with complaints from anywhere in the province of Manitoba.
11. The Metropolitan Toronto Police Force Complaints Project Act, 1981. In December 1984, this Act was revised.
12. Preamble to the Metropolitan Toronto Police Force Complaints Project Act, 1981.
13. *Second, Third and Fourth Annual Reports* of the Public Complaints Commissioner and Police Complaints Board, 1983, 1984 and 1985 respectively.
14. See Public Complaints Commissioner, *First Annual Report,*1982, Table 23; *Second Annual Report*, 1983,Table 16; *Third Annual Report*, 1984, Table 18; *Fourth Annual Report*, 1985, Table 8.
15. See Table 23 in *Second and Third Annual Reports*.
16. See Tables 24, 17 and 18 in the Public Complaints Commissioner's 1982, 1983 and 1984 *Annual Reports* respectively.
17. The figures upon which this conclusion is based were provided by the Toronto Police Association and Public Complaints Commissioners, *Second Annual Report*, 1983, Table 17; *Third Annual Report*, 1984, Table 18.
18. Blumberg's findings also support this conclusion. Specifically, he found that when the officer's assignment, e.g., traffic, narcotics, etc., was controlled "younger officers and those with fewer years of

police service were observed to be more likely to become involved in a shooting." Blumberg (1983).

19. In 1982, the Canadian Bill of Rights was replaced by the Canadian Charter of Rights and Freedoms. One major difference between the Bill and the Charter is this: whereas the former was an ordinary statute that could be changed by Parliament, the Charter can be changed only by constitutional amendment. Another important difference between them is that the Charter goes much further than the Bill in protecting individual citizens against the illegal use of power by the state. Arguments for and against the need for such protection are presented by the Canadian Civil Liberties Association. *The Effective Right to Counsel in Ontario Criminal Cases*, brief presented November 30, 1972 and D. Mackintosh, *Charter of Rights: A Trojan Horse for the Courts, The Globe and Mail*, September 22, 1981, page 7.

20. For a more detailed analysis of the Metro Toronto hold-up squad, see Henshel (1982).

21. This is an estimate. It assumes plea bargaining and therefore a prison sentence for each officer that is less than the statutory maximum. Plea bargaining is an informal arrangement or exchange worked out, not in open court, but between the Crown attorney and defence counsel, in which the reward for a guilty plea is a shorter prison term or less serious punishment. The vast majority of criminal cases that come to court are dealt with informally, via the process of plea bargaining. The maximum and minimum sentences for each of the crimes listed is contained in the Canadian Criminal Code.

22. Front de Libération du Québec.

23. James Hunt worked on the Vancouver narcotics squad for ten years. These comments are taken from a lecture Hunt presented at Glendon College, York University, in the winter term of 1980.

24. According to sociologist Box (1983, ch. 3), deviance is endemic to police work.

25. The percentage of officers named in complaints will actually vary with recidivism. That is to say, the greater the number of police officers who are mentioned in more than one civilian complaint, the smaller will be the percentage of different officers mentioned in civilian complaints. These data were not provided in the relevant table (Table 21), 1983 Report.

26. Source: Table 21 *Public Complaints Commissioners Second Annual Report* (Toronto: Office of the Public Complaints Commissioner, 1983). Table 17 of this same report indicates that 1 058 officers were involved in complaints. Why four more officers were included in Table 21 is not explained.

27. The major reasons given for this were "no action warranted," pre-

sumably because the officer's conduct was legally authorized, and "informal resolution." An informal resolution occurs where the officer *and* the complainant agree to resolve the matter and sign a form to this effect.

28. These are 69 completed reviews. A completed review is one that was ended or closed during the reporting year. In the present case, this was 1982. Where a case had been reviewed by the PCC and the PCC had ordered a Complaints Board hearing, the case was regarded as closed only if the Board hearing had been completed during 1982. Thus, five cases that were still before the Board at the end of the reporting year were not included among the complete reviews. A review takes place only when a citizen who knows that he is entitled to request a review by the PCC actually does request one.

29. Reasons for doing this include having the case dealt with in court and advice by their lawyers.

30. See Table 22. Public Complaints Commissioner, *Second Annual Report,* 1983.

31. This Board hears cases referred to it by the Public Complaints Commissioner. It is the Board and not the Commissioner that hears cases and metes out sanctions where necessary.

32. Judgement on an appeal to the Judicial Committee of the Privy Council. For a more general discussion, see Shearing (1981b).

33. Lord Denning. Cited in Nova Scotia Police Comm. (1984, 124).

34. This makes it more difficult to obtain a conviction. Even so, the Metro Toronto Police Union has set-up a "war chest" of $250 000 to abolish the Office of the Public Complaints Commissioner. According to Union President Paul Walter, police officers just want the same rights as criminals, the rights to a fair and impartial trial, to be afforded the full and due process of law in a regular court. *The Toronto Star,* November 21, 1985, page A7.

35. For example, in the process of investigating the 23 separate allegations against officers assigned to the hold-up squad, the Commissioner noted that "in only two cases were the allegations brought to the attention of any public authority within one month of the alleged incident. In ten cases, it was at least one year before a complaint was filed." PCC (1984, 3).

36. See *The Toronto Star,* Thursday, May 3, 1984, page A6. See also Judge Crossland's remarks about "police lies" in *The Toronto Star,* February 28, 1986, page A12.

37. Evidence provided by Box (1983, ch. 3) for England and Wales supports the same conclusions. Data provided by Chappell and Graham (1985) suggests that this conclusion also applies when Canadian police officers kill civilians "in the line of duty."

38. For a more detailed discussion of police subcultural expectations as "rules of thumb" guiding police behaviour, see Manning (1977).

39. Subcultural explanations of police deviance have also been formulated by E. Stoddard (1971) and L. Sherman (1974, 165–205).

40. For a time, the Metro Toronto hold-up (robbery) squad achieved notoriety for its reliance on force and fraud in obtaining confessions from suspects. See Henshel (1983) and *Third Annual Report*, Public Complaints Commissioner, Toronto (1984), pp. 24–26. By contrast, Ericson (1981) discovered that because the law itself was so vaguely worded and the working conditions were so private, the detectives he studied had no need to use violence. They could get what they wanted legally, even if it meant using unethical means.

41. For example, the Bail Reform Act lays down rules regulating pre-trial detention of suspects by the police. One reason for not granting bail is that the police have "reasonable and probable grounds" for believing that the individual, if released, would pose a threat to the "public interest." The criteria to be used in deciding what constitutes "reasonable and probable grounds" are, however, not defined. See Hagan and Morden (1981).

42. For a legalistic and formalized treatment of the process of social control and its relevance to police deviance, see Black (1984).

43. For a further discussion of wider societal constraints on policing the police, see Rumbaut and Bittner (1979).

44. For example, see Rubington and Weinberg (1981).

45. For more details, see Silberman (1978).

46. The latter part of Punch's quotation is taken from Brittan (1973, 23).

47. Left-handing a search warrant refers to the practice of detectives forging signatures of justices of the peace. Presumably, a right-handed detective uses his left-hand to forge the JP's signature in order to conceal the fact that he was responsible. Hence the name.

48. Ratner, a Marxist sociologist, regards Ericson as an "exemplary of the interactionist perspective" and one who "shows that . . . detectives and the police divest processed individuals of any significant autonomy (and who use) the criminal law to 'order justice' in ways that buttress state authority." Whether this is done legally or not, it makes them deviant in Ratner's eyes (1985, 19).

49. For a description of police accounts of their role in capitalist society, see Reiner (1980) and the introduction to any randomly selected Annual Report of any major police department in Canada. For a more detailed description of the "police myth," see Manning (1977, 323–331).

50. In a later book, *State, Class and Crime* (1977), Quinney seems to have moved in the direction of conferring more autonomy on the state.

Thus, on pages 89-90, he notes that the state is a "complex apparatus with its own direction and its own contradictions." For an opposed Marxist view of the police as a group that may well play a part in bringing about a socialist revolution, see Harring (1985, 134–141).

51. Other important historical studies of policing include Miller (1977), Parks (1970) and Silver (1966).

52. In this connection, see also Parks (1970) and Stedman-Jones (1984).

53. For evidence concerning the relationship between police killings, social class, and social inequality, see Tagaki (1979); Harring, Platt, Spiegleman and Tagaki (1977); Jacobs and Britt (1979). The Chappell and Graham (1985) study of the police use of deadly force in Canada is useful descriptively. The same thing cannot be said for its theoretical contribution, since it is atheoretical.

54. To Marxists such as Poulantzas, Box's "Marxist" explanation is confusing because of his tendency to use "elites" and "social classes" interchangeably. Elite and class conflict theories are not the same.

55. For a more detailed analysis of "police vigilantes," see Kotecha and Walker (1976).

56. Reiner's conception of social class is influenced by Poulantzas. Central to Poulantzas' conception was his opposition to "economism," i.e., the reduction of the political and the ideological to the economic realm. For Poulantzas, class position is influenced by position in the production of surplus value (economic factors) but also by political and ideological factors which are not a simple and direct reflection of economic factors. See Poulantzas (1975).

CHAPTER FIVE

WIFE ABUSE:

GENDER AT HOME

WHAT IS WIFE ABUSE?

IN MORE POLITICIZED AREAS of social inquiry, definitions are used in both a technical and political sense. Technically, definitions influence measurement and are used to identify or delimit theory and research. Politically, definitions are used as weapons in social struggles. Together with poverty, unemployment, racism and terrorism, wife abuse is a highly politicized topic of study. Current definitions of wife abuse reflect this fact.

In defining wife abuse, politics seem to merge with technical considerations in three ways. These are: the breadth of the definition (broad versus narrow), whether it emphasizes interaction or victimization (*spousal* violence versus *wife* abuse) and whether it is objective or subjective (quality inherent in an act or label applied to an act).

Broad vs Narrow Definitions

Some definitions of wife abuse are so broad as to lead one to conclude that almost all women who live with men are abused by them. Therefore, major social and legal changes should be initiated right away in order to put a stop to a serious and widespread social problem. Other, very narrow definitions suggest that wife abuse is a relatively rare social phenomenon. For this reason, the educational, therapeutic and punitive resources of the state should not be diverted from more serious problems (e.g., youth unemployment) in order to deal with it.

One of the best examples of a very broad definition of wife abuse is the one formulated by Stark-Adamec and Adamec. Attached to the Department of Psychiatry, Wellesley Hospital, Toronto and the University of Toronto, they offer a definition that represents an amalgam of the definitions of Straus, Hotaling, and Carr: spousal violence refers to anything one spouse has done or not done to the other that is perceived as psychologically, socially, economically, or physically harmful. Measures of spousal violence derived from this definition include a search for "fractures, stitches, bruises, semen in the vagina and/or anus, browbeating, restriction of educational and employment opportunities, economic threats . . . adultery." According to this definition, wife abuse in Canada is "frighteningly pervasive" (Stark-Adamec 1982, 8). A much narrower definition has been formulated by Canadian researchers working for the ministry of the federal Solicitor General. The definition implied by the measures they use is this: Spousal violence involves the intentional use of verbal threats of physical injury or the infliction of physical injury by one spouse against another. When only threats of an assault and/or actual assaults are used as measures, we are led to conclude that between one and three percent of wives resident in Canada are abused by their mates (Solicitor General 1982, 2).

Spousal Violence vs Wife Abuse

Spousal violence and wife abuse have this in common: both have to do with suffering. Macleod and Cadieux (1980) describe a typical example of the kind of suffering involved. Karen married Richard shortly after she graduated from high school. Three months later, Karen was pregnant. Shortly afterwards, she and Richard went to a party. When they got home Richard accused her of flirting with other men and beat her. More beatings followed. Karen got pregnant again. The beatings continued for about two and a half years. Then, on the advice of her parents, she left Richard and went to stay at a women's shelter. In the meantime, Karen's father persuaded Richard to leave the house so that Karen and the two children could return. They did. Two weeks later, Richard also returned. He broke into the house, locked the children in a bedroom, beat Karen, shot her dead and then killed himself.

A number of names have been applied to this kind of incident. Included among these are "marital violence," "spousal violence," "conjugal violence," "violence between mates," "domestic violence," "wife abuse," "wife assault" and "wife battering." The last three names, those with the word "wife" in them, clearly identify the woman as victim. All the others conceal this fact. Terms such as spousal violence suggest, instead, that violence results from ordinary, everyday social interaction that has "gone wrong" and that females are as responsible for this as males (Small 1981). After all, a woman who hits or abuses her mate because he hits her must expect the interaction to escalate to the point of being violent. Almost all feminist scholars use the term wife abuse or assault. Some non-feminists also use this term. Others do not. They use one or other of the gender-neutral interactional terms noted above.

Included among those whose definitions identify the women as victim are Macleod and Cadieux. The title of their book is *Wife Battering in Canada: The Vicious Circle (1980)*. According to them, wife battering is an example of "normative violence."

Normative violence is violence that is supported by the "traditions, laws and attitudes prevalent in the society in which we live" (Macleod and Cadieux 1980, 7). Violence includes the intentional infliction of physical and/or psychological damage. Wife abuse occurs when the victim of this kind of violence is a woman who has lived with or is now living with a man with whom she was or now is sexually intimate. Wife abuse includes pushing, kicking, burning, strangling, knifing, hitting, shooting, name calling, threatening.

Activist-scholar Shirley Small is highly conscious of the possibility that "names change attitudes." Therefore, she feels it is very important to use the term wife assault rather than "spousal violence" because it does a better job of describing what actually goes on (Small 1981, 4). On the basis of statistics she cites and her own involvement with abused women, Small concludes that women are more frequently injured, more seriously injured and more likely to be killed. Wife assault is the appropriate term because it describes this reality more accurately and also because it changes attitudes towards the victimization of women. For the same reasons, nuns, housewives and feminists in Quebec have provided shelters for "battered women" and not "participants in spousal violence" (Beaudry 1985).

In their book, *Behind Closed Doors* (1980), American scholars Straus, Gelles and Steinmetz state that *"wives as victims"* should be "the focus of social policy" (1980, 43). Yet, their definition of the phenomenon is gender-neutral.[1] This kind of definition diverts attention from the harmful *consequences* actually experienced by women who are victimized by male violence or aggression. Thus, they define "abusive violence" as "an act which has the high potential for injuring the person being hit" (1980, 22). Whether an individual is hit or hurt and how badly is not covered by this definition, a definition used by them to develop their violence-measuring instrument, the Conflict Tactics Scale. According to this measure, "a man who pushes, grabs, shoves or slaps his wife is not counted as a wife-beater." Yet, those who work with assaulted women report shoves resulting in broken bones and slaps that draw blood (Small 1981, 5). Canadian scholars who embrace a gender-neutral definition include Chan (1978), Chimbos (1978), Fleming (1975) and Prus (1978). All are males.

Objective vs Subjective Definitions

Most sociologists define wife abuse objectively. In addition to theoretical reasons, there are also political considerations to explain why this is so. Thus, to call a man who assaults his wife a wife abuser is to show greater support for women and greater opposition to violence against women than would be the case if one were to limit this term (wife abuser) only to wife assaulters who have been publicly identified as wife abusers. In the latter subjective-societal reactions definition, men who are secret wife beaters, whose violence is not known outside the home, are not really wife abusers. An attempt to avoid the political implications of offering a subjective definition of wife abuse may be one of the reasons why subjectively oriented sociologists abandon subjective definitions when it comes to wife abuse. Thus, in order to emphasize the seriousness and pervasiveness of woman battering, subjectivist Schur cites findings based on sociological surveys employing objective definitions (Straus 1978). In his subjectively oriented text entitled *Labeling Women Deviant* (1984), Schur apparently sees no inconsistency in providing an objective definition of woman battering (p. 157).

WIFE ABUSE: HOW MUCH

Some, perhaps many abused women suffer in silence (Pizzey 1974). Others relate their experiences to researchers by responding to questions asked of them in victim surveys. Here a relatively few women (or couples) are selected in such a way (probability sample) as to enable the researchers to generalize his results to the entire population (city or country) from which the sample was selected.[2] In other cases the police are informed. Usually fewer cases of wife abuse or assaults are reported to police than to interviewers conducting victim surveys.[3] One major exception to this is the very serious crime of murder. Most murders, including the murders of women who live or lived with men, are known to the police. Police statistics on lethal wife abuse are among the most accurate statistics produced by the police. Because they provide the most accurate estimates available, victim survey data and national police statistics on "domestic homicide" will be used to answer questions about the amount and distribution of wife abuse in Canada.

"Spousal Homicide"

In the United States and Canada, the most serious form of family violence investigated by the police is the type they classify as "domestic homicides" (Straus 1980). Between 1971 and 1981, Canadian police classified 3 343 homicides as domestic homicides. Of this number, 2 153 or 64.4 percent involved "husbands and wives as suspect or victim."[4] The 2 153 victims included 1 198 female victims who were wives and 855 male victims who were husbands. The ratio of wives to husbands killed was 1.3:1. For every husband killed, then, 1.3 wives died violently.

The husbands and wives referred to here were killed, but not necessarily by their spouses. Spousal homicide, a sub-category of domestic homicides, refers specifically to homicides in which a husband or wife murders his or her spouse. Between 1971 and 1981 there were 694 cases of spousal homicide in Canada. This figure represents almost one-third of the 2 153 domestic homicides noted earlier. In approximately 82 percent (565) of the spousal homicides, husbands were suspects in the murder of their wives. This means that for every wife who is suspected of murdering her husband, four husbands are suspected of murdering their wives.

Before leaving spousal homicide, one further question remains to be answered. Between 1971 and 1981, 565 wives died, and their husbands were suspected of killing them. What proportion of the total number of wives in Canada does this figure represent? Assuming their husbands did actually do what they were suspected of doing, the average number of wives killed per year during this period was 56.5. During the same period, the average number of women classified as spouses by Statistics Canada was almost 5.5 million. From these figures, we may tentatively conclude that one wife in every 96.6 thousand is killed by her husband.[5]

Wife Assault

In 1982, researchers working for the Solicitor General of Canada (Statistics Division) published the results of a victim survey in seven major Canadian cities.[6] In this seven-city survey, a random (probability) sample of 61 000 residents were asked about "any previous victimization they may have suffered during the previous year" (Solicitor General 1983). Although the survey was not specifically designed to produce information that could be used as a basis for estimating the incidence of wife assault in these cities, some relevant information was provided because "respondents were asked to state what their relationship to the offender(s) was" (Solicitor General of Canada, 1983).

Based upon the sample data, it was estimated that the combined male and female rate of violent victimization per 1 000 population aged 16 and over was 70. The male rate per 1 000 was 90. The female rate per 1 000 females was 53. The male rate is 1.7 times greater than the female rate. Now what happens to these rates when we focus on assaults against husbands and wives respectively?

Approximately 1 790 (5 percent) of the 352 000 violent incidents involved family members as aggressors or victims. In 77 percent of all assaults occurring among family members, the victim was female. When spousal assaults occurred, the wife was the victim in 90 percent of the incidents. When assaults between ex-spouses were reported, the ex-wife was the victim in 80 percent of the cases. Among married women, 8 percent of the assaults reported by them were committed by their husbands. Separation markedly increases this percentage. Thus, 54 percent of all assaults against separated women were committed by former marital partners (Solicitor General of Canada 1985, 4).

Turning next to series assaults, that is, assaults that had occurred "five or more times within the year," women are much more likely to experience series assaults in the home and men more likely to experience them at work. Among women reporting series assaults in the home, the assaulter was, in over one-third of the cases, a spouse or ex-spouse. From this we may conclude, not only that husbands and ex-husbands are much more likely to assault their wives than vice versa, but also that they are more likely to be recidivist wife-beaters. Moreover, when husbands beat their wives, they are likely to injure them more seriously than strangers would (Solicitor General of Canada 1985).

The Seven Cities study was a general victimization survey that focussed on a variety of personal and property crimes, including assaults. This study was not specifically designed to study either wife assault or the more general category of wife abuse. More recently two researchers, Jane Ursel and Mike Smith, have conducted victim surveys of wife abuse.

Wife Abuse

Ursel's study (1984) took place in Winnipeg. Here a random sample of 573 household residents was selected for a survey on wife abuse. The household members interviewed were reasonably representative of all members of households listed in the city's tax assessment file. One of the questions respondents were asked was this: What is your best estimate of the number of women who are married or have common-law relationships who have been abused by their husbands? Seventy-seven percent of the sample answered "most or many." A difference between men and women in the sample is evident: 84 percent of the women and 68 percent of the men answered "most or many." These estimates lead the principal investigator, Jane Ursel, to conclude that wife abuse is "seen as a pervasive social problem" (1984, 8).

A second major finding of Ursel's survey has to do with whether women in the sample "know of another woman who was abused." Overall, 46 percent of the sample answered "yes." More women than men answered "yes": 51 percent of the women and 38 percent of the men reported knowing personally of at least one woman who had experienced wife abuse (1984, Table 3a).

Moving from estimates of incidence to estimates of prevalence,[7] Ursel's findings indicated that 44 percent of the sample believe that in an abusive relationship, abusive events occur "frequently." This finding is used to support the conclusion that "abusive behaviour is recurrent and habitual" (1984, Table 6).

Finally, Ursel wanted to find out how serious a problem wife abuse was compared with the harm caused by other kinds of crimes. Wife abuse ranked third in seriousness, after child abuse and drunk driving. The average estimates of harm caused by these three offences — child abuse, drunk driving, wife abuse — were quite similar, (9.3, 9.3 and 8.9 respectively) concluding that "respondents viewed wife abuse as a serious and pervasive social problem" (1984, 7).[8]

The Ursel study is a major improvement upon the oft-quoted, but methodologically unsound Macleod and Cadieux (1980) survey. Their conclusion that "every year, one in ten Canadian women who are married or in a relationship with a live-in lover are battered" (1980, 17) is based on very poor transition-house and divorce-petition data. Mike Smith's Toronto survey is a major improvement on both the Ursel and Macleod and Cadieux studies.[9]

Smith (1985) selected a (probability) sample of 315 Toronto residents. These were interviewed by telephone. Just over 18 percent reported being abused at least once by a male they had lived with *at any time.* When the women were asked whether or not they had been abused *"during the past year,"* 11 percent said yes.

Self reports of wife abuse also vary by marital status. Thus, almost 43 percent of separated or divorced women report being abused. This compares with 14 percent of those who are presently married and 18 percent of those who never married. Remember that the figure for all respondents, i.e., for the sample as a whole is 18 percent.

This percentage is based on the self reports of women sampled. These reports refer to their *own* experiences. When they were asked whether they *personally knew of other women* who had been abused by the men they lived with 46 percent said they had. While it is difficult to know how reliable this kind of evidence is, it suggests to Smith, that "the true prevalence of wife abuse is considerably higher than the figure (18 percent) derived solely from self-reports" (1985, 29).[10] Finally, it may be interesting to compare estimates of wife abuse in the United States and Canada. The best known and most widely cited U.S. wife-abuse surveys are those conducted by Straus, Gelles and Steinmetz. Their first national survey was conducted in 1975–1976. Their major finding was that 12.1 percent of married or cohabiting women report being abused by the man they lived with (Straus et al. 1980). In 1985, Straus and Gelles (1986) replicated their earlier study, 3 520 households containing married or cohabiting couples were interviewed by telephone. Just over 11 percent (11.3 percent) of the women reported being abused by their male partners during the previous year. The corresponding figure of Toronto was 11 percent (Smith, 1985, 29). Toronto and U.S. national-based estimates of wife abuse among the "presently married" and "separated/divorced" are very similar.[11]

In sum, Canadian and U.S. victim-survey data on wife abuse indicate that approximately 11 percent of women who live with men are abused by them in any given year. Evidence presented by women who personally know of other women who have been abused, suggests that the actual figure may be higher than this. Separations and divorce are associated with a much higher incidence (43 percent) of man-to-woman abuse.

The statistics presented here might lead one to conclude that the phenomenon of men abusing women is confined to the United States and Canada during the 1970s and 1980s. This is not so (Davidson 1977; French 1985). Not only does wife abuse have a long history, it also occurs in many different kinds of society. In 1869 John Stuart Mill wrote *The Subjection of Women*. Here he noted: "From the earliest twilight of human history, every woman . . . was found in a state of bondage to some man . . . . How vast is the number of men . . . who are little higher than brutes, and . . . this never prevents them from being able, through the laws of marriage, to obtain a victim . . . The vilest malefactor has some wretched woman tied to him, against whom he can commit any atrocity except killing her and even that he can do without too much danger of legal penalty."

The law's relative lack of interest in punishing wife beaters has its roots in social customs that go back over 2 000 years to pre-biblical times. The Bible, principally the story of Adam and Eve, only amplified the cultural process of defining women as legitimate targets of male violence. Compared with what men were permitted to do to women earlier in history, the oft-cited 19th century British rule-of-thumb was a major humanitarian achievement. Instead of bashing his wife with anything he could lay his hands on, the amended British common-law section on wife beating restricted the husband to "a rod not thicker than his thumb." So long as the intention was to chastise his wife, the British husband could legally beat her.

One reason why the British husband might want to chastise his wife might be his suspicion that she was "'aving if off" (sex) with their male lodger while he was at work. In Nigeria, suspicions regarding female sexual promiscuity are associated with a very damaging, culturally legitimated male reaction — clitoridectomy. Clitoridectomy refers to the surgical removal of a young girl's clitoris. According to Teresa Hibbert (1986), a graduate student who did her field-work in Nigeria, Nigerian men believe that if a women's clitoris were not removed, she "will . . . masturbate . . . take many lovers and be sexually active" (1986, 130). Hibbert's conclusion was that clitoridectomy "has to be understood in the context of traditional systems of gender inequality and belief systems" (1986, 130). Here it should be noted that clitoridectomy is only one of a number of sexual mutilations to which women's bodies are subjected in first, second and third world countries (Thiam 1985). Like Topsy, these have "just growd" in most societies because in them, the rulers are mainly men. This is Hibbert's thesis.

PERSPECTIVES ON WIFE ABUSE

Cultural Theories

Two of the most widely cited theories of wife abuse were formulated by scholars working under the auspices of the Family Violence Research Programme, University of New Hampshire. These are the "violence-begets-violence" and "marriage-licence-is-a-hit-licence" theses.

According to Straus (1977) the violence-begets-violence thesis expresses the idea that violence in one family role is associated with violence in other family roles. Thus, husbands become wife beaters as part of a normal progression from using physical punishment against their children to abusing their wives. Minor forms of wife abuse gradually change to more serious forms. Central to this theory is the notion that husbands learn that violence in one role is part of a "way of life" that condones violence in other male roles. In other words, violence in one male role begets violence in other roles because the culture (cultural norm) permits or even requires men in these roles to behave aggressively in order to maintain their superordinate status.

The violence-begets-violence thesis focusses on violent or aggressive *behaviour.* This behaviour, according to Straus and his co-workers, is rule- or norm-governed. The marriage-licence-is-a-hit-licence thesis focusses on the *norms* governing spousal and more generally, family violence. Thus Gelles maintains that, "violence between spouses is often viewed as normative and, in fact, mandated in family relations" (Gelles 1974). From this perspective, wife abuse is not an example of deviant behaviour but one of conforming behaviour. In beating their wives, husbands are conforming with cultural norms condoning, if not actually requiring, violence under a broad range of circumstances. "She did not have my dinner ready when I arrived home" appears to be one frequently mentioned circumstance.

Central to this thesis is the idea that "the family has different rules about violence than do other groups." Whereas other groups such as monasteries, the country club, and sociology departments have rules prohibiting the use of force in interpersonal relations, rules governing families permit or oblige parents to beat their children and each other. Parental and spousal violence is legitimate under these conditions: a family member is "doing something wrong"; he or she will not "listen to reason"; the violence administered as a teaching technique is not excessive in relation to the alleged wrong. Although members of different ethnic and social groupings disagree about what constitutes a good reason for administering a beating, our culture in general makes the marriage licence a hit licence.[12]

As was true of the violence-begets-violence thesis, the hit-licence thesis is widely accepted by Canadian scholars and activists. To their credit, Macleod and Cadieux do attempt to ground their acceptance of the thesis in history. "Wife beating," they note, "has been condoned throughout history." Their historical analysis reveals a number of enduring cultural norms. These are: men own their wives; wives should obey their husbands; the wife's place is in the home and her home role involves denying herself so that she can better serve her husband and children (1980, 27–30). According to Macleod and Cadieux, then, history explains why marriage is a licence for men to hit their wives.

Both of these theories are cultural theories. Both suffer from the defect of taking culture or cultural norms as *given*. That is to say, they do not attempt to explain why norms condoning or requiring wife abuse were created or emerged in the first place *and* why they continue to exist (if indeed they do). Strain-subcultural theories of wife abuse attempt to do this.

Strain-subcultural Theories

In the strain-subcultural theory formulated by Stark-Adamec and Adamec (1982), wife abuse occurs in a special kind of cultural setting. Specifically, "there has to be a climate in which aggression is both condoned and reinforced; a climate in which asymmetrical sex roles are adopted and the female devalued, for men to choose aggression as a response to stress and to choose women as the target of the aggression" (1982, 10). The primary cause of this cultural climate is "gynaephobia" (1982, 11). Gynaephobia refers to men's "fear and loathing of women based on their ability to create life, to arouse powerful sexual urges in men and the fact of their bleeding, once-a-month, condition." Men, it seems, loathe women but they also need them.

For Stark-Adamec and Adamec then, the major cause of the strain that causes men to create and maintain a subculture that condones wife abuse is *ambivalence*. Men fear and devalue women but they also need and want them. Subcultural norms condoning wife abuse solve this problem by inculcating in men the belief that it is not wrong to beat the women you live with, loathe, fear and need. Beating and abuse generally, simultaneously demonstrate love and fear/loathing.

In contrast to the foregoing bio-social formulation, Walter Miller

(1958) and Bowker (1983) offer accounts that emphasize the social determinants of aggressive masculinity and toughness. According to Miller, males in lower-class families are more likely than middle-class males, to be brought up in father-absent homes. Mothers, often deserted by their husbands, are left to bring up the children on their own. For lower-class boys reared in father-absent homes, the perception of being "feminized" is stressful. Strain is reduced by creating norms requiring toughness and a demonstration of masculinity in dealings with other men and especially women. One result is wife-abuse.

A third variant of the strain-subcultural theory of wife abuse has been offered by Schur (1984) and by Diana Russel (1982). Their contributions can be called a "backlash thesis." Central to this thesis is the idea that wife abuse, including wife rape and rape generally, is a reaction to the strain experienced by men threatened by the advance of feminism. Here, wife abuse and norms justifying it, are part of an "anti-feminist backlash" (Schur, 1984, 156). In the dependency thesis that follows, low dependency, facilitated perhaps by feminism, is associated, not with an increased but with a lowered risk of wife abuse.

Control Theories

Dependency and deterrence represent two major theories of wife abuse to which the process of social control is central.

DEPENDENCY THEORY   Women who are abused by the men with whom they live have to remain in the relationship in order to be beaten regularly. Put another way, "career wife abusers" need an ever-present target. Assuming a woman is beaten more than once, the question that some theorists ask is: Why does she stay around to get beaten? Dependency, one major basis of social control, represents an answer to this question.

The dependency thesis has been formulated by Kalmuss and Straus (1982) and Gelles (1976). Women who remain with men who abuse them increase their time-at-risk. The effect of dependency on time-at-risk varies with the kind of dependency involved and the severity of the abuse. Kalmuss and Straus identify two kinds of dependency, subjective and objective. *Subjective dependency* refers to a psychological state that indicates how emotionally tied to the marriage a wife feels. *Objective dependency* refers to economic and other conditions (e.g., the presence of young children) that make a wife economically dependent upon her husband.

The severity of violence varies between "minor" and "major."

Minor acts of violence include cutting remarks, shoves, pushes, and slaps. When bruises, cuts, stitches, and hospitalization are the result, major violence is involved. Subjectively dependent women tend to stay with husbands who inflict minor violence upon them. As the severity of violence increases, they tend to leave. Objectively dependent wives tend to stay with their husbands even when they are subjected to repeated acts of major violence. Table 5-1 describes the relation between these two variables.

As a result of progress towards equality, wives may, to an increasing degree, become less dependent upon and therefore less controlled by their husbands. Will this mean a decrease in career spousal violence? Kalmuss and Strauss believe that, in the long run, it will. In the short run, changes in female/male dependency may, by posing a threat to husbands, actually increase the number of wives who are abused. Changes in the dependency of wives on their husbands, then, may instigate violence directed against wives. In sum, high dependency helps explain career wife abuse and changes in dependency from high to low, help explain a short-term increase and a longer-term decrease in wife abuse.

TABLE **5-1** *Severity of Violence*

		High	Low
Dependency	Subjective	Go	Stay
	Objective	Stay	Stay

DETERRENCE THEORY   An influential group of therapists-scholars (psychiatrists, psychologists, social workers) have, since the mid 1970s, worked very hard to assist abused and battered women. The general focus of their approach has been to improve the response to wife abuse adopted by various agents of the state. The agents they had in mind included policemen, social workers, psychologists, the counsellors employed in various community agencies.[13]

Initially, it was thought that the policing of wife abuse would be improved if policemen were trained in crisis-intervention techniques specifically geared to domestic violence. Policemen trained in this way were made part of a team that included social workers from community agencies responsible for the welfare of Canadian families (Levens 1978; Jaffee and Thompson 1979). More recently, the focus seems to have shifted toward a more specifically law-enforcement response to wife abuse. Thus, police chiefs and attorneys general in various jurisdictions have issued directives requiring policemen to make arrests in wife-abuse cases, and the law has been changed to require abused women to testify in court.[14]

The earlier state response, implemented by Jaffee and Thompson (1979) in London, Ontario, involved the creation of family service consultant teams. The second, also implemented by the police force in London, Ontario, involved arresting and charging more abusive husbands (Burris 1981). The first strategy was based on the assumption that a more understanding and knowledgeable approach would reduce wife abuse. The second was based on the idea that deterrence works best to achieve the same objective. Does arresting wife abusers reduce wife abuse?

Answers to this question using Canadian data are in the process of being formulated.[15] For the time being, the only evidence comes from U.S. sources. Evidence from a well-designed U.S. field experimental study (conducted in Minneapolis, Minnesota) indicates that arresting wife assaulters does deter them. Sherman and Berk (1984) found that ten percent of arrested wife assaulters repeated their assault during a six-month period following their arrest. This compares with nineteen percent of assaulters who were counselled by the police and twenty-four percent who were asked by the police to leave the home for a short period of time.

To the extent that arresting a wife abuser attaches the label 'wife abuser' more firmly to him than either of the other police-response modes ("advise" and "send away"), labelling theorists would predict an increase in wife abuse. Yet, those arrested were less likely to continue their violent ways during the six-month observational period.

The authors of the Minneapolis Domestic Violence Experiment are cautious about concluding that arrest and arrest alone will deter all kinds of wife abusers and all kinds of abuse in all kinds of settings. Minneapolis, they point out, is a city with a special combination of characteristics. These may limit the generalization of their findings. In other words, their findings may apply only to cities with large native-American populations, with low unemployment and violence rates, where winters are severe and where suspected wife abusers are kept in jail overnight. In cities that are similar to Minneapolis, their findings apply only to minor forms of domestic violence. Finally, Sherman and Berk provide no evidence to refute the possibility that, for certain kinds of individuals, arrest may actually increase the seriousness of assaults on their wives.

Conservative supporters of a more punitive criminal justice

system as well as more liberal critics of it are agreed on one thing: "If an offence occurs so seldom that deterrence scarcely seems needed, then and only then, will deterrence work well" Pepinsky, 1980, 130–131; also Palmer 1977). So, deterrence works best where it is needed least. This "master" social control irony results from three conditions. First, wife abuse occurs *frequently*. It is not a scarce phenomenon. Second, punishment, if it is to deter the abuser effectively, must be *severe*. Third, the more *swiftly* punishment follows the wife assault, the more effectively punishment acts as a deterrent. Now, the more serious the punishment for this offence, the longer the time period between arrest and conviction will be. Offences for which serious punishments are provided simply take longer to dispose of than offences for which minor punishments are mandated. The average murder trial takes fourteen months, while the average traffic violation is disposed of in about four weeks.

On the other hand, if the time period between the offence of wife assault and punishment is reduced to, say, three days from the current four to five months, then the chances of making mistakes increase. More husbands who did not actually assault their wives will be arrested, and more husbands who did beat their wives will not be arrested. This will weaken the link between wife assault and punishment. Any deterrent effect that might have operated because of swift punishment will be vitiated by errors in linking wife assault and punishment. Beyond this, the immorality of a justice system that punishes innocent husbands and ignores guilty ones may weaken the "general deterrence" effect. This is an effect that applies not to the individual wife assaulter, but to husbands generally.

With respect to wife assault, then, deterrence at both the individual and general levels may not work as effectively as the findings of Berk and Sherman suggest. An additional and important reason for this state of affairs may be that the state itself maintains the cultural and structural conditions that reproduce wife assault.

Interactionist Theories

Interactionist theories of wife abuse are not numerous. Edwin Schur and Patricia Morgan are two sociologists who have formulated interactionist accounts. Their respective contributions are quite different. Schur's focus is on the relations between gender norms and woman battering, while Morgan analyses the societal reaction of the state to wife abuse. Schur's account is ahistorical, Morgan's is historical.

GENDER NORMS AND THE POLITICS OF MARITAL INTERACTION   In his book *Labelling Women Deviant* (1984), Schur formulates an explanation of woman battering that interrelates the concepts of gender norms, marital relations, dependency and woman battering.

Gender, according to Schur, "refers to the socio-cultural and psychological shaping, patterning and evaluating of male and female behaviour" (1984, 10). Gender norms are the rules that regulate "masculine" and "feminine" role behaviour. Taken together, gender norms form a system whose organizing principle is the maintenance of male superordination and female subordination in the home, at work, at school, at church and even on Sesame Street (Greenglass 1982; Burstyn 1985).

Reflecting society's gender norms, the marital relation encourages husbands to use force in controlling the behaviour of their wives. Also working in the same direction is the fact that the marital relation is generally regarded as involving both intimacy and privacy. Gender norms governing occupational roles are biased in favour of men — they get more of the higher paying jobs available and are also less likely to be unemployed. This tends to make women economically dependent upon the men with whom they live. The "romantic myth" emphasizing the traditional role of the "loving, self-sacrificing wife" is also part of the gender system. This myth tends to make women emotionally dependent on their partners. Dependency leads men to devalue women. Devalued women are easier for men to hit and hurt.

Hitting and hurting are implicated in the politics of the marital relation. Gender norms require it. Marital interaction "becomes the battlefield where the early war between the sexes is fought. It is here that women are constantly reminded where their 'place' is and that they are put back in their place, should they venture out" (Henley and Freeman 1979, 474). In turn, constantly reminding women of their subordinate status reinforces gender norms that define males as superior and women as inferior. Far from being deviant, woman battering is quite normal. It is an example of conformity not deviance, an example of "normative" and not "deviant" violence (Ball-Rokeach, 1980).

IMAGES OF WIFE ABUSE: THE ROLE OF SOCIETAL REACTION   During the early part of the 1970s, women in various communities across Canada and the United States attempted to help abused women and their children by providing temporary shelters of various kinds. Here, an abused wife could find safety, sympathy and empathy. The women running the earliest shelters also propagated a theory that explained why men abused the women with whom they lived and why and how their shelters help battered women.

According to Morgan (1981), shelter theorists linked wife abuse with male gender domination. Their theory was a structural one. That is to say, gender domination or social inequality based on gender differences, was part of the very fabric of society. Men occupied most of the most important positions (educational, religious, economic, military, governmental) in society and also believed that this was how things ought to be. This is called patriarchy. Patriarchy legitimated the male use of almost any means in controlling "their" women. To formulate a theory of wife abuse attacking patriarchy was to offer a major challenge to male domination.

As time went on, the shelter movement needed more funds than they could obtain from private sources. So, funds were requested from various state agencies. Funds were made available. So too were professionals (psychiatrists, psychologists, social workers) who worked for various state welfare and law-enforcement bureaucracies. These bureaucracies work best when the problems they deal with are diagnosed as *individual* problems or pathologies, rather than as manifestations of deep societal or structural problems. An individualized diagnosis and definition of wife abuse also *depoliticizes* wife abuse. Gradually, apolitical, individualized images or definitions of abused women who use shelters, replaced the earlier women-as-an-abused-group definition of wife abuse.

The individual pathology used to bring about this change of labels was alcoholism. Alcohol caused otherwise gentle men to beat their wives. Alcohol explained why interaction between spouses "goes wrong." If the problem of "problem drinking" could be solved, wife abuse would be reduced. Therefore shelters should include therapies designed to deal directly with the problem of boozing and therefore indirectly with the problem of women battering.

As a result of changing the image of wife abuse, professionals gained more work. The state gained too. More control and a political problem depoliticized. In the meantime, women who created and ran the earliest shelters became a sideshow. Occupying centre stage was the state, a state whose constituent agencies and bureaucracies publish volumes describing their contribution towards reducing wife abuse.[16]

Conflict Theories

In almost all of the theories reviewed here, inequality between men and women is, in one way or another, implicated in violence directed against women by the men with whom they live. At the same time, these theories tend to ignore both the fundamental causes of inequality and the role of the capitalist state as facilitator or promotor of wife abuse. By contrast conflict theories are characterized by an emphasis on the fundamental sources of inequality between men and women and a view of the state as working on behalf of those responsible for beating women.

The two characteristics that help separate conflict from non-conflict theories, may also be used to distinguish between "class" and "gender" theories. In class conflict theories, a capitalistic economy is viewed as a fundamental cause of social inequality. The state serves as an instrument of class rule. Gender theorists replace "capitalist domination" with "masculine domination" and retain the conception of the state as instrument, but have the state working as an instrument of male rule instead of class rule.

Gender theories of wife abuse may themselves be sub-divided into "gender conflict" and "gender class conflict" theories. The first are non-Marxist formulations, the second tend to be influenced by Marx and Engels.

GENDER CONFLICT THEORY   In its original meaning, patriarchy referred to "a specific form of masculine domination and privilege" that flourished under certain historically specific (feudal) modes of production. In feudal society, patriarchy referred to the absolute rule of the father over the men and women in a kin group. Female members produced material things (e.g., food) and reproduced the kin group by bearing children. The patriarch ruled both their productive and reproductive labour.

In advanced capitalist societies patriarchal rule becomes more complex. As a regime it consists of three interrelated elements or parts. Role differentiation is the first of these. Role differentiation means that male roles and female roles are separated from each other. So, men work, and women stay at home; men go off to fight, and women stay at home. Men go off to bars, and women stay at home.

Second, the concept refers to the stratification of gender roles. This means that any male role, even the one ranked lowest in terms of status, power and wealth, is superior to the highest-ranked female role. In capitalist societies, political and economic roles ranked highest in terms of status, wealth and power are, for the most part, male roles. Third, patriarchy refers to an ideology or set of cultural norms and values that legitimizes the pattern of gender role differentiation and role stratification extant in society. When males occupy most positions of power, most people in society, men and women alike, accept patriarchy as "natural."

The domination of husbands over their wives is as definitive of patriarchy in advanced capitalist societies as it was and is in agrarian-feudal societies. In both kinds of society, the family is the locus of patriarchy, a cell socially and historically constructed by men commanding all the important positions of power (political, economic, religious, educational, military) in a wider society. Wife abuse, according to Dobash and Dobash (1979, 15), is simply "an extension of the domination and control of husbands over their wives." Patriarchy then, is the fundamental cause of both inequality and wife abuse.[17] Wife abuse and patriarchy are maintained because they are "supported by the economic and political institutions and by a belief system that makes (them) seem natural, morally just and sacred" (Dobash and Dobash 1979, 45).

Together with the Dobashes, Wilson (1977) provides numerous examples of the support given to wife abuse by state policies. For example welfare policies define wives and children as "dependents." Family policies promise but do not really help women to perform the "dual role" of mother and worker. Without adequate and affordable child care, many women cannot work outside the home. Housing policies encourage women to remain with the husbands who beat them because separation might mean that the state would have to bear the cost of housing them. Law-enforcement policies tend to be subordinated to the view that a family that stays together is socially more desirable than one that may be broken up by police interference in a "private" fight in which the wife gets hurt.

For these reasons, the Dobashes reach the following conclusion: "If women's place in history has been at the receiving end of a blow, the capitalist state has done little to change the course of history" (1979, 58). Instead, it has functioned as a "male protection racket" (1979, 64).

GENDER-CLASS CONFLICT THEORY   Vadya Burstyn (Queen's University) agrees with the main thrust of the Dobash and Dobash thesis. At the same time, she introduces changes that she believes would improve it. To this end, she replaces the concept of patriarchy with that of "masculine dominance." This term is preferred because "it allows us to name both the relation (dominance) and the agent (the gender men)" (Burstyn 1985, 50). Next, she introduces us to "gender classes." This concept refers to two major socially-constructed groupings, the gender men and the gender women. These classes stand in a relation of conflict to each other. The basis of opposition of the feminine gender-class is their "appropriation and domination" by members of the masculine gender-class.

The origin of a major social hierarchy composed of a superordinate and subordinate gender-class is the male appropriation of the surplus produced by women and the use of this surplus to increase their wealth, power and privilege vis-a-vis other men.[18] The cause of men's ability to appropriate what women produce is the *sexual division of labour*. This predates capitalism.

The women's labour referred to in the sexual division of labour has a two-fold character. First, women produce material things such as food and clothing. Second women engage in "reproductive labour," i.e., they bear and produce people. Men appropriate both forms of women's labour. They take and use what they produce, and they control (via inheritance laws and so on) their children. In order to do this and live as a relatively "leisured gender class," men had first to control women's bodies, their sexuality.

One major way in which men attempted to do this was by socially constructing the feminine gender class. This involved the creation and maintenance of invidious differences between masculine and feminine gender classes. In the process of creating these differences—differences that legitimate gender inequality— Burstyn (1985, 54) identifies "the physical body of the woman . . . as one of the most contested terrains." Effective masculine control of women's bodies is the key to the routine appropriation of women's labour by men. Rules or norms of monogamy and compulsory heterosexuality are central to the task of ensuring that women will use their bodies to produce things and services and reproduce children for their male kin, and that they will not use them to do the same thing for other men or women. Wife abuse is a way of controlling women's bodies, a way of trying to make unthinkable the possibility of using their bodies to serve the material and sexual interests of other men (Burstyn 1985, 54).

Based partly on their domination and use of women, men in agrarian societies occupied all or most of the positions of power and authority. The same situation exists in advanced capitalist societies. Men are in charge of society's command posts — military, economic, political and so on. Burstyn sees the capitalist state as being "condensed . . . out of these (male dominated) . . . networks and systems of power" (1985, 56). Naturally, the state reflects and expresses the politics of masculine domination. This is why she refers to the capitalist state as the "genderic state" (1985, 57). One important item of business of the generic state is gender oppression. Gender oppression comes naturally to state agencies, because most of the people in charge of the state welfare, health, finance and criminal-justice agencies, are men.

For Burstyn, then, the capitalist state is an instrument for the maintenance of the long-term interests of the masculine gender-class. These are associated with continued masculine dominance. If concessions will help achieve this objective, concessions will be made. On closer inspection, these often turn out to be merely different ways (e.g., welfare) of "regulating women in the interests of continued male dominance" (1985, 65). In supporting male dominance the state is also supporting the efforts of members of the married masculine gender-class to control the bodies, hearts and minds of members of the feminine gender-class by beating them up.

SUMMARY

Definitions of wife abuse fuse political with technical considerations. Broad definitions of wife abuse focussing on the quality of the act appear to be preferred by those who are for women and against men who beat women and a state that facilitates such conduct. U.S. and Canadian evidence indicates that, in any given year, approximately 11 percent of women who live with men are abused by them. This figure increases to over 40 percent for separated and divorced women.

In strain-subcultural explanations, wife abuse is seen as a solution to problems of strain or stress caused by ambivalence, feminization or feminism. Control explanations take two forms, dependency and deterrence. In the former, wives who are most seriously abused are those who are forced to stay with their husbands because they are dependent on them for food and shelter. Deterrence theorists contend that wives who are least likely to be beaten are those who report their husbands to police officers who take notice, come to the house and arrest or summons the perpetrator. If he is a male, the police officer who attends and the husband who beats his wife are both influenced by cultural norms permitting men to hit their wives. These gender norms figure prominently in interactionist accounts of wife abuse. In another version of this perspective, the role of the state in diverting attention from the real societal sources of wife abuse is emphasized. Finally, two versions of conflict theory were presented, gender conflict and gender-class conflict. Both emphasize the connection between male dominance and wife abuse. Patriarchy is central to the former, the genderic state to the latter.

SUGGESTED READINGS

M. **Beaudry,** *Battered Women* (Montreal: Black Rose Books, 1985).
M. **French,** *Beyond Power: Women, Men and Morals* (New York: Jonathan Cape, 1985).
J. **Hanmer and Sheila Saunders,** *Well Founded Fear: A Community Study of Violence to Women* (London: Hutchinson, 1984).
National Institute of Justice, *Confronting Domestic Violence* (Washington, D.C. Superintendent of Documents, 1986).

NOTES

1. In fairness to Straus, it should be noted that he does use the term "wife beating" in his more recent publication (1984). However, the interactional emphasis is retained.
2. These results are usually stated within statistically estimated degrees of error. So, one may say, 20 percent of all Canadian women now living with men were beaten at least once during their relationship, and this estimate is accurate to plus or minus two percentage points. This means the actual percentage could vary between 18 and 22 percent.
3. Included among the reasons for not reporting threats and assaults to the police are fear of future violence, a view of wife assault as a private matter, embarrassment and the wife's belief that she was partly to blame. (Solicitor General 1985).
4. *Domestic Homicides 1961–1981,* Canadian Centre for Justice Statistics, Publications 5540-2, Ottawa, Ontario. The analysis done by CCJS was based upon data collected by Statistics Canada. The figures on domestic homicides and spousal homicides presented here are taken from this source.
5. The numbers from which the average number of spouses were derived were taken from the census, 1961, 1971, 1981, Statistics Canada. The number of spouses, including women in the married and separated categories, for the three years was actually 5 460 461.
6. The seven cities surveyed were Greater Vancouver, Edmonton, Winnipeg, Toronto, Montreal, Halifax-Dartmouth, and St. John's.
7. See footnote 10.
8. In evaluating the results of this survey, it is relevant to note that "wife abuse" and "abusive events" were left undefined. This means

that some respondents might have had in mind "cutting remarks" as an example of an abusive event while others might have restricted the meaning of the concept to some sort of physical assault. The contribution made to the findings by respondents holding different conceptions of abusive events is not known. The larger the proportion that include minor assaults and hurtful remarks or jokes as abusive events, the larger will be the proportion of respondents whose answers suggest that wife abuse is frequent and pervasive.

9. For a methodological review of these studies see Smith (1985). By contrast, Smith's own wife-abuse survey is, methodologically speaking, a very sound one. This increases the reliability of the estimates he provides.

10. Incidence estimates and prevalence estimates are not the same thing. Incidence figures tell us how many spouses are assaulted or abused in a stated time period. They do not tell us how many times any given husband or wife is assaulted or abused. That is to say, they do not tell us how *prevalent* wife abuse is. Prevalence figures provided this information. Thus Straus reports that the 148 violent husbands he discovered during his national survey committed an average of seven violent acts against their wives during the year. For wives the corresponding figure was almost the same, 6.8 acts per year. In the Straus et al., 1980 study, incidence rates were devised by "defining a couple as violent if one or more violent incidents occurred during the year." Prevalence measures are derived from "how many times each violent act occurred during the year." M. Straus, "Victims and Aggressors in Marital Violence" *American Behaviour Scientist* 23, 5 (May/June, 1980): 684–685.

11. This conclusion is also supported by the findings of Schulman (1979); Stachura and Teske (1979).

12. Straus (1980, 690–695). The MLHL thesis is also described in Gelles and Straus (1979, 15–39) and Gelles (1974, 59–61).

13. See, Dutton and Levens (n.d.); Levens (1978); Byles (1980); Jaffee and Thompson (1979); and Jaffee and Burris (1984).

14. In August 1982, Robert Kaplan, Solicitor General of Canada, directed all Crown attorneys to treat domestic assault cases as seriously as they treated assaults among strangers. For a brief historical account of these changes, see Canadian National Clearinghouse on Family Violence, "A Community Responds to Wife Assault," *Response* 5, 6.

16. For confirmation, write for information on wife abuse to either the Research Division, Solicitor General of Canada, Ottawa or Ministry of Community and Social Services, Toronto, Ontario. For further elaboration of this thesis see Loeske and Cahill (1984) and Stark and Flitcraft (1983).

17. For a good discussion of patriarchy, see Beechey (1979).
18. The model for this process was provided by Marx. For Marx the appropriation by capitalists of the surplus produced by labour played an important part in the formation of the capitalist and proletarian social classes.

CHAPTER SIX

VANDALISM: YOUTH

AS TROUBLE-MAKERS

WHAT IS VANDALISM?

ON THE BASIS OF A reading of Chapter 1 (Definitions), one would expect definitions of vandalism to fall into two groups, objective and subjective. As we shall shortly discover, this expectation is met. At the same time, similarities and differences among definers, as well as conceptions influencing their definitions, vary in ways that are unique to vandalism. Thus, we find adults who are in the business of social control (legislators, police officers, judges), as well as the adolescents they are trying to control, defining vandalism objectively, while some sociologists who study vandalism define it subjectively. Here, sociologists offering objective definitions stand closer to the vandals' own definition of vandalism than do those formulating subjective definitions. In addition to these similarities and differences, definitions of vandalism are influenced by either a "sensible" or a "senseless" conception of the phenomenon. As conceptions come before definitions, we shall deal with this specific conceptual difference before discussing objective and subjective definitions of vandalism.

Senseless vs Sensible

In law, vandalism is legally punishable when a person intentionally damages someone else's property. It does not matter what this person's motive was. All that is needed for a conviction is a finding that the person had the intention to cause damage.

Motives for this behaviour may vary all over the lot. The law is not interested in them. However, adults generally, and especially their media representatives, appear to be exclusively interested in the motives for vandalism. What appears to irk them most is that they cannot discover any motives that make sense to those who own or control property or who are carriers of a middle-class aesthetic concerning the "look" of things. Kids who destroy or deface private and public property rather than steal it are engaging in a senseless form of behaviour because they don't gain anything material, and in the process, all they do is to make a nice school, statue, phone booth, bus, or subway station look ugly. In the meantime, taxpayers and innocent people (like us) have to pay for the damage.[1]

Support for the idea that adolescent vandals conceive of their behaviour sensibly, comes from sociological studies of youth in general and of vandalism in particular. One of the most extensive and costly surveys of vandalism in Canada was undertaken by Ontario's Task Force on Vandalism. This task force commissioned a self-report survey of vandalism among a non-random sample of students aged 9–19 years. These students were enrolled in ten primary and two secondary schools in Metropolitan Toronto. As part of this study, students were asked to comment on vandalism. These revealed adolescent conceptions of vandalism. One of these conceptions is stated by a 17-year-old vandal who broke the aerial of a police cruiser. "I didn't want to cause damage to friends, just foes." One obvious foe of this lad was a 17-year-old female who did not engage in vandalism. She said, "vandalism is a terrible offence against the freedoms and rights of people. I feel that it should be stopped. Vandalism gives a bad name to many innocent people because of a few terrorists. People who do this should be punished severely" (Ontario Task Force 1981, 283–287). Clearly, both he and she share a political conception of this phenomenon.

Much the same idea is conveyed by the adolescents studied by Friedenberg. In his book *The Vanishing Adolescent* (1962), Friedenberg describes how adolescents feel, think and behave. Within this larger context, he discovered that adolescents regard vandalism as a form of rebellion against an oppressive system of gerontocratic rule, the rule of adults over young persons. The values, attitudes, and anxieties of adults, especially middle-class teachers and school officials, not only batter the self-esteem of adolescents but are "insulting to the process of adolescence" (1962, 42). Vandalism is one way of gaining esteem by fighting back.

Friedenberg's conception reveals a trace of romanticism, a "wallowing in the youth culture, (of) going native by adopting the poses and symbols (of youth) as if they were his own." Stanley Cohen, the British author of this statement, did not apply it to Friedenberg. He is much more interested in not having it applied to him (Cohen 1974a, 276). He sees himself as being vulnerable because of his conception of vandalism as symbolic gesture and/or a form of problem-solving behaviour. Evidence supporting this conception of vandalism, says he, can be obtained by anyone who studies vandalism in the context of the total life styles of adolescents, especially working-class adolescents in their own local social environments. Vandalism is the most pervasive form of rule (law) breaking these adolescents engage in. Some types of vandalism solve the problem of boredom; others express hostility motivated by adult hypocrisy and so on. All types are motivated and make sense to the vandals themselves (Cohen 1974a).

Objective and Subjective Definitions

In law, vandalism is defined as behaviour that "damages or destroys property or renders it useless by tampering with it" (Canadian Criminal Code). A similar objective definition is offered in the report of Ontario's Task Force on Vandalism (1981).[2] In these definitions vandalism is a quality of the act. The same thing is true of the sensible definitions offered by adolescent vandals.

Joining legislators, task force researchers and vandals is sociologist John Hagan. As you may recall from Chapter 2, Hagan defines vandalism as a crime because the norm or rule prohibiting it is included in the Canadian Criminal Code. Having objectively defined vandalism as a crime, Hagan then faces the problem of deciding whether it is a consensual or a conflict crime. The test is the degree to which Canadian citizens agree that vandalism should be a crime. According to this test, vandalism is a consensus crime.

In Hagan's definition, vandalism is treated as a homogenous category. The term covers any kind of damage to property, every way of rendering it useless. Stanley Cohen feels that a heterogenous definition, a typology of vandalism, is more valid and useful because different types of vandalism are associated with "different meanings and motives" (Cohen, S. 1974a, 260). To this end, he offers an objectively-defined typology of vandalism. The sub-types included in this typology are: "acquisitive vandalism," "tactical vandalism," "ideological vandalism," "vindictive vandalism," "play vandalism" and "malicious vandalism" (Cohen, S.

1974a, 260–261). Many actual incidents of vandalism may involve more than one sub-type, and different sub-types may involve different kinds of costs.

Based on the distinction between monetary and social (psychological) costs, Vestermark and Blauvelt (1980, 223) derive the following four-fold typology. Type one, vandalism characterized by low social and high monetary costs. Type two, involving high social and high monetary costs. Type three, involving high social and low monetary costs and type four, involving low social and low monetary costs. Examples given for the four types respectively are, destruction of a science lab, broken windows, racial graffiti and tire tracks on the school lawn.

Although his vandalism sub-types are objectively defined, Stanley Cohen does also alert us to the fact that not all incidents involving "the illegal destruction or defacement of property belonging to someone else . . . leads to its classification as the deviant act, vandalism" (1974a, 260). Thus, on Grey Cup Day in Canada, the fourth of July in the United States and Guy Fawkes Day in the United Kingdom, destruction of property may occur without the label being applied. Again on Rag Days in England, university students are "permitted" to destroy property. Obviously, the same behaviour is being labelled in different ways. The loose fit between destructive behaviour and the label vandalism is central to subjective definitions of vandalism.

When Howard Becker's subjective definition is applied, vandalism is not a quality of the act the person commits, but rather a consequence of the application of rules and sanctions to an "offender" (1963, 8). The vandal becomes an individual to whom the label "vandal" has been successfully applied. According to this definition, an individual who wilfully damages property but is not discovered doing so or is discovered but is not punished for his behaviour is not a vandal. A person who wilfully damages property becomes interesting to the student of vandalism only *after* that behaviour is discovered and the person is punished and labelled a vandal.

VANDALISM: HOW MUCH?

In Canada, questions about the amount of wilful damage or vandalism nationally can only be answered by examining police statistics. When these are tabulated, they indicate that for every 100 000 inhabitants of Canada, 127 acts of vandalism become known to the police (Table 6-1). This table also indicates that the rate of vandalism or violence against property is 1.8 times greater than is the police-reported rate for violence against persons (127.1 to 69.3). One particular kind of violence against property, arson, has a much lower reported rate, although the vandalism rate is lower than the reported rate for such economically motivated offences as break and enter, and theft. In addition, Table 6-1 indicates that almost half of all offences known to the police are theft offences. This compares with 8 percent for violent offences against the person and 14 percent for violence against property.

TABLE 6-1 *Selected Offences for Canada, 1982*
Rates per 100 000 inhabitants

Offence	Number of Offences[a]	Rate	Percentage of all Known Offences
Vandalism[b]	309 437	127.1	14.0
Arson	8 881	3.6	0.4
Break and Enter	369 882	151.9	17.0
Theft[c]	1 074 211	441.3	49.0
Violent[d]	168 646	69.3	100.0
Total Criminal Code	2 203 668	905.3	100.0

Source: Statistics Canada, *Crime and Traffic Enforcement Statistics, 1982* (Ottawa: Minister of Supply and Services Canada, 1983), Table 2.
Notes: a. These refer to offences actually known to the police.
b. This offence refers to wilful damage to public and private property.
c. This offence includes all thefts, that is, of and from vehicles, shoplifting, under and over $200 000 as well as frauds.
d. Violent offences include homicide, attempted murder, wounding, assault and rape.

On the basis of the findings presented in this table, we may conclude that vandalism offences reported by the police occur less frequently than economically motivated crimes, but more frequently than violent offences against persons.

Violent offences against property occur in all provinces, albeit not with equal frequency. Table 6-2 shows that acts of wilful damage known to the police are higher in some provinces than others. Yukon and the Northwest Territories have very high reported rates of vandalism.[3] The western provinces, Saskatchewan excepted, have high rates. Ontario has a reported rate that is quite close to the national rate, while Quebec, Nova Scotia and New Brunswick have relatively low wilful damage rates. Among eastern provinces, Prince Edward Island and Newfoundland have rates that are well above those for the other provinces in this region. On the basis of these findings, we may conclude that: (a) no

TABLE **6-2** *Wilful Damage for Canada and the Provinces and Territories, 1982*

Rates per 100 000 inhabitants

Offence	Canada	Nfld.	P.E.I.	N.B.	N.S.	Que.	Ont.	Man.	Sask.	Alta.	B.C.	Yukon & N.W.T.
Total Criminal Code	8 500	6 200	6 100	6 500	6 800	6 600	8 858	10 400	8 400	10 400	13 700	20 000
Wilful Damage	127.1	110.1	136.0	66.2	80.2	76.0	126.3	126.2	157.7	128.6	197.9	2 517.6

Source: Statistics Canada, *Crime and Traffic Enforcement Statistics, 1982* (Ottawa: Minister of Supply and Services Canada, 1983), Table 2.

clearly-established pattern characterized provincial variations in rates of wilful damage against property; (b) there appears to be no clear connection between the total amount of reported crime in a province and its reported rate of wilful-damage offences. Thus PEI has the lowest rate of criminal code offences, but the third highest rate of wilful-damage offences. In fact, seven of the ten provinces do not occupy an equal ranking on both offence rates.

All of the offences reported by the police actually occur more frequently than the police statistics presented in tables 6-1 and 6-2 suggest. Some indication of the size of the gap between what actually occurs and what the police establish as having occurred is provided by Table 6-3. This table indicates that household dwellers in seven of Canada's cities report to the police only about one-third of all acts of vandalism directed against their households. This compares with 70 percent of motor vehicle thefts, 64 percent of break and enter offences, and 44 percent of household thefts.

TABLE 6-3 *Selected Types of Household Victimization in Seven Canadian Cities*
Total Number of Households in 7 cities = 2 424 900

Type of Incident	Rate per 100 000 Households	Percentage of Estimated Incidents	Percentage Unreported
All Household Incidents	369	100	47
Break and Enter	94	25	36
Motor Vehicle Theft	17	5	30
Household theft	172	46	56
Vandalism	88	24	65

Source: Table 1, Canadian Urban Victimization Survey, Bulletin #1, 1983, Programmes Branch, Research and Statistics Group, Ministry of the Solicitor General, Ottawa, Canada. The seven cities included in the survey are Greater Vancouver, Edmonton, Winnipeg, Toronto, Montreal, Halifax-Dartmouth and St. John's.

Perhaps if victims, witnesses, and citizens generally believed that vandalism was increasing, they would report more offences to the police in the hope that this would prevent a "crime wave" of violence against property. Actually, citizens do seem to believe that vandalism is increasing.[4] Yet they appear to be reluctant to report to the police a greater proportion of the offences they are aware of. Thus, for Canada as a whole, violent offences against public property known to the police decreased by about three percent between 1978 and 1982.[5] A decrease of roughly the same magnitude also occured in Ontario.[6] Based on insurance data collected during an earlier five-year period and included in Ontario's task Force Report on Vandalism, Julian Roberts concluded that "vandalism is not costing Ontario communities more now than it did five years ago" (Roberts 1981, 27). Although dollar losses due to vandalism were higher in 1979 than in 1974, a large part of this increase was due to inflation. Thus, one may conclude that between 1978 and 1982, both nationally and in Ontario, vandalism was decreasing, albeit very gradually.

In Ontario, a major exception to this general trend was Metropolitan Toronto. Table 6-4 indicates that the wilful damage rate was 168 percent greater in 1979 than it was in 1970. During the same period the reported violent crime rate increased by 45 percent and the break and enter rate by 36 percent. Whether this large increase was due to an increase in the actual incidence of wilful damage offences, to increases in the reporting of such offences, or to changes in police recording and reporting procedures cannot be ascertained either from figures presented in Table 6-4 or any other figures presented in the task force report.

TABLE **6-4** *Selected Offences, 1970–1979 for Metropolitan Toronto Rates per 100 000 inhabitants*

	Offences		
Year	Wilful Damage	Violent[a]	Break and Enter
1970	40.8	38.4	70.4
1972	47.8	42.8	67.8
1974	63.8	46.5	71.2
1976	79.0	48.1	83.2
1978	92.6	56.6	95.8
1979	106.2	58.3	94.7

Source: Ontario Task Force on Vandalism (Toronto, Queen's Printer, 1981), *Vandalism: Responses and Responsibilities* (Report). Table 1, page 365.
Note: a. Includes assaults and robberies.

WHO ARE THE VANDALS?

Any attempt to identify the vandals is hampered by the absence of relevant information. No government agency, research organization, or individual social scientist has conducted a self-report survey containing questions on such things as ethnicity, social class, religion and so on to a random sample of the Canadian population. Official or police statistics tell us only that young males tend to be over-represented among those charged: in Canada, 44 percent of those charged with wilful damage in 1982 were juveniles, although the population between the ages of 7 and 16 contained only about 25 percent of the total population. Similarly, females constituted about 50 percent of the population between the ages of 7 and 16, but they represented only about seven percent of the young persons charged.[7]

As a matter of fact, statistics on persons charged may *underestimate* the degree to which young persons commit acts of vandalism. For one thing, the police are likely to be more lenient with juveniles, preferring to deal with them informally rather than charging them with a criminal offence. Secondly, Ann Cavoukian's self-report study of vandalism indicates that almost 90 percent of the 1 222 students in her school sample admitted committing at least one act of vandalism (Cavoukian 1981, Appendix 1). These findings, she notes, "are consistent with previous self-report studies of vandalism."[8]

Most studies of vandalism do indicate that the incidence of vandalism among young people is very high.[9] At the same time, the prevalence of vandalism among this group is not equally high. More specifically, the average or mean number of acts of vandalism committed increases steadily from age 9 to ages 15 and 16 and then decreases among 17, 18, and 19 year olds. Cavoukian's findings indicate that 9 year olds admit committing an average of 6 acts of vandalism during the preceding 12 months. This figure increases to 13 for 12 year olds and 16 for 15 year olds. The average then starts decreasing until it reaches its second lowest value, 8, for 19 year olds.[10]

In addition to being young and male, vandals also tend to come from lower- and working-class homes. This conclusion is supported by the results of a study conducted by Stephen Tribble (1972). Tribble's sample consisted of 60 households selected from four socio-economic areas in Fredericton, New Brunswick. Using a self-report measure of law-violative behaviour, including damage to property, he discovered that a young person's involvement in vandalism varied with the rank or status of the father's occupation. The higher the father's occupational status, the lower the child's reported involvement in the criminal and delinquent activities included in the survey. Thus, of the 32 juveniles whose fathers had the lowest-ranked occupations, 26 were self-reported offenders. The corresponding figures for juveniles whose fathers had middle- and highly-ranked occupations were 4 out of 7 and 5 out of 15 respectively. Additional support for concluding that lower- and working-class juveniles are more likely to engage in acts of vandalism than middle- or upper-class juveniles comes from Tribble's survey of 60 households in New Brunswick, from Vaz's (1965) study of high-school students in Hamilton, Ontario; Elliott and Huizinga's (1973) self-report survey of a national sample of youth in the U.S.A.; and from Gladstone's (1978) self-report survey of youth in England.[11]

The results of studies conducted in all three countries also indicate that the vandal is usually a young person who does poorly at school, who dislikes school, and who is subject to relatively lax supervision and control by his parents. Thus, among secondary-school students, Cavoukian found that the average number of self-reported acts of vandalism by students who like school was 9.4. This compares with an average of 26.6 for those who don't like school. Again, among "A" or "B" students, the self-reported average was seven acts per student. For "D" or "F" students, the corresponding figure was 25.4. Finally among those students who report spending zero to one hour on the streets, the average number of self-reported acts was 7.6. Those spending two or more hours on the streets report an average of 16.5.

On the basis of the results presented here and a more general review of the Canadian literature, two major conclusions seem warranted. The first refers to vandals. Vandals are mainly lower-class males who are doing poorly at school, who do not like school and who are subject to weak parental control in their homes. The second refers to vandalism. Most acts of vandalism are minor in nature and tend to increase with age up to the age of sixteen. Thereafter, they decrease in frequency. There seems to have been no major increase in either the seriousness or the frequency of vandalism over the past few years.

PERSPECTIVES ON VANDALISM

Strain Theories

In Canada, one well-known strain theoretic explanation of delinquency in general and vandalism in particular, is provided by Memorial University anthropologist Elliot Leyton (1979). For Leyton, vandalism consists of senseless acts mainly engaged in by adolescents from lower-class homes characterized by poverty and unemployment. An uncaring society routinely creates and maintains such homes. Vandalism, according to Leyton, is caused by parents who instil feelings of being rejected in their children. They do this by blaming them for their own troubled situation. Like delinquency in general, vandalism is an attempt on the part of juveniles to become reintegrated with their families. Ultimately then, society and parents are to blame, because they are the sources of the strain that vandalism attempts to reduce.

Leyton's triple theory of delinquency (society, family and delinquent), is described by Gordon West (University of Toronto) as "unsophisticated" (West 1985, 81). More than this, he sees Leyton as dangerous to youth because his therapy for delinquency, "compulsory family counselling," extends the control of the state over members of lower socio-economic groups. Neither of these criticisms applies to Stinchombe's (1964) strain explanation of "rebellion" among high school students.

According to Stinchombe, middle- and not lower- or working-class boys experience the greatest amount of strain in high school. The source of their greater strain lies in their commitment to academic success *and* their involvement in a course of studies that does not appear to them to be related to the kinds of jobs they expect to get later on. The *ambiguity* of the link between curriculum choice and job prospects constitutes a pressure-inducing ambivalence. They have internalized middle-class success values and have also accepted the idea that education is their ticket to success, and now their school, via its curricula, has let them down. The resulting ambivalence and strain induces a rebellious stance. Interaction with others having similar experiences is associated with rebellious behaviour, including acts of vandalism.

In another variant of the strain thesis, vandalism is seen as a way of creating a hazard (getting caught) in order to "manufacture excitement" (Matza, 1964, 108). Vandalism, in short, is a form of risk-taking behaviour, one that has the dual advantage of being exciting and conferring status within the group of adolescent peers. Adult authorities are responsible for making society safe and predictable and for ensuring that adolescents are kept out of the mainstream of (occupational) life until they become adults. A sense of strain induced both by boredom and an isolated, subordinated marginal status, is meliorated by the "gesture" (Cohen 1980, 86) of vandalism. The gesture is directed at the private and public property of adults for a variety of reasons, including getting back at the perceived sources of their troubles.[12]

Control Theories

FEATHERING, FLOCKING AND VANDALISM   There exist in our culture a number of "common-sense" theories of delinquency. One of the most popular of these is the belief that "bad companions" are a major cause of deviant behaviour. The average parent, teacher, policeman, judge, scout leader and newspaper editor share the belief that a young person who goes around with deviant or delinquent peers will get into trouble. Whether this individual does actually cause trouble or not, he or she will be regarded as a troublemaker because "birds of a feather flock together."

Included in this common-sense belief are two variables or factors and a statement of relationship between them. The first variable is "feather" or feathering. It refers to what the individual brings to the peer group. The second variable is "flock" or flocking, and it refers to what the group does for or to its members. The statement of relation implies that someone who brings "goodness" or other attributes to a deviant group will soon become deviant, and in order to remain a group member will have to continue to behave in deviant or delinquent ways. The statement also implies that individuals who are already delinquent or deviant go around with others who behave in the same way. They do this because conformist peers do not wish to include deviants in their groups.

The two variables figure prominently in subcultural and social control theories of delinquency in general and of vandalism in particular. The same variable is, however, not given primacy in each of the two theories. Moreover the contribution made by the group to the individual member is seen differently by each theory. Finally, the way in which the two variables are related to each other and to vandalism is also different in each theory.

For Travis Hirschi, the key theoretical problem in the field of delinquency is "how much feathering precedes how much flocking" (1971, 159). Thus the student who is doing poorly at school has a relatively low stake in conforming with either school rules or legal ones. Having less to lose than students who are successful, such students are also less likely to be deterred from committing acts of vandalism by the prospect of getting caught. Therefore, they are more likely to damage property willfully, and, in general, they exhibit a less docile stance towards school authorities. Conformist students tend to disassociate themselves from troublemakers. They have their own school careers, reputations and parents to think of. For the individual vandal, this narrows the choice of associates to other troublemakers, since they are the only group of peers whose members have little to lose by associating with him. In itself, going around with deviant associates does not induce the individual to engage in acts of vandalism. It is feathering or the low stake in conformity that does this.

Figure 6-1 describes the relation between feathering (e.g., failing at school), flocking (delinquent associates), and vandalism in Hirschi's social control model.

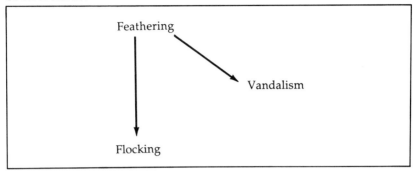

In Albert Cohen's subcultural theory, the one-way relationship between feathering and flocking is replaced by a two-way one. Having delinquent associates is, like feathering, also related to vandalism (Figure 6-2).

FIGURE **6-2** *Feathering, Flocking and Vandalism: Cohen's Subcultural Theory.*

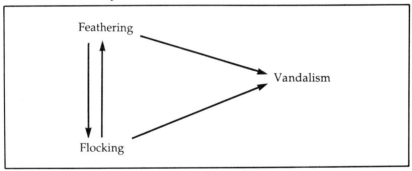

According to Albert Cohen, working-class boys are more likely than middle-class boys to do poorly at school and therefore experience status frustration. They tend to gravitate toward other boys who are also failing at school. The peer group supports its members. It also rewards those who demonstrate, by their attitudes and behaviour, acceptance of the group's inversion of the values of the school and of its middle-class teachers. For example, teachers value attendance and punctuality; therefore, the peer group values tardiness and truancy. Teachers value property; the peer group rewards vandals with status. Truancy and vandalism represent ways of acquiring status in a peer group composed of deviants of various kinds, including poor academic achievers. By making status contingent upon vandalism, truancy, defiance, and so on, the peer group solves the problem of status frustration for its members. It also diverts the attention of members away from compliance with school rules in general and academic achievement in particular. Poor achievers become school failures and then dropouts. Having invested less and achieved less, their stake in conforming with the school's rules and society's laws decreases. Students who have relatively little to lose and who also go around with delinquent associates are more likely to engage in acts of vandalism than are students with conformist associates who are doing well at school.

For Cohen then, feathering and flocking are equally important causes of vandalism, in contrast to Hirschi, who maintains that feathering is far more important than flocking. Indeed, Hirschi believes that flocking is either unrelated to vandalism or that engaging in vandalism leads to association with other vandals.[13]

Flocking, we now know, refers to going around with others. These others, the peer group, are regarded quite differently by Hirschi and by Cohen. For Hirschi, lonely students, the ones who tend to keep to themselves, are more likely to engage in acts of vandalism than are students who associate with others, conformist or deviant.[14] By contrast, Cohen maintains that boys who associate with delinquent or deviant peers are more likely to become vandals than are boys who keep to themselves or those who go around with conformist peers. Who is right? Theories formulated by other sociologists and the results of recent research findings on vandalism support Cohen. Almost all the studies conducted during the past ten years indicate that vandalism is largely a group activity.[15] The lonely vandal, then, figures more prominently in Hirschi's theory than he or she does in reality.

In Hirschi's control theory, the influence that deviant associates have upon deviant behaviour is underestimated while the influence of conformist associates upon conforming behaviour is overestimated. Two Canadian sociologists, Linden and Fillmore (1980), have attempted to build upon and improve social-control theory by integrating it with a theory (differentiated association) that does emphasize the influence of deviant peers. In their integrated theory, ties to conventional others, such as Boy Scout friends, parents and teachers, and to conventional institutions such as the school, decrease the likelihood of vandalism, while ties to unconventional others increase it. Ties to conventional others decrease vandalism for two reasons: (i) The individual's stake in conforming with the expectations of conventional others such as parents is strong, and (ii) the individual is diverted from associating with unconventional or delinquent peers. Conversely, delinquent associates make vandalism more probable because acts of vandalism are approved of and rewarded. Naturally, the individual who is diverted from associating with delinquent peers cannot be easily influenced by them. Therefore, feathering precedes flocking in the integrated theory of Linden and Fillmore (Figure 6-3).

FIGURE **6-3:** *Feathering and Flocking — Linden and Fillmore*

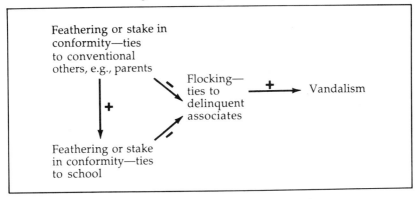

Figure 6–3 describes a situation in which juveniles who are strongly attached to their parents do not choose to become involved with delinquent peers because this might jeopardize their relations with their parents. It may also jeopardize the material support parents provide. On the other hand, doing well at school is likely to be rewarded by parents. Hence, effort is put into academic tasks and involvement in various conventional school activities and activity groups. Ties to parents and to school authorities divert students from associating with delinquent peers. This reduces the likelihood of delinquency.

Having developed their theory, Linden and Fillmore tested it by using data obtained from samples of students enrolled in schools in Richmond, California and Edmonton, Alberta. The findings confirmed their theory. "Association with delinquent peers," they concluded, "is preceded by a weakening of ties to the conventional order" (1980, 159). This conclusion also supports Albert Cohen's subcultural theory because both of his feathering variables — working-class position and failing at school — are associated with each other and with vandalism. Going around with delinquent associates is also associated with vandalism.[16]

In specifying feedback between feathering and flocking, Cohen is formulating a dynamic theory, one that explains what happens over a period of time. By contrast, Linden and Fillmore present a static theory, one that holds time constant. Thus for them, feathering influences flocking because students already belong to different social classes; they already come from different kinds of families before they enrol in school, and flocking occurs after they enrol. To this Cohen would reply, "yes, but working-class boy who gets C grades prior to hanging around with deviant associates will probably obtain Ds and Fs after his involvement with deviant associates." Hence, flocking further reduces the boy's stake in conformity.

ADOLESCENTS AS A LONELY GROUP Adolescent vandals who flock together in groups may not be lonely as individuals. However *as a social category*, they are segregated from the mainstream of social life. Norwegian criminologist Nils Christie's (1965) social control formulation directs attention away from Hirschi's lonely adolescent and towards the lonely adolescents as a category. More than this, he identifies the structural conditions associated with the segregation of adolescents and, therefore, the pervasiveness of vandalism and other forms of deviance among youth in capitalist societies.

Christie's major hypothesis is that segregated groups are more difficult to control because they have less to lose should deviance be discovered. In other words, they have a lower stake in conformity. Two societal factors help explain why adolescents are segregated and therefore less effectively controlled. First, because they do not have full-time jobs, they are not controlled by work-related rewards and punishments, e.g., they can't lose their jobs. Second, schools congregate adolescents and facilitate peer-group formations. Membership in these groups tends to reduce the salience and relevance of adult rewards and punishments. Peer-group mediated rewards and punishments become more important. The influence of conformist adults who already have a stake in conformity is thus attenuated or made less effective.

For these reasons, an adolescent who does *not* engage in vandalism is, like true love, hard to find. In Christie's own words, "it is difficult to imagine a situation better designed for giving a group a greater risk in society" (1965, 10). Adolescents, in short, engage in vandalism because the structure of society makes youth a "crime-generating phenomenon."

Interactionist Theories

Interactionist theories of vandalism are quite varied. These theoretical variations can be placed under three headings: labelling, resistance to labelling and deviance amplification. The focus of these theories is usually lower- and working-class males. The societal context is invariably one in which they are "compelled to go to school in order to receive an education for a society which does not need them" (Cohen, S. 1980, xxix). In deviance amplification theory, vandals are socially constructed "folk devils." Teachers would be too, if working class lads controlled the mass media; this is what the first two theories suggest.

LABELLING AND RESISTANCE TO LABELLING   According to Stanley Cohen vandalism or "smashing up" is a way of "staking a claim to an identity other than that which you have been offered" (1974b, 61). Cohen admits that there is a spontaneous, spur-of-the-moment element in incidents of vandalism, but there are also more stable social interactional processes at work that influence meanings as well as the targets selected. Schools are often selected as targets because in them working-class lads are not rewarded for aspiring to working-class-based identities and are not offered a fair chance of achieving identities valued by middle-class school authorities — even if they wanted them.

Teachers assigned the responsibility for inculcating middle-class norms and values in their charges, work best with those who have already internalized them, i.e., middle-class students. These students are labelled "bright," "hardworking," "punctual," "clean" and "responsible." Their future academic path or track is one for which such students are well suited on grounds of ability and motivation. By contrast, working-class lads have deficiencies in both motivation and ability attributed to them. These students make teachers work much harder, at a task that will probably bear no fruit because they are likely to drop out and go to work in a factory or grocery store. A technical or non-academic track is viewed as being more suitable to those less likely to succeed because they just cannot or will not use the educational opportunities made available to them.

The identity problem here does not stem from the fact that working-class lads are denied the middle-class identities they aspire to. Rather, the school, unlike their peers and the non-school leisure context, (clothes, music, soccer, hanging around, etc.), does not provide identities valued by them. In Stanley Cohen's interactionist account, then, vandalism is one way of being somebody, one way of establishing an identity by making a prohibited "gesture" against the property of those with the authority to make their labels stick.

The "stuff" out of which the labels vandalism and vandal are made has, according to Newman and Newman (1980), been around in schools for a long time, since the Middle Ages at least. This stuff includes children as a group separate from adults. Later, about the middle of the 19th century, "adolescent" as a subordinate and distinct social type was constructed by psychologists (Musgrove 1964).[17] In addition, school authorities have always had to deal with a "crisis of discipline," an alleged crisis that includes not only acts of destruction for which students have been responsible, but also all *unexplained* acts of destruction involving school property. Finally, schools are responsible not only for taking students in, but also for moving them on and out. To the extent that schools themselves have always played some part in influencing student decisions to play truant or to drop out of school, they create "phantom students" who return to contribute to the school's crisis of discipline. Thus students who are least often present in school, i.e., phantom students, are responsible for a disproportionate amount of school vandalism, especially of the more serious kind (Scherer 1979, 69; Birman and Nattrieloo 1980, 167; Ellis and Choi 1984).

To say that the stuff out of which the labels "vandalism" and "vandals" are made has always been present, is not to say that such labels were actually created and used with equal enthusiasm and zeal in different historical periods. Since the mid-1970s, vandalism has received a great deal of attention. In one specific year, the dollar cost of studying it must have come close to the dollar cost of the damage done by vandals.[18] What stimulated all these special investigations? Partly an increase in property destroying/defacing incidents (especially in schools) but mainly, "more extensive reporting" of these kinds of events (Newman and Newman 1980, 43; Rubel 1979, 88). The role of the mass media in amplifying youth deviance is the focus of Stanley Cohen's "folk devil" thesis.

THE VANDAL AS FOLK DEVIL   Cohen's transactional (interactional) account begins with the concept of "moral panic." A moral panic is:

> "a condition, episode, person or group of persons . . . (that becomes) defined as a threat to societal values and interests; its nature is presented in a stylized and stereotypical fashion by the mass media. The moral barricades are manned by editors, bishops, politicians . . . (and) . . . socially credited experts; ways of coping are evolved or (more often) resorted to; the condition then disappears, submerges or deteriorates and becomes more visible (Cohen, S. 1980, 9).

The targets of moral panics are occasionally new or novel persons, groups and so on. At other times, these have been around for ages but are suddenly seen or interpreted as a new, threatening phenomenon, group or type. Since the end of the Second World War in 1945, the social category of "youth," especially, but not exclusively, working-class youth associated with violence of one kind or another, have been the target of one moral panic after another. Specifically, Mods and Rockers, Teddy Boys, Skinheads and soccer hooligans in Britain, the Hells Angels and street gangs in the United States, rock concert goers in Canada, and vandalism of various kinds in all three societies, have been the object of recurring moral panics.

If it is successful, a moral panic *amplifies* fears about the amount and seriousness of the group or phenomenon that is its target. In the process of deviancy amplification, a moral panic creates folk devils. A folk devil is a socially constructed, stereotypical carrier or source of significant social harm or evil. The creation of this social type stabilizes deviance. It helps make it more permanent than it otherwise might have been. Moral panics, then, amplify and stabilize the deviance they intend to regulate.

Those who profit from running moral enterprises are called moral entrepreneurs. The mass media are identified by Cohen as the moral entrepreneurs who ran the moral panics that transformed minor vandals into folk devils. In addition to selling newspapers, those who controlled the mass media also spoke for adults, property owners, tax payers in general and middle-class values in particular. Both discipline and utilitarian values were, or seemed to be, threatened by the vandal. Vandalism itself was regarded as contagious, as something that might infect youth as a whole, including their children.[20]

Cohen's description of the entire process leading to the construction of the vandal as folk devil can be summed up in the following terms: The structural (segregated) and cultural (different and oppositional norms) position of working class youth causes a problem for them. They are redundant outsiders who are offered no valued action or identity by society. Vandalism is one way of attempting to stake a claim to a more valued identity, to enhance oppositional meanings within their own group. Society reacts by sensitizing the general population to the threat posed by vandalism. The mass media also dramatize and escalate incidents of vandalism. Vandalism increases and the mass media helps polarize the conflict by taking an "us versus them" line. In the process, they confirm the stereotypes they help construct (Cohen, S. 1980, 199).[21]

Conflict Theories

Research results suggest that vandals are usually young and tend to come mainly from lower- and working-class homes.[22] Some conflict theorists of vandalism emphasize age differences. Others make class differences central to their theories or try to include both age and class differences in their formulations.

AGE (GENERATIONAL) CONFLICT   A major starting point for sociologists formulating generational conflict theories is the finding of "maturational reform" among vandals. As adolescents get older and more out of adolescence and into adulthood, their involvement in acts of vandalism decreases. Since this finding applies to vandals from both working- and middle-class homes, it suggests that generational conflict is present in all social classes (Richards 1979).

This view is shared by generational conflict theories that differ from each other in a number of ways. A review of these differences yields the conclusion that generational conflict theories can be subdivided into two groups. One group of theories attempts to explain why adolescence, in highly industrialized societies such as Canada, is a period of transition during which conflict, delinquency and deviation peak. A second group attempts to explain why moving from the age status of adolescent to that of adult is associated with a marked decrease in deviance in general and vandalism in particular.

Prominent among the first group of theories is the "generational conflict" theory of Kingsley Davis (1968). In this theory, Davis identifies two factors that characterize parents and adolescents in all societies. These are: "decelerating socialization" and "physiological differences." The first concept refers to the process whereby socialization of children by parents decreases as children get older. The potential for conflict associated with these changes varies with the rate or pace of social change. In rapidly changing societies, such as ours, what the parents (as adolescents) learned from their parents may not be perceived as relevant or even appropriate by their own adolescent children. The attempt by parents to instil "out-of-date" parental values, attitudes and ways of behaving on their adolescent children creates conflict, one manifestation of which is vandalism.

Physiological differences refer to differences in the external appearance, strength, and internal organs of the bodies of adolescents and parents. As adolescents are reaching their peaks sexually and physically, their parents are going downhill. In a society that places a high value on youth and looking young and that also maintains that the achievement of high status is based on accomplishment and not age, sex, or race, adolescents believe themselves to be ready to compete successfully for positions that give status, such as jobs. They become frustrated and angry because adults do not allow them to do this. Instead they are forced to remain in school. For their part, adults, as well as being envious of the vitality of the young, can become jealous of opportunities young people now have that they did not have. In addition, they are fearful of an energetic group that "does not speak their language" and does not seem to want to wait their turn to enter the mainstream of life.

Adults, according to Friedenberg (1962), envy adolescents but feel threatened by them and therefore fear them as well. Major causes of adult fear and hostility towards adolescents are fear of aging and fear that adolescents will successfully struggle to evade, avoid or rebel against adult authority. Parental attempts to deal with these feelings by dealing more firmly with their adolescent children, actually facilitate rebellion, including the form it takes in vandalism.

Schools are frequently selected as targets of vandalism because the effects of bureaucracy are added to or interact with the effects of adult-youth conflict based on fear and envy. Schools are bureaucracies. Adherence to the rules (designed to ensure predictable, stable, co-ordinated, superordinate/subordinate role relations among students and between teachers and students) are its essence. Adolescents, however, emphasize the *personal* as a basis of respect, affection and commitment. They value spontaneity over planned bureaucratic arrangements they never made. If to adults in general, adolescent spontaneity, individuality and disorderliness are terrible because they are uncontrolled, then the adults who run schools must deal simultaneously with two major sources of conflict with adolescent subordinates. One is located in adult/teacher-adolescent-student power relations, the other in the disjunction between spontaneity and bureaucracy.

The power of parents over their adolescent children also contributes to generational conflict. The family is a primary group, a small, informally organized group, in which the authority of the parent touches all aspects of the child's life. One reason why the all-inclusive power of the parent is not experienced as unbearable by the child, is the child's intellectual, physical, and emotional dependence on the parent. However, as childhood gives way to adolescence, this dependence decreases. Peers now become important as objects of emotional attachment, and other adults outside the home, such as rock musicians, teachers, writers, and film stars all constitute alternative sources of authoritative knowledge and worthy values. As a result, the power structure of the family is weakened. The age inequality that is associated with adult-adolescent conflict in families and schools tends to facilitate vandalism in three ways (Richards 1979).

First, a relation in which adolescents are always subordinate influences adolescents to select conflict tactics as a way of establishing for themselves a sense of self or identity for which, at this period of their lives, they so desperately search. Vandalism tends to be selected by most adolescents precisely because it represents a "conflictual validation of the self." Even middle-class adolescents, adolescents with reputations and school positions to lose, may engage in acts of vandalism when they believe they are unlikely to be discovered by school authorities or the police, while their violence is likely to be appreciated by the peers in whose company they behaved as vandals.

Second, one consequence of parent-adolescent conflict is mutual alienation. This occurs at a time when adolescents are reaching the height of their physical and sexual development and are most willing to take the risk involved in various kinds of behavioural experimentation. Vandalism may be included among these novel or experimental forms.

Third, angry and frustrated adolescents, as Goodman (1956) and Albert Cohen (1955), have pointed out, attempt to get back at adults in various ways. Included among these is the wilful damage of "adult property."

As was indicated earlier, much of this damage occurs in schools. Schools, according to such sociologists as Bloch and Neiderhoffer (1958), contribute to delinquency by acting as a barrier to access to the mainstream of social life. Central to social life is work. For most people, paid, full-time employment is the major source of income and status. Adolescents are required by law to attend school. The law, made by adults, segregates students from the world of work and concentrates them in schools. By concentrating them, schools facilitate the process of peer-group formation. Since vandalism is mainly a group activity, schools, by helping create peer groups, also facilitate vandalism. By keeping students out of employment, schools also remove adolescents from a major locus of social-control rewards our society has to offer. By their being kept out of the work force, the behaviour of potential adolescent vandals is regulated neither by wages earned nor by the possible loss of earnings contingent upon getting captured.

In conclusion, age is significant to the sociologists, not because of biology, but because of the *social consequences* of age in society.

Age categories and their hierarchical ranking are socially created (Musgrove 1964). Adults make the rules that govern the lives of teenagers. The institutions and power relationships constructed by adults constitute structural factors that, in a rapidly changing, youth-valuing society, have made "outsiders" out of adolescents. Included among the social consequences of being made an outsider in a property-owning society is the wilful damage of the property owned or managed by adults.

The risk of youth-adult conflicts decreases as adolescents become adults. One reason for this is that adolescent outsiders are now adult insiders. They are more integrated into the mainstream of life and therefore are more effectively controlled. Having a job, a family, a car, a home and a reputation means having more to lose if one should be discovered behaving in criminal ways. For theorists, such as Briar and Piliavin, Hirschi and Toby, the inverse association between vandalism and age is, in part, caused by the increase in the adolescents' stake in conformity as they move from the status of segregated adolescent to that of integrated adult. Coterminous with this transition is the movement by adolescents out of a rather intense period of conflict with their parents.

Class Conflict Theory   The class conflict theory advanced by Muncie and Fitzgerald focusses on youth as a social category but ignores the effects of age, inequality and conflict. For them, "social class provides the primary mediating role in the genesis and development of youth subcultures" (1981, 407). Unlike American subcultural theorists such as Albert Cohen and David Matza, Muncie and Fitzgerald see vandalism, and working-class youth crime in general, as part of a broader attempt by a "subordinate (working class) to wrest more control from the dominant class or otherwise improve its position" (1981, 409). To be properly understood then, vandalism must be viewed in the context of class conflict. While adults who work may use the strike and individual sabotage as weapons in the class struggle, working-class youth use such subculturally supported responses as vandalism and soccer hooliganism.

Another example of class conflict theory is provided by Messerschmidt (1981). According to Messerschmidt, "the school is . . . a miniature society, resembling the one students would eventually be participants in." The school, in other words, helps reproduce the prevailing social class system. The primary mechanisms responsible for achieving this objective are grading and "tracking." Students are assigned grades partly on the basis of their submission to authority. Middle-class students are more submissive and receive higher grades. Middle-class students also tend to be assigned to "college-bound tracks," while students from working-class homes are assigned to "trade," "vocational" and other tracks. For these reasons, lower- and working-class students are, according to Messerschmidt, disproportionately represented among school failures. Students from these social class groupings are not only subject to relatively lax parental supervision, but they have also been socialized to believe that violence is a means of solving problems. Schools and school teachers, in preparing working- and lower-class children to do the same sorts of jobs their parents do, create problems. By failing and tracking these students and then by attempting to inculcate in them the submissive stance that will be required of them in their jobs, teachers invite the violence directed against them as individuals as well as violence directed against school property.

CLASS, AGE AND VANDALISM   David Greenberg (1977) has formulated an integrated theory that includes both age and social class as variables. This theory has been constructed out of parts borrowed from Cohen's subcultural theory, Hirschi's social-control theory, Marx's class-conflict theory, Bloch and Neiderhoffer's structural theory and the labelling perspective of Becker.

Greenberg interrelates two kinds of factors. The first are universal factors that apply to all adolescents, e.g., physiological status, puberty. The second are variable factors that apply more to some adolescents than to others, e.g., educational achievement. The variable factors are those whose effects vary with the social-class position of parents. For example, parental supervision and control decrease during adolescence, but they decrease more for working- and lower-class adolescents than for middle-class adolescents. If universal factors help explain why most adolescents engage in vandalism, variable factors help explain class differentials in the frequency and seriousness of vandalism.

In addition to including both kinds of variables, Greenberg also attempts to interrelate the personal thoughts and feelings of adolescents with membership in such large social groupings as social classes and with involvement in bureaucracies such as schools. Thus, the school bureaucracy suppresses novelty and spontaneity in behaviour, while teachers humiliate and degrade students in the process of controlling them. Vandalism represents a challenge to bureaucratic rules and also helps establish a sense of self-respect in the vandal.

Finally, Greenberg's theory indicates factors that allegedly cause adolescents to engage in acts of vandalism as well as factors that help explain the delinquency-producing reactions of adults. Thus, the exclusion of adolescents from the work force weakens the adolescent's bond to society and therefore increases the likelihood of vandalism. Ironically, the material things adults acquire as a result of working are damaged by the youths they have segregated from the world of work.

When all of the major variables included in Greenberg's theory are interrelated, we discover that the heightened motivation toward deviance during adolescence stems from the structural location of adolescents in society. Structural location refers to their segregation from work, their temporary subordinate status with respect to adults and their legally-enforced membership in school bureaucracies.

As part of the process of locating adolescents in society, adults create labels such as "teenager." These labels constitute part of a rationale for the segregation of adolescents and help bring about or increase the kinds of troublesome behaviour the labels allegedly describe. Moreover, by segregating and concentrating adolescents, schools help create subcultures that are hostile to adults and adult-controlled institutions. One manifestation of adolescent hostility is vandalism.

As adolescents age and move into the social category of adults, their motivation to behave illegally decreases because the costs of behaving in criminally deviant ways are much greater. A marriage, a job, a house, and a reputation, as well as a prison sentence or fine, may all have to be included in the cost of being convicted for a criminal offence. Because they now have more to lose, adults are not as likely to engage in criminal acts as they were when they were adolescents.

From Greenberg then, we learn that structural location is responsible for increasing the motivation toward criminal deviance during adolescence. We also learn that this motivation is not equally distributed across class groupings. Compared with lower- and working-class adolescents, adolescents who come from middle-class homes are less motivated to deviate. Unlike most of those in the lower-class groupings, middle-class adolescents can see themselves improving upon or at least not falling below the class level of their parents and teachers. Hence, the rewards for conforming are greater. So are the costs for deviating because middle-class adolescents have more to lose, including a "bright future." Major increases in the costs of destroying or defacing property also explain why the motivation to engage in vandalism decreases markedly as adolescents become adults.

An integrated theory of vandalism, based on Greenberg's theory is described in Figure 6-4. Here adolescence is associated with parental conflict. This gives rise to alienation among adolescents. Adolescents are subjected to less effective forms of social control by their parents. Because of this, they are more likely to engage in acts of vandalism. Alienated adolescents are also more likely to come under the influence of their peers. Membership in peer groups tends to increase the likelihood of vandalism.

FIGURE **6-4** *An Integrated Theory of Vandalism*

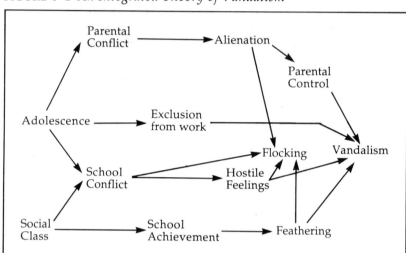

Adolescence also means exclusion from work and inclusion in schools. This facilitates the formation of peer groups. Peer-group membership, as noted earlier, tends to make vandalism more probable.

Adolescence is also associated with conflict at school. Conflicts with school authorities give rise to hostile feelings. This turns students away from teachers and toward association with others who share their feelings. Flocking increases the likelihood of vandalism. Also, hostile feelings may instigate acts of vandalism among individuals who do not belong to peer groups.

Adolescents who come from lower- or working-class homes are more likely to experience conflicts with school authorities. Such conflicts give rise to hostile feelings. Hostile students are more likely to engage in acts of vandalism. Lower- and working-class students are more likely than middle-class students to do poorly at school. This reduces their stake in conforming with school rules and regulations. The lower the stake in conformity, the greater the likelihood of vandalism. Finally, students with a low stake in conformity tend to go around with each other. Flocking increases the likelihood of vandalism.

SUMMARY

Senseless and sensible are two ways of conceiving of vandalism. To vandals and to many of the sociologists who study them, vandalism makes sense. It is a motivated form of behaviour, a symbolic act of resistance. Subjectively defined, vandalism refers to acts labelled as such. Acts that destroy property or render it useless constitute an objective definition of vandalism. The evidence indicates that most adolescents engage in acts of vandalism. Most of these cause minor damage.

Strain explanations of vandalism point to rejection, ambivalence and boredom as important sources of the strains that vandalism helps reduce. In control theories, adolescents are least likely to conform with laws prohibiting vandalism because of their low stake in conformity. By contrast, interactionist accounts emphasize labelling, resistance to labelling and the process of deviance amplification. In the amplification thesis, the vandal emerges as a socially constructed folk devil, a devil created by a moral panic. Finally, age and social class figure prominently in conflict accounts of vandalism. Generational conflict explains why vandalism is most frequently engaged in by adolescents. As adolescents age, they acquire an increased stake in conformity. Adult status and an increasing stake in conformity tend to increase conformity with laws prohibiting vandalism. In class conflict theories, vandalism is seen as an act of working-class resistance to control by members of the dominant class. Class, age and vandalism are interrelated in Greenberg's integrated theory.

SUGGESTED READINGS

Stanley Cohen, *Folk Devils and Moral Panics* (Oxford: Martin Robertson, 1980).

F. Musgrove, *Youth and the Social Order* (Bloomington: Indiana University Press, 1965).

A. Sillitoe, *The Loneliness of the Long Distance Runner* (New York: Signet, 1959).

W. Gordon West, *Young Offenders and the State* (Toronto: Butterworth and Co., 1985).

NOTES

1. For examples of this conception read almost any newspaper or magazine article on vandalism. For example, *The Toronto Star* September 25, 1984, page A/3. The research reports of teachers' groups and boards of education are another major source of senseless conceptions. For example, see the Ministry of Education (Ontario) Report (1980). For a criticism of this conception, see Stanley Cohen (1974) and Zimbardo (1982).
2. Here, vandalism is defined as, "the wilful damage or destruction of the property of another" (Ont. Task Force 1981, 15).
3. We cannot conclude from these figures either that there are more vandals in the west and northwest or that this part of Canada contains a disproportionate number of vandals who commit many violent offences against property. The statistics refer neither to the actual number of offences nor to the number of vandals by offence, but only to offences known to police. Variations in police knowledge and activity could explain provincial variations in vandalism.
4. See Ontario Task Force on Vandalism (1981, Ch. 2, Subsection B).
5. Statistics Canada, *Crime and Traffic Enforcement Statistics, 1982,* (Ottawa: Minister of Supply and Services Canada, 1983), p. 40.
6. *Crime and Traffic Enforcement Statistics,* 1978, Table 2 and 1982, Table 2. (Ottawa: Statistics Canada).
7. This is a rough estimate because, in 1982, the definition of a juvenile varied from province to province. In most, it included persons aged 7–16. In some, the age range was 7–18 and in others, 7–17. Source: *Crime and Traffic Enforcement Statistics* (Ottawa: Statistics Canada 1982).
8. It is relevant to note here that adults were not included in Cavoukian's survey. Therefore, we do not know whether the incidence of vandalism among adults is equally high.
9. See Gaudet and Doyle (1979); Boggs (1980); Tross (1977); Winnipeg Police Department (1980).
10. Ontario Task Force on Vandalism (1981, 35).
11. Vaz (1965); Elliott and Huizinga (1983); Gladstone (1978); Tribble (1972).
12. Vaz (1965) also draws attention to the role of risk-taking in adolescent subcultures. Christie (1965) describes the criminogenic structural position of adolescents in capitalist societies. Note that the strain-risk vandalism relation forms only one line of theorizing in Stanley Cohen's work. His main thrust is in another direction.
13. On page 152 of his *Causes of Delinquency* (1969), Hirschi provides evidence in support of this statement. Specifically, he asserts that, "holding the delinquency (or worthiness) of friends truly constant at

any level, the more one respects or admires one's friends, the less likely one is to commit delinquent acts."

14. See Ontario Task Force on Vandalism (1981); National Institute of Education (1977); Gladstone (1978); Richards (1979).

15. Gottfredson's research (1982) supports Hirschi's social control hypothesis.

16. Control theories that have been tested using Canadian data include Gomme (1982) and Leblanc (1981).

17. Musgrove goes on to note that, "Having invented the adolescent, society was faced with two major problems how and where to accommodate him in the social structure and how to make his behaviour accord with this specification" (1964, 33).

18. See National Institute of Education (1977).

19. In the last sentence, the word "more" should perhaps be replaced by "less." This makes more sense. I suspect a typographical error. Originally applied to Mods and Rockers, the thesis has here been extended to vandals and vandalism.

20. A good Canadian example of what Cohen had in mind is provided in the social construction of the Parkdale Gang by police and magistrates and reported in *The Globe and Mail*, April 28, 1977. For a British example see Chesshyre (1985). *Time* magazine can be relied upon to provide a U.S. example.

21. This process is not always successful. For an unsuccessful attempt to transform unemployed Canadian youth into political radicals, see Tanner et al. (1985).

22. See Home Office Research Unit (1978) and National Institute of Education (1977).

C H A P T E R   S E V E N

CONCLUSION

THIS BOOK OPENED WITH definitions of deviance (Chapter 1), moved on to a consideration of theoretical perspectives on deviance (Chapter 2) and concluded with an application of these perspectives to four substantive topics (Chapters 3–6). A review of what has been included under these three major headings yields a number of conclusions. One of the most obvious of these is that the sociology of deviance is characterized by a rich variety of definitions, approaches and theoretical perspectives. There is a lot of room for disciplined choice within this sociological sub-field.

With respect to the choice of definition, scholars whose work was included in *The Wrong Stuff* seem to fall into two major groups, those who define deviance objectively and those who define it subjectively. Those defining deviance objectively tend to work with statistics on fairly large numbers of people, organizations, cities or societies and so on. By contrast, sociologists offering subjective definitions tend to actually observe people, listen to them or join them in the activity they are studying. Their aim is to get at processes going on in the minds of individuals interacting in rather small-scale situations such as bars, massage parlours, beauty salons and so on. How one defines deviance, then, helps determine the research strategy that is adopted as well as the type of theory that is used in the collection, analysis or interpretation of data. Definitions, in short, constitute a primal sociological act or decision.

One decision that is infrequently made by either subjectively or objectively oriented sociologists is to study deviance and social control historically. Of all the studies included in this book for example, only two or three (e.g., *Wayward Puritans* and *Whigs and Hunters*) are historical studies.

The fact that Erikson and Thompson provide subjective and objective definitions of deviance respectively, suggests that historical research on deviance, crime and social control are open to those offering either definition. In this connection, Thompson's *Whigs and Hunters* and Erikson's *Wayward Puritans* stand as models of what can be accomplished.

This conclusion, one that is appropriately applied to the above mentioned historical studies, cannot be legitimately extended to any one of the four major theoretical perspectives included in this text. Instead, we discover that some theories do a better job of explaining some forms of deviance than others. For example, deterrence theory does a fairly good job of explaining corporate and police deviance, but it cannot explain why its major variables, certainty, celerity and severity of punishment operate in one way for corporate executives and police officers and in another way for vandals and ordinary street criminals. Again, the bond version of control theory works better with vandals than it does with police deviants. There appears to be no single major theoretical perspective that does the best job of explaining all of the four types of deviance included in this text. The same conclusion would probably apply if sexual deviance, child abuse or other major types of deviance were included in this book.

Many of the topics included in deviance texts elicit highly politicized conceptions and definitions. This is certainly true of the topics included in *The Wrong Stuff*. For most of the studies examined, conceptions and definitions of corporate crime, police deviance, wife abuse and vandalism have clear political implications. If, as Sartre suggests, "all writing is political" (1969, 29), then these conceptions and definitions are political in a more primal sense, that is, in the sense that they precede theory and research and so focus attention on certain aspects of the social world while diverting attention from others. Thus, a sociologist who conceives of murder as a rational, predatory act will focus on punishment as deterrence and divert attention from improving the quality of life as a preventive measure. More generally, the conceptions and definitions presented in this text reveal who and what the author is for or against. Thus a sociologist who is for youth and against corporate criminals will conceive of and define vandalism in such a way as to include corporate vandals and then go on to explain why corporations that tear down beautiful, historically significant buildings and replace them with parking lots are legally ignored, while youthful vandals are the targets of a great deal of law enforcement activity. In sum, the study of deviance and the advancement of political views go together.

From the preceding conclusion, one may derive the following penultimate conclusion: adequate sociological explanations of socially significant forms of deviance require an adequate theory of the state. Socially significant forms of deviance include all forms that are associated with superordinate and subordinate relations or positions. Thus corporate crimes are "crimes of the powerful." So is police deviance because the police are part of the state's social control apparatus. Wife abuse is a manifestation of gender and gender-class conflict. Age and class inequality are implicated in vandalism. State action and reactions to these forms of deviance appear to be guided by a number of strategic concerns. Minimally, these include avoiding actions and reactions that work against the long run interests of men, adults, parts of itself (police) and those who are viewed as being mainly responsible for the process of accumulating capital, i.e., corporate executives. An adequate theory of the state would be one that recognizes the dependence of the state on various social groupings as well as its independence from them.

The kind of sociological theory in which a theory of the state should be included, is one that focusses simultaneously on deviant behaviour or action and on societal, including state, reactions to it. This is the final conclusion to be drawn from a reading of the theoretical perspectives included in *The Wrong Stuff.*

REFERENCES

Akers, R. (1968). "Problems in the Sociology of Deviance: Social Definitions and Behavior." *Social Forces* 46: 1–11.

_____ (1977). *Deviant Behavior: A Social Learning Approach.* Belmont, Calif.: Wardsworth.

Allen, S. (1979). *Ripoff: The Corruption that Plagues America.* Secaucus, N.J.: Lyle Stuart.

Andenaes J. (1972). Deterrence and Specific Offences. In J. Susman (ed.), *Crime and Justice, 1970–1971.* New York: AMS Press.

_____ (1974). *Punishment and Deterrence.* Ann Arbor: University of Michigan Press.

Anderson, Perry. (1974). *Lineages of the Absolutist State.* London: Verso Press.

Antony, A.E.C. (1980). Radical Criminology. In R. Silverman and J. Teevan (eds.), *Crime in Canadian Society.* Toronto: Butterworth and Co.

Balbus, I. (1973). *The Dialectics of Legal Repression.* New York: Russell Sage.

Ball-Rokeach, S.J. (1980). "Normative and Deviant Violence from a Conflict Perspective." *Social Problems* 28: 45–59.

Beaudry, M. (1985). *Battered Women.* Montreal: Black Rose Books.

Becker, H. (1953). "Becoming a Marijuana User." *American Journal of Sociology* 59: 242–253.

_____ (1963) *Outsiders: Studies in the Sociology of Deviance.* New York: Free Press.

_____ (1974) Labeling Theory Revisited. In *Outsiders.* 2nd ed. New York: Free Press.

Beechey, V. (1979). "On Patriarchy." *Feminist Review* 3: 66–82.

Bell, Bowker J. (1979). *A Time of Terror: How Democratic Societies Respond to Revolutionary Violence.* New York: Basic Books.

Bierne, P. (1979). "Empiricism and the Critique of Marxism on Law and Crime." *Social Problems* 26: 373–385.

Birman, B. and G. Nattrieloo. (1980). Perspectives on Absenteeism in High Schools: Multiple Explanations for an Epidemic. In K. Baker and R. Rubel (eds.), *Violence and Crime in Schools.* Lexington, Mass.: D.C. Heath.

Bittner, E. (1970). *The Functions of the Police in Modern Society.* Rockville, Md.: National Institute of Mental Health.

Black, D. (1968). *Police Encounters and Social Organization: An Observation Study.* Ph.D. dissertation, University of Michigan.

_____ (1984). Social Control as a Dependent Variable. In D. Black (ed.), *Toward a General Theory of Social Control. Vol. 1, Fundamentals.* New York: Academic Press.

Bloch H. and A. Neiderhoffer. (1958). *The Gang.* New York: Philosophical Library.

Blumberg, M. (1983). *The Use of Firearms by Police Officers: The Impact of Individuals, Communities and Race.* Ph.D. dissertation, School of Criminal Justice, State University of New York at Albany.

Blumenthal, M., R. Kahn, F. Andrews and K. Head. (1975). *Justifying Violence: Attitudes of American Men.* Ann Arbor, Mich.: Institute for Social Research.

Boggs, M. (1980). *Report on Vandalism.* Burlington, Ont.: Board of Education.

Boritch, H. (1984). *Policing Public Order in Toronto: 1859-1959.* Paper presented at the annual meeting of the Social Science History Association, Toronto, October.

Bowker L. (1983). *Beating Wife Beating,* Lexington, Mass: D.C. Heath.

Box, S. (1981). *Deviance, Reality and Society.* 2nd ed. London: Holt, Rinehart and Winston.

——————— (1983). *Power, Crime and Mystification.* London: Tavistock Publications.

Braithwaite, J. and G. Geis. (1981). "Increasing Community Control Over Corporate Crime: A Problem in the Law of Sanctions." *Yale Law Review* 71: 60–72.

Breines, W. and L. Gordon. (1983). "The New Scholarship on Family Violence." *Signs: Journal of Women in Culture and Society* 8: 490–531.

Briar, S. and I. Piliavin. (1970). Delinquency, Situational Inducements and Commitment to Conformity. In H. Voss (ed.), *Society, Delinquency and Delinquent Behaviour.* Boston: Little, Brown and Co.

Brittan, A. (1973). *Meanings and Situations.* London: Routledge and Kegan Paul.

Brown, L. and C. Brown. (1973). *The Unauthorized History of the R.C.M.P.* Toronto: James Lewis and Samuel.

Burstyn, V. (1985). Masculine Dominance and the State. In V. Burstyn and D. Smith, *Women, Class, Family and the State.* Toronto: Garamond Press.

Byles, J. (1980). "Family Violence in Hamilton." *Canada's Mental Health* 28: 4–6.

Campbell, D. (1961). Conformity in Psychology's Theories of Acquired Behavioral Dispositions. In I. Berg and B. Bass (eds.), *Conformity and Deviation.* New York: Harper and Row.

Canadian Centre for Justice Statistics (1982). *Domestic Homicides, 1961-1981.* Ottawa: Solicitor General of Canada.

Canadian Civil Liberties Association, Education Trust. (1971). *Due Process Safeguards and Canadian Criminal Justice - A One Month Inquiry.* Toronto: Canadian Civil Liberties Association, Education Trust.

Canadian National Clearinghouse on Family Violence. (1982). "A Community Responds to Wife Assault." *Response* 5: 4–6.

Cavoukian, A. (1981). Vandalism. A Self Report Study. Appendix I in *Task Force Report on Vandalism.* Toronto: Queen's Printer.

Chambliss, W. (1966). "The Deterrence Influence of Punishment." *Crime and Delinquency* 12: 70–75.

_____ (1973). "The Saints and the Roughnecks." *Society* 11: 22–31.

_____ (1982). *On the Take: From Petty Crooks to Presidents.* Midland Book Edition. Bloomington, Ind.: Indiana University Press.

Chan, K. (1978). *Husband-Wife Violence in Toronto.* Ph.D. thesis, York University, Department of Sociology.

Chappell, D. and L. Graham. (1985). *Police Use of Deadly Force: Canadian Perspectives.* Research report, Centre of Criminology, University of Toronto.

Chesshyre, R. (1985). "A Brutishness Shapes the Mood of Britain." Toronto: *The Globe and Mail,* October 24: A7.

Chimbos, P. (1978). Marital Violence: A Study of Husband-Wife Homicide. In K. Ishwaran (ed.), *The Canadian Family.* Toronto: Holt, Rinehart and Winston.

Christie, N. (1965). "Youth as a Crime Generating Phenomenon." *New Perspectives in Criminology* 12: 1–10

Cicourel, A.V. (1973). *Cognitive Sociology.* London: Penguin Books.

Clement, W. (1975). *The Canadian Corporate Elite: An Analysis of Economic Power.* Toronto: McClelland and Stewart.

_____ (1983). *The Corporate Elite, the Capitalist Class and the Canadian State.* In W. Clement, *Class, Power and Property.* Toronto: Methuen.

Clinard, M. (1983). *Corporate Ethics and Crime: The Role of Middle Management.* Beverly Hills Calif.: Sage Publications.

Clinard, M. and R. Meier. (1985). *Sociology of Deviant Behaviour.* Toronto: Holt, Rinehart and Winston.

Clinard, M. and R. Quinney. (1967). *Criminal Behavior Systems,* New York: Holt, Rinehart and Winston.

_____ (1973). Corporate Criminal Behavior. In M. Clinard and R. Quinney, *Criminal Behavior Systems: A Typology.* rev. ed. New York: Holt, Rinehart and Winston.

Clinard, M. and P. Yeager. (1980). *Corporate Crime.* New York: Macmillan.

Cloward, R. and L. Ohlin. (1960). *Delinquency and Opportunity: A Theory of Delinquent Gangs.* New York: Free Press.

Cohen, A. (1955). *Delinquent Boys.* New York: Free Press.

_____ (1972). "Social Control and Subcultural Change." *Youth and Society* 3: 259–276.

Cohen, Percy (1980). "Is Positivism Dead?" *Sociological Review* 28: 141–153.

Cohen, P. (1984). Subcultural Conflict and Working Class Community. In S. Hall, D. Hobson, A. Lowe and P. Willis (eds.), *Culture, Media, Language.* London: Hutchinson.

Cohen, S. (1968). "The Politics of Vandalism." *New Society* (December): 872–878.

_____ (1974a). "Breaking Out, Smashing Up and The Social Context of Aspiration." *Working Papers in Cultural Studies* 5 (Spring): 37–63.

_____ (1974b). "Directions for Research on Adolescent Group Violence and Vandalism. *British Journal of Crime, Delinquency and Deviant Social Behaviour* 11: 319–340.

_____ (1980). *Folk Devils and Moral Panics.* 2nd ed. Oxford: Martin Robertson.

Colvin, M. and J. Pauley. (1983). "A Critique of Criminology: Toward an Integrated Structural-Marxist Theory of Delinquency Production." *American Journal of Sociology 89:* 513–551.

Cook, P. (1980). Research in Criminal Deterrence: Laying the Groundwork for the Second Decade. In N. Morris and M. Tonry (eds.), *Crime and Justice: An Annual Review of Research.* Vol. 2, Chicago: University of Chicago Press.

Corsi, J. (1981). "Terrorism as a Desperate Game." *Journal of Conflict Resolution* 25: 47–85.

Couchiching Conference, 53rd. (1984). *Free Enterprise and the State.* Toronto: CBC Enterprises.

Crawford, T. 1984. "Firm Shirking Pension Duties." *Toronto Star,* May 15: A8.

Cressey, D. (1972). *Criminal Organization.* New York: Harper and Row.

Cullen, F. and J. Cullen. (1978). *Toward a Paradigm of Labeling Theory.* Lincoln: University of Nebraska Press.

Dahrendorf, A. (1957). *Class and Class Conflict in Industrial Society.* Stanford, Calif.: Stanford University Press.

Davidson, T. (1977). Wifebeating: A Recurring Phenomenon Throughout History. In M. Roy (ed.), *Battered Women.* New York: Van Nostrand Reinhold.

Davis, K. (1937). "The Sociology of Prostitution." *American Sociological Review* 2: 36–48.

_____ (1968). "The Sociology of Parent-Youth Conflict." *American Sociological Review* 5: 523–535.

Deaton, R. (1973). The Fiscal Crisis of the State in Canada. In D. Roussopoulos (ed.), *The Political Economy of the State.* Montreal: Black Rose Books.

Dentler, R. and K. Erikson. (1959). "The Functions of Deviance in Groups" *Social Problems* 7: 98–107.

Dion, R. (1982). *Crimes of the Secret Police.* Montreal: Black Rose Books.

Dixon, M. (1978). *Women in Class Struggle.* San Francisco: Synthesis Publications.

Dobash, R. and R. Dobash. (1979). *Violence Against Wives: A Case Against Patriarchy.* New York: Free Press.

Doern, G. Bruce. (1978). *The Regulatory Process in Canada.* Toronto: Macmillan.

Doob, A. (1985). *Police Use of Deadly Force: Canadian Perspectives.* Introduction by D. Chappell and L. Graham. Research report, Centre of Criminology, University of Toronto.

Douglas, J. (1970). Deviance, Respectability and Moral Meanings. In J. Douglas (ed.), *Social Respectability and Moral Meanings.* New York: Basic Books.

_____ (1984a). The Problematic Meanings of Deviance: What (Who) is Deviant? In J. Douglas (ed.), *The Sociology of Deviance,* 13–14, Toronto: Allyn and Bacon.

_____ (1984b). Introduction to the Interactionist Theory of Deviance. In J. Douglas (ed.), *The Sociology of Deviance,* Newton, Mass.: Allyn and Bacon.

Douglas, J. and J. Johnson (eds.). (1977). *Official Deviance.* Toronto: J.B. Lippincott.

Dowie, M. and C. Marshall. (1982). The Bendectin Cover-up. In D. Ermann and R. Lundman (eds.), *Corporate and Governmental Deviance.* 2nd ed. New York: Oxford University Press.

Downes, D. and Paul Rock. (1982). *Understanding Deviance.* Oxford, England: Clarendon Press.

Dubin, C.J. (1981). *Report of the Commission of Inquiry on Aviation Safety.* Ottawa: Ministry of Supply and Services Canada.

Durkheim, E. (1947). *The Division of Labor in Society.* Glencoe, Ill.: Free Press. (Originally Published in 1893.)

_____ (1950). *Rules of Sociological Method.* Translated by S. Solovay and J. Mueller. New York: Free Press. (Originally published in 1895.)

_____ (1951). *Suicide.* Glencoe, Ill.: Free Press. (Originally published in 1897.)

Dutton, D. and B. Levens. (n.d.). *Crisis Intervention Training for Police: A Prescriptive Package.* Ottawa: Solicitor General of Canada, File #62-6/1-35.

Edgerton, R. (1973). *Deviant Behavior and Cultural Theory.* Warner Modular Publication #37. Reading, Mass.: Addison-Wesley.

Edleson, J. (1984). "Violence is The Issue: A Critique of Nedig's Assumptions." *Victimology* 9: 483–489.

Eisenstein, Z. (1984). *Feminism and Sexual Equality.* New York: Monthly Review Press.

Elliott, D, and D. Huizinga. (1983). "Social Class and Delinquent Behavior in a National Youth Panel." *Criminology* 21: 149–177.

Ellis, D. (1971). "The Hobbesian Problem of Social Order: A Critical Appraisal of the Normative Solution." *American Sociological Review* 36: 692–703.

Ellis, D. and A. Choi. (1984). *Video Arcades and Student Behaviour.* Toronto: Board of Education.

Ellis, D., H. Grasmick and B. Gilman. (1974). "Violence in Prisons: A Sociological Analysis." *American Journal of Sociology* 80: 16–43.

Engels, F. (1963). Eulogy. In E. Fromm (ed.), *Marx's Concept of Man,* 258–260. New York: Frederick Ungur.

_____ (1972). *The Origin of the Family, Private Property and the State.* New York: International Publishers. (Originally published in 1884.)

Erchak, G. (1984). "The Escalation and Maintenance of Wife Abuse: A Cybernetic Model." *Victimology* 9: 247–253.

Ericson, R. (1983). *Making Crime: A Study of Detective Work.* Toronto: Butterworth and Co.

_____ (1982). *Reproducing Order: A Study of Police Patrol Work.* Toronto: University of Toronto Press.

Erikson, K. (1962). "Notes on the Sociology of Deviance." *Social Problems* 9: 307–314.

_____ (1966). *Wayward Puritans: A Study in the Sociology of Deviance.* New York: John Wiley and Sons.

Erlich, I. (1975). "The Deterrent Effect of Capital Punishment: A Question of Life and Death." *American Economic Review* 63: 397–417.

Ermann, M.D. and R. Lundman. (1982). Overview. In M. Ermann and D. Lundman (eds.), *Corporate and Governmental Deviance.* New York: Oxford University Press.

Farrell, R. and V. Swigert. (1982). *Deviance and Social Control.* New York: Scott, Foresman.

_____ (1985). "The Corporation in Criminology: New Directions for Research." *Journal of Research in Crime and Delinquency* 22: 83–94.

Federal Bureau of Investigation. "FBI Analysis of Terrorist Incidents in the U.S. — 1982." *Victimology* 7: 87–117.

Fleming, T. (1975). *Violent Domestic Assault.* Master's thesis. Centre of Criminology, University of Toronto.

Fox, J. and M. Ornstein. (1986). "The Canadian State and Corporate Elites in the Post-War Period." *The Canadian Review of Sociology and Anthropology* (Forthcoming.)

French, M. (1985). *Beyond Power: Women, Men and Morals.* New York: Jonathan Cape.

Friedenberg, E. (1962). *The Vanishing Adolescent.* New York: Dell Paperback.

_____ (1985). The Punishment Industry in Canada. In T. Fleming (ed.), *The New Criminologies in Canada.* Toronto: Oxford University Press.

Fyfe, J. (1982). "Blind Justice: Police Shootings in Memphis." *Journal of Criminal Law and Criminology* 73: 707–722.

_____ (1984). "Administrative Interventions on Police Shooting Discretion: An Empirical Examination." *Journal of Criminal Justice* 7: 13–19.

Gaudet, M. and P. Doyle. (1979). *Vandalism: An Overview, Prince Edward Island and Elsewhere: A Basis for Concern.* Charlottetown, P.E.I.: Department of Justice.

Geis, G. (1982). "The Heavy Electrical Equipment Antitrust Cases of 1961." In D. Ermann and R. Lundmann (eds.), *Corporate and Governmental Deviance.* New York: Oxford University Press.

Gelles, R. (1974). *The Violent Home.* Beverly Hills, Calif.: Sage Publications.

_____ (1976). "Abused Wives: Why Do They Stay?" *Journal of Marriage and the Family* 38: 659–668.

Gelles, R. and M. Straus. (1979). "Violence in the American Family." *Journal of Social Issues* 35: 15–39.

Gibbons, D. (1965). *Changing the Law Breaker: The Treatment of Delinquents and Criminals.* Englewood Cliffs, N.J.: Prentice-Hall.

Gibbs, J. (1966). "Conceptions of Deviant Behavior: Old and New." *Pacific Sociological Review* 9 (Spring): 9–14.

_____ (1968). "Crime, Punishment and Deterrence." *Social Science Quarterly* 48: 515–530.

_____ (1972). *Social Control.* Andover, Mass.: Warner Modular Publications.

Gibbs, J. and M. Erickson. (1975). "Major Developments in the Sociological Study of Deviance." *Annual Review of Sociology* 1: 21–42.

Gladstone, F. (1978). Vandalism Amongst Adolescent Boys. In *Tackling Vandalism.* Home Office Research Study #47. London, England.

Glaser, D. (1956). "Criminality Theories and Behavioral Images." *American Journal of Sociology* 61: 433–444.

Glassbeek, H. (1984). *Why Corporate Deviance is not Treated as a Crime.* Downsview, Ont., Osgoode Hall Law School, York University.

Glassbeek, H. and S. Rowland. (1979). "Are Injuring and Killing at Work Crimes?" *Osgoode Hall Law Journal* 17: 507–594.

Goff, C. and C. Reasons. (1976). "Corporations in Canada: A Study of Crime and Punishment." *Criminal Law Quarterly* 18: 479–484.

_____ (1978). *Corporate Crime in Canada.* Scarborough, Ont.: Prentice-Hall.

Goffman, E. (1957). *Stigma: Notes on the Management of Spoiled Identity.* Englewood Cliffs, N.J.: Prentice-Hall.

Gomme, I. (1982). *A Multivariate Analysis of Self-Reported Delinquency Among Students.* Ph.D. dissertation, Ontario Institute for Studies in Education, University of Toronto.

Goodman, P. (1956). *Growing Up Absurd.* New York: Random House.

Gottfredson, M. (1982). *Role Models, Bonding and Delinquency.* Paper presented at the annual meeting of the American Society of Criminology, Toronto, November.

Gouldner, A. (1968). "The Sociologist as Partisan: Sociology and the Welfare State." *American Sociologist* 7: 103–116.

Gove, W. (1975). *The Labeling of Deviance: Evaluating a Perspective.* New York: Russell Sage.

—————— (1970). "Societal Reaction as an Explanation of Mental Illness: An Evaluation." *American Sociological Review* 35: 873–884.

Graham, C. (1986). RCMP Widens Probe of Corrupt Grain Trading. Toronto: *The Toronto Star.* June 19: 5.

Gramsci, A. (1972). *Selections From the Prison Notebooks.* Q. Hoare and G.N. Smith (eds. and trans.). New York: International Publishers.

Greenberg, D. (1977). Delinquency and the Age Structure of Society." *Contemporary Crises* 1: 189–223.

—————— (1980). *Crime and Capitalism: Readings in Marxism Criminology.* Palo Alto, Calif.: Mayfield.

Greenblatt, C.S. (1983). A Hit, is a Hit is a Hit . . . is it?: Approval and Tolerance of Physical Force by Spouses. In D. Finkelhor et al. (eds.), *The Dark Side of Families.* Beverly Hills, Calif.: Sage Publications.

Greenglass, E. (1982). *A World of Difference: Gender Roles in Perspective.* Toronto: John Wiley and Sons.

Greenspon, L. (1986). "Charter Hasn't Restricted the Police." Toronto: *The Toronto Star.* September 5: A14.

Greisman, H. (1977). "Social Meanings of Terrorism: Reification, Violence and Social Control." *Contemporary Crises* 1: 303–318.

Gronau, A (1985). Women and Images: Feminist Analysis of Pornography. In C. Vance and V. Burstyn (eds.), *Women Against Censorship.* Toronto: Douglas and McIntyre.

Guettel, C. (1982). *Marxism and Feminism.* Toronto: The Women's Press.

Hackler, J. (1975). Theories of Deviance and Social Policy. In R. Silverman and J. Teevan (eds.), *Crime in Canadian Society.* Toronto: Butterworth and Co.

Hagan J. (1982). "Corporate Advantage: A Study of the Involvement of Corporate and Individual Victims in a Criminal Justice System." *Social Forces* 60: 993–1022.

—————— (1984). *The Disreputable Pleasures.* 2nd ed. Toronto: McGraw-Hill Ryerson.

_____ (1985). *Modern Criminology: Crime, Criminal Behaviour and its Control.* Toronto: McGraw-Hill Ryerson.

Hagan, J. and P. Morden. (1981). The Police Decision of Detain: A Study of Legal Labelling and Police Deviance. In C. Shearing (ed.), *Organizational Police Deviance.* Toronto: Butterworth and Co.

Haliechuk, R. (1986). "Right to Talk to a Lawyer First Isn't Absolute." Toronto: *The Sunday Star.* May 11: 114.

Hall, S., C. Critcher, T. Jefferson, J. Clarke and B. Roberts. (1978). *Policing the Crisis: Mugging, the State and Law and Order.* London: Macmillan.

Hall, S. and T. Jefferson (eds.). (1976). *Resistance Through Rituals: Youth Subcultures in Post-War Britain.* London: Hutchinson.

Hanmer, J. and S. Saunders. (1984). *Well Founded Fear.* London: Hutchinson and the Explorations in Feminism Collective.

Harring, S. (1985). The Contradiction Between Professionalization and Taylorization in the Modern American Police Institution. In B. Maclean (ed.), *The Political Economy of Crime.* Scarborough, Ont.: Prentice-Hall.

Harring, S., T. Platt, R. Speigleman and P. Tagaki. (1977). "Management of Police Killings." *Social Justice* (Fall/Winter): 34–43.

Harris, M. (1985). "Spy Agency Obeys Laws, Watchdog Body Reports." Toronto: *The Globe and Mail,* June 28.

Harrison, F. (1983). *The Modern State: An Anarchist Analysis.* Montreal: Black Rose Books.

Hartnagel, T. and J. Tanner. (1982). "Class, Schooling and Delinquency: A Further Examination." *Canadian Journal of Criminology* 24: 155–173.

Hay, D., P. Linebaugh, J. Rule, E.P. Thompson and Cal Winslow. (1975). *Albion's Fatal Tree: Crime and Society in Eighteenth Century England.* New York: Pantheon.

Heilbronner, R.L. (1985). *The Nature and Logic of Capitalism.* New York: W.W. Norton.

Henley, N. and Jo Freeman. (1979). The Sexual Politics of Interpersonal Behavior. In Jo Freeman (ed.), *Women: A Feminist Perspective.* 2nd ed. Palo Alto, Calif.: Mayfield.

Henry, S. (1985). "Corporate Ethics and Crime: The Role of Middle Management, M.B. Clinard (1983): A Review." *British Journal of Criminology* 35: 70–73.

Henshel, R. (1982). *Police Misconduct in Metropolitan Toronto: A Study of Formal Complaints.* A report prepared for the LaMarsh Research Programme on Violence, York University, Downsview, Ont.

Henton, D. (1985). "Why Did Policeman Investigate Himself, Complaints Board Asks. Toronto: *The Toronto Star,* June 22: A13.

Hepburn, J. (1976). "Testing Alternative Models of Delinquency." *Journal of Criminal Law and Criminology* 67: 450–460.

Herman, E.S. (1982). *The Real Terror Network*. Montreal: Black Rose Books.

Hibbert, T. (1986). *Clitoridectomy: Men's Control of Women's Sexuality: The Nigerian Case*. Ph.D. dissertation. York University, Department of Sociology, Downsview, Ont.

Hinch, R. (1985). Marxist Criminology in the 1970s: Clarifying the Clutter. In T. Fleming, *The New Criminologies of Canada*. Toronto: Oxford University Press.

Hindelang, M. (1973). "Causes of Delinquency: A Partial Replication and Extension." *Social Problems* 18: 471–487.

Hirschi, T. (1969). *Causes of Delinquency*. Berkeley, Calif.: University of California Press.

Hirschi, T. and M. Gottfredson. (1985). "Age and Crime, Logic and Scholarship: Comment on Greenberg. *"The American Journal of Sociology* 91: 22–27.

Hirschi, T. and E. Lemert. (1975). Debate. Annual meeting of the American Sociological Association, Washington, D.C.

Hirst, P. (1975). "Marx and Engels on Law, Crime and Morality." In I. Taylor, P. Walton and J. Young (eds.), *Critical Criminology*. London: Routledge and Kegan Paul.

Hobbes, T. (1963). *Leviathan*. New York: Meridian Books (Originally published in 1651.)

Hollander, E. and R.H. Willis. (1967). "Some Current Issues in the Psychology of Conformity and Nonconformity." *Psychological Bulletin* 68: 62–76.

Home Office Research Unit. (1978). *Tackling Vandalism*. Study #47. London: Home Office Research Unit.

Horowitz, J.L. (1973). "Political Terrorism and the State." *Journal of Political and Military Sociology*. 1: 147–157.

Hyman, H. (1953). The Value Systems of Different Classes. In R. Bendix and S. Lipset (eds.), *Class, Status and Power*. New York: Free Press.

Jacobs, D. and D. Britt. (1979). "Inequality of Police Use of Deadly Force: An Empirical Assessment of a Conflict Hypothesis." *Social Problems* 26: 403–412.

Jaffee, P. and C. Burris. (1984). *An Integrated Response to Wife Assault: A Community Model*. A working paper prepared for the Solicitor General of Canada, File #1984-27, Ottawa.

Jaffee, P. and J. Thompson. (1979). *Family Consultant Service and the London Police Force*. Ottawa: Solicitor General of Canada.

Jessop, B. (1985). *Nicos Poulantzas, Marxist Theory and Political Strategy*. New York: St. Martin's Press.

Johnson, E. (1961). "Sociology of Confinement, Assimilation and the

Prison 'Rat'." *Journal of Criminal Law, Criminology and Police Science* 51: 528–533.

Kalmuss, D. and M. Straus. (1982). "Wife's Marital Dependency and Wife Abuse." *Journal of Marriage and the Family* 44: 277–286.

Keable Commission. (1975), *Commission d'enquète sur les operations policiers en territoire Québécoise.* Quebec: Canadian Government.

Kitsuse, J. (1962). "Societal Reaction to Deviant Behavior: Problems of Theory and Method." *Social Problems* 9 (Winter): 253.

Kitsuse, J. and D. Dietrick. (1959). "Delinquent Boys: A Critique." *American Sociological Review* 24: 208–215.

Kornhauser, R. (1978). *Social Sources of Delinquency.* Chicago, Ill.: University of Chicago Press.

Kotecha, K. and J. Walker. (1976). "Police Vigilantes." *Society* 13: 33–37.

Labour Canada. (1979). *Fatalities in Canadian Industry, 1969–1979.* Ottawa: Occupational Health and Safety.

_____ (1982). *Employment Injuries and Occupational Illnesses: 1972–1981.* Ottawa: Ministry of Supply and Services Canada.

Law Reform Commission of Canada. (1976). *Corporate Responsibility for Group Action.* Ottawa: Ministry of Supply and Services Canada.

_____ (1980). *Damage to Property: Vandalism.* Working Paper #31. Ottawa: Ministry of Supply and Services Canada.

LeBlanc, M. (1981). *"An Integrative Control Theory of Delinquent Behaviour."* Paper presented at the annual meeting of the American Society of Criminology, Washington, D.C., November.

Lederer, L. (ed.). (1980). *Take Back the Night.* New York: Wm. Morrow.

Leger, G. (1983). *Criminal Charges as a Means of Assisting Victims of Wife Assault.* Ottawa: Research Division, Solicitor General of Canada.

Lemert, E. (1951). *Social Pathology.* New York: McGraw-Hill.

_____ (1967). *Human Deviance, Social Problems and Social Control.* Englewood Cliffs, N.J.: Prentice-Hall.

_____ (1974). "Beyond Mead: The Societal Reaction to Deviance." *Social Problems* 21: 457–468.

_____ (1982). Issues in the Study of Deviance. In M. Rosenberg, R. Stebbins and A. Turowetz (eds.), *The Sociology of Deviance.* New York: St. Martin's Press.

Levens, B. (1978). "Domestic Disputes, Police Response and Social Agency Referral." *Canadian Police College Journal* 2: 13–26.

Leyton, E. (1979). *The Myth of Delinquency: An Anatomy of Juvenile Nihilism.* Toronto: McClelland and Stewart.

Levy, M.J. (1952). *The Structure of Society,* Ch. 4. Princeton, N.J.: Princeton University Press.

Linden, R. and C. Fillmore. (1980). "A Comparative Study of Delinquency Involvement." In R. Silverman and J. Teevan (eds.), *Crime in Canadian Society.* Toronto: Butterworth and Co.

Lockwood, D. (1958). *The Black Coated Worker.* London: Routledge and Kegan Paul.

Loeske, D. and S. Cahill. (1984). "The Social Construction of Deviance." *Social Problems* 31: 296–307.

Loving, N. (1980). *Responding to Spouse Abuse and Wife Beating.* Washington, D.C.: Police Foundation.

Luna-Gardinier, E. (1983). *Hearing on Police Use of Deadly Force.* A report submitted to the Subcommittee on Criminal Justice, Berkeley, Calif.

Lundman, R. (1985). Police Misconduct. In A. Blumberg and E. Neiderhoffer (eds.), *The Ambivalent Force.* New York: Holt, Rinehart and Winston.

Maclean, B. (1986). Critical Criminology and Some Limitations of Traditional Inquiry. In B. Maclean (ed.), *The Political Economy of Crime.* Scarborough, Ont.: Prentice-Hall.

Macleod, L. and A. Cadieux. (1980). *Wife Battering in Canada: The Vicious Circle.* Ottawa: Ministry of Supply and Services Canada.

Mahon, R. (1977). Canadian Public Policy: The Unequal Structure of Representation. In L. Panitch (ed.), *The Canadian State.* Toronto: University of Toronto Press.

_____ (1980). Regulatory Agencies: Captive Agents or Hegemonic Apparatuses. In J. Paul Grayson (ed.), *Class, State, Ideology and Change.* Toronto: Holt, Rinehart and Winston.

Mair, J. and D. LeClaire. (1984). *A Police Response to Domestic Assaults.* Ottawa: Solicitor General of Canada.

Malarek, V. (1984). *Hey Malarek!* Toronto: Macmillan.

Mann, E. (1981). Introduction. In C. Shearing (ed.), *Organizational Police Deviance.* Toronto: Butterworth and Co.

Mann, E. and J. Lee. (1979). *R.C.M.P. vs. The Police: Inside Canada's Security Service.* Don Mills, Ont.: General Publishing.

Manning, P. (1977). *Police Work.* Cambridge, Mass.: MIT Press.

Manning, P. and L. Redlinger. (1976). Invitational Edges of Corruption: Some Consequences of Narcotic Law Enforcement. In P. Rock (ed.), *Politics and Drugs.* New York: Dutton.

Marshall, M. (1979). *Weekend Warriors.* Palo Alto, Calif.: Mayfield.

Martin, D. (1979). What Keeps a Woman Captive in a Violent Relationship?: The Social Context of Battering. In D.M. Moore (ed.), *Battered Women,* Beverly Hills, Calif.: Sage Publications.

Marx, G. (1981). Social Control: Divergent and Convergent Interpretations." *Social Problems* 28: 221–246.

Marx, K. (1959). *Manifesto of the Communist Party.* Moscow: Foreign Languages Publishing House. (Originally published in 1872.)

_____ (1963). The Economic and Philosophical Manuscripts. Translated by T. Bottomore. In E. Fromm (ed.), *Marx's Concept of Man.*

New York: Frederick Ungar. (Originally published in 1844.)

_____ (1968). The Eighteenth Brumaire of Louis Bonaparte. In K. Marx and F. Engels, *Selected Works, Vol. 1.* New York: International Publishers. (Originally published in 1852.)

_____ (1984). *A Contribution to the Critique of Political Economy.* Chicago: Charles H. Kerr. (Originally published in 1859.)

Marx, K. and F. Engels (ed.). (1939). *German Ideology.* New York: International Publishers. (Originally published in 1846.)

_____ (1942). *Selected Correspondence, 1846–1895.* New York: International Publishers.

Matsueda, R. (1981). Control Theory, Differential Association and Causal Modelling. Paper presented at the annual meeting of the American Sociological Association, Toronto, August.

Matza, D. (1964). *Delinquency and Drift.* New York: John Wiley and Sons.

Maynard, M. (1985). "The Response of Social Workers to Domestic Violence." In J. Pahl (ed.), *Private Violence and Public Policy.* London: Routledge and Kegan Paul.

MacDonald, L. (1967). *The Sociology of Law and Order.* Boulder, Colo.: Westview Press.

McDonald Commission. (1977). *Royal Commission of Inquiry Into Certain Activities of the Royal Canadian Mounted Police.* Ottawa: Ministry of Supply and Services Canada.

McIntosh, M. (1975). *The Organization of Crime.* London: Macmillan.

McLaren, C. (1982). "New Definition Urged for Death." Toronto: *The Globe and Mail,* June 15: 7.

McMullan, J. and R. Ratner. (1982). "Radical versus Technocratic Analyses of Crime: Critique of Criminal Justice in Canada." *Canadian Journal of Criminology* 24: 483–495.

Mead, G.H. (1918). "The Psychology of Punitive Justice." *American Journal of Sociology* 23: 577–602.

_____ (1934). *Mind, Self and Society,* Chicago: University of Chicago Press.

Melossi, D. (1985). "Overcoming the Crisis in Critical Criminology: Toward a Grounded Labeling Theory." *Criminology* 23: 193–208.

Merton, R. (1957). *Social Theory and Social Structure.* New York: Free Press.

Messerschmidt, J. (1981). "Marginalization, Reproduction and Assaults Against Teachers: Ideas on the Contradictions of Ideological Social Control." *Contemporary Crises* 5: 83–101.

Miller, W. (1958). "Lower Class Culture as a Generating Milieu of Gang Delinquency." *Journal of Social Issues* 14, 3 (1958): 5–19.

_____ (1977), *Cops and Bobbies: Police Authority in New York and London, 1830–1870.* Chicago: University of Chicago Press.

Miliband R. (1969). *The State in Capitalist Society.* London: Wiedenfeld and Nicholson.

_____ (1983). *Class Power and State Power.* London: Verso Press.

Mills, C.W. (1963). *Power, Politics and People.* New York: Oxford University Press.

Ministry of Education (1980). *Violence and Vandalism in Ontario Schools.* Toronto: Ontario Ministry of Education.

Mitford, J. (1979). My Short and Happy Life as a Distinguished Professor. In J. Mitford, *Poison Penmanship.* New York: Random House.

Mohr, H. (1973). "Facts, Figures, Perceptions and Myths — Ways of Describing and Understanding Crime." *Canadian Journal of Criminology and Corrections* 15: 39–49.

Monahan, J., R. Novaco and G. Geis. (1979). Corporate Violence: Research Strategies for Community Psychology. In D. Adelson and T. Sorbin (eds.), *Challenges for the Criminal Justice System.* New York: Human Sciences Press.

Morand, D.R. (1976). *Report of the Royal Commission into Metropolitan Toronto Police Practices.* Toronto: Queen's Printer.

Morgan, P. (1981). *Constructing Images of Deviance: A Look at State Intervention into the Problem of Wife Battery.* Paper presented at the annual meeting of the American Sociological Association, Toronto, August.

Muncie, J. and M. Fitzgerald. (1981). Humanizing the Deviant: Affinity and Affiliation Theories. In M. Fitzgerald, G. McLennan and J. Pawson (eds.), *Crime and Society.* London: Routledge and Kegan Paul.

Musgrove, F. (1964). *Youth and the Social Order.* Bloomington, Ind. Indiana University Press.

National Institute of Education. (1977). *Safe Schools Study.* Washington, D.C.: National Institute of Education.

Newman, J. and G. Newman. (1980). Crime and Punishment in the Schooling Process: A Historical Analysis. In K. Baker and R. Rubel (eds.), *Violence and Crime in Schools.* Lexington, Mass.: D.C. Heath.

Noble, K. (1985). "Job-Linked Illnesses and Injuries Rose in 1984." New York: *The New York Times,* November 14: 11

Nova Scotia Police Commission. (1984). *Report of the Inquiry into the Kentville Police Department.* Halifax, N.S.: Nova Scotia Police Commission.

O'Connor, J. (1973). *The Fiscal Crisis of the State.* New York: St. Martin's Press.

_____ (1975). "Productive and Unproductive Labor." *Politics and Society* 5: 297–336.

O'Connor, W.D. (1972). "The Manufacture of Deviance: The Case of the Soviet Purge" *American Sociological Review* 37: 403–413.

Ontario Federation of Labour. (1982). *Occupational Health and Safety: A Training Manual.* Toronto: Copp Clark Pitman.

Ontario New Democrat Caucus. (1986). *Second Task Force Report on Occupational Health and Safety.* Elie Martel MPP, Chairperson. Toronto.

Ontario Task Force on Vandalism. (1981). *Vandalism: Responses and Responsibilities.* Toronto: Queen's Printer.

Ouston, J. (1984). "Delinquency, Family Background and Educational Attainment." *British Journal of Delinquency* 24: 2–26.

Palmer, J. (1977). "Economic Analysis of the Deterrent Effect of Punishment: A Review." *Journal of Research in Crime and Delinquency* 14: 4–21.

Panitch, L. (1977). The Role and Nature of the Canadian State. In L. Panitch (ed.), *The Canadian State: Political Economy and Political Power.* Toronto: University of Toronto Press.

Parks, E. (1970). "From Constabulary to Police Society: Implications for Social Control." *Catalyst* (Summer): 76–97.

Parsons, T. (1937). *The Structure of Social Action.* New York: McGraw-Hill.

Pearce, F. (1978). *Crimes of the Powerful.* London: Pluto Press.

Pearson, G. (1982). *Hooligan: A History of Respectable Fears.* London: Macmillan.

Pepinsky, H. (1980). *Crime Control Strategies.* New York: Oxford University Press.

Pizzey, E. (1974). *Scream Quietly or the Neighbours Will Hear.* Toronto: Penguin Books.

Platiel, R. (1986). "Indian Bingo Promoter, 'not your average savage'." Toronto: *The Globe and Mail,* August 18: A11.

Plummer, K. (1979). Misunderstanding the Labelling Perspectives. In D. Downes and P. Rock (eds.), *Deviant Interpretations,* Oxford: Martin Robertson.

Poland, J. (1978). "Subculture of Violence: Youth Offender Value Systems." *Criminal Justice and Behaviour* 5: 159–164.

Polsky, H. (1969) A Sociological Theory of Pornography. In H. Polsky, *Hustlers, Beats and Others.* New York: Doubleday-Anchor.

Poulantzas, N. (1969). "The Problem of the Capitalist State." *New Left Review* 58: 67–78.

_____ (1972). "On Social Classes." *New Left Review* 61: 27–55

_____ (1973). *Political Power and Social Classes.* London: Verso Press.

_____ (1975). *Classes in Contemporary Capitalism.* London: New Left Books.

Prus, R. (1978). From Bar Rooms to Bedrooms: Towards a Theory of

Interpersonal Relations. In A. Bayer-Gammon (ed.), *Violence in Canada*. Toronto: Methuen.

Prus, R. and S. Irvine (1980). *Hookers, Rounders and Desk Clerks*. Toronto: Gage Publishing.

Pryce, K. (1979). *Endless Pressure: A Study of West Indian Life Styles in Bristol*. Harmondsworth: Penguin Books.

Public Complaints Commissioner. (1983). *Second Annual Report*. Toronto: Office of the Public Complaints Commissioner.

——————— (1984a). *Third Annual Report*. Toronto: Office of the Public Complaints Commissioner.

——————— (1984b). *Summary of Report and Recommendations Concerning the Hold-up Squad*. Toronto: Office of the Public Complaints Commissioner.

Punch, M. (1985). *Conduct Unbecoming: The Social Construction of Police Deviance and Control*. London: Tavistock Publications.

Quinney, R. (1970). *The Social Reality of Crime*. Boston: Little, Brown and Co.

——————— (1974). *Critique of the Legal Order*. Boston: Little, Brown and Co.

——————— (1980). *Class, State and Crime*. New York: Longmans.

Radzinowicz, L. and J. King. (1977). *The Growth of Crime: The International Experience*. Toronto: Penguin Books.

Rapaport, A. (1966). *Two-Person Game Theory*. Ann Arbor: University of Michigan Press.

Rapaport, D. (1984). "Fear and Trembling: Terrorism in Three Religious Traditions." *American Political Science Review* 78: 658–677.

Ratner, R. (1985). Inside the Liberal Boot: The Criminological Enterprise in Canada. In T. Fleming (ed.), *The New Criminologies in Canada*. Toronto: Oxford University Press.

Ratner, R. and J. McMullan. (1983). "Social Control and the Rise of the 'Exceptional State' in Britain, the United States and Canada." *Crime and Social Justice* 15: 31–43.

Reasons, C. (1982). Organizational Crime. In M. Rosenberg, R. Stebbins and A. Turowetz (eds.), *The Sociology of Deviance*. New York: St. Martin's Press.

Reasons, C., L. Ross and C. Patterson (1981). *Assault on the Worker: Occupational Health and Safety in Canada*. Toronto: Butterworth and Co.

Reiman, J. (1979). *The Rich Get Richer and the Poor Get Prison*. New York: John Wiley and Sons.

Reiner, R. (1978). "The Police in the Class Structure." *British Journal of Law and Society* 5: 166–184.

——————— (1980). "Fuzzy Thoughts: The Police and Law and Order Politics." *Sociological Review* 28: 377–413.

Reiss, A. (1968). "How Common is Police Brutality?" *Transaction* (July/Aug.): 10–19.

Reschenthaler, G. (1972). *The Performance of Selected Independent Regulatory Commissions in Alberta, Saskatchewan and Manitoba.* A Study Commissioned by the Canadian Consumer Council. Ottawa: Ministry of Supply and Services Canada.

Resnick, P. (1978). Political Economy and Class Analysis: A Marxist Perspective on Canada. In J. Redekop (ed.), *Approaches to Canadian Politics.* Scarborough, Ont.: Prentice-Hall.

Richards, P. (1979). "Middle Class Vandalism and Age-Status Conflict." *Social Problems* 26: 489–497.

Roberts, J. (1981). The Costs of Vandalism: A Survey of Insurance Data, Appendix 4. Ontario: Task Force on Vandalism.

Rosenbluth, G. and H. Thorburn. (1972). *Canadian Anti-Combines Legislation, 1952–1960.* Toronto: University of Toronto Press.

Rubel, R. (1979). *Theoretical Perspectives on School Crime and Poverty: Summary Volume.* Prepared for Assistant Secretary, Planning and Evaluation (HEW), Washington, D.C.

Rubington, E. and M. Weinberg (eds.). (1981). *Deviance: The Interactionist Perspective,* 4th ed. Toronto: Macmillan.

Rumbaut, R. and E. Bittner. (1979). Changing Conceptions of the Police Role. In N. Morris and M. Tonry (eds.), *Crime and Justice: An Annual Review of Research.* Vol. 1. Chicago: University of Chicago Press.

Russell, D. (1982). *Rape in Marriage.* New York: Macmillan.

Sagarin, E. and F. Montanino. (1976). "Anthologies and Readers on Deviance." *Contemporary Sociology* 5: 259-267.

Sagarin, W. and R. Kelly. (1982). Collective and Formal Promotion of Deviance. In M. Rosenberg, R. Turowetz and R. Stebbins (eds.), *The Sociology of Deviance.* New York: St. Martin's Press.

Samuelson, L. (1985). New Parallels Between Marxist and Non-Marxist Theories of Law and State. In T. Fleming (ed.), *The New Criminologies in Canada.* Toronto: Oxford University Press.

Sawadsky, J. (1980). *Men in the Shadows.* Toronto: Doubleday.

Scheff, T. (1966) *Being Mentally Ill: A Theory.* Chicago: Aldine.

——————— (1975) "The Labeling Theory of Mental Illness." In T. Scheff (ed.), *Labeling Madness.* Englewood Cliffs, N.J.: Prentice-Hall.

Scherer, J. (1979). School Community Linkages: Avenues of Alienation or Socialization. In E. Wenk and N. Harlow (eds.), *School Crime and Disruption.* Davis, Calif.: Responsible Action.

Schlesinger, B. (1980). "Abused Wives: Canada's Silent Screamers." *Canada's Mental Health* 28: 17–20.

Schrager, L. and J. Short. (1977). "Toward a Sociology of Organizational Crime." *Social Problems* 25: 407–419.

Schrieber, J. (1979). *The Ultimate Weapon: Terrorists and World Order.* New York: Wm. Morrow.

Schulman, M. (1979). *A Survey of Spousal Violence Against Women in Kentucky.* Kentucky Commission on Women. Washington, D.C.: U.S. Government Printing Office, Study #792701.

Schur, E.M. (1971). *Labeling Deviant Behavior.* New York: Harper and Row.

——————— (1984). *Labeling Women Deviant: Gender, Stigma and Social Control.* New York: Random House.

Sewell, J. (1985). *Police: Urban Policing in Canada.* Toronto: James Lorimer.

Shearing, C. (1981a). Deviance and Conformity in the Reproduction of Order. In C. Shearing (ed.), *Organizational Police Deviance.* Toronto: Butterworth and Co.

——————— (1981b). *The Legal Status of the Police.* Ottawa: Law Reform Commission of Canada.

Sherman, L. (1974). Moral Careers of Corrupt Policemen. In L. Sherman *Police Corruption.* New York: Doubleday.

——————— (1982). Deviant Organizations. In D. Ermann and R. Lundman (eds.), *Corporate and Governmental Deviance,* New York: Oxford University Press.

Sherman, L. and R. Berk. (1984). "The Specific Deterrence Effects of Arrest for Domestic Assault." *American Sociological Review* 49: 261–272.

Shook, L. (1983). *Aberrant Sexuality: A Model for All Sexual Behavior.* Paper presented at the annual meeting of the American Society of Criminology, Denver, Colorado, November.

Silberman, C. (1978). *Criminal Violence, Criminal Justice.* Toronto: Random House.

Sillitoe, A. (1959). *The Loneliness of the Long Distance Runner.* New York: Signet Paperback.

Silver, A. (1966). The Demand for Order in Civil Society: A Review of Some Themes in the History of Urban Crime, Police and Riot. In D. Bordua (ed.), *The Police in Sociological Essays.* New York: John Wiley and Sons.

Simon, D. and S. Eitzen (1986). *Elite Deviance.* Toronto: Allyn and Bacon.

Skeoch, L. (1956). "The Combines Investigation Act: Its Intent and Application." *Canadian Journal of Economics and Political Science* 22: 17–37.

Skogan, W. (1981). *Issues in the Measurement of Victimization.* Washington, D.C.: Department of Justice, NCJ–74682.

Small, S. (1981). *The Interactionist Perspective on Wife Assault: A Sociological Rule of Thumb.* Paper presented at the annual meeting of the

Sociology and Anthropology Association, Halifax, May 28–31.

Smandych, R. (1984). Marxism and the Creation of Law: Re-examining the Origins of Canadian Anti-Combines Legislation, 1890–1910. In T. Fleming (ed.), *The New Criminologies in Canada*. Toronto: Oxford University Press.

Smith, M. (1985). *Woman Abuse: A Telephone Survey*. A report prepared for the LaMarsh Research Programme on Violence, York University, Downsview, Ont.

Smith, W. and A. Smith. (1975). *Minimata*. New York: Holt, Rinehart and Winston.

Snider, L. (1980). Corporate Crime in Canada. In R. Silverman and J. Teevan (eds.), *Crime in Canadian Society*. Toronto: Butterworth and Co.

Snider, L. and G. West. (1980). A Critical Perspective on Law in the Canadian State: Delinquency and Corporate Crime. In R.J. Ossenberg (ed.), *Power and Change in Canada*. Toronto: McClelland and Stewart.

Solicitor General of Canada, Research Division. (1982). *Domestic Homicides: A Report*. Ottawa: Ministry of Supply and Services Canada.

_____ (1983). *Seven Cities Victim Survey*. Ottawa: Ministry of Supply and Services Canada.

_____ Statistics Division. (1985). *Female Victims of Crime*. Bulletin #4. Ottawa: Ministry of Supply and Services Canada.

Sparks, R. (1980). A Critique of Marxist Criminology. In N. Morris and M. Tonry (eds.), *Crime and Justice: An Annual Review of Research*. Vol. 2, Chicago: University of Chicago Press.

Spector, M. (1977). *Constructing Social Problems*. Menlo Park, Calif.: Cummings.

Spitzer, S. (1975). "Toward a Marxian Theory of Deviance." *Social Problems* (June): 638–651.

Stachura, J. and R. Teske. (1979). *A Special Report on Wife Abuse in Texas*. Huntsville, Tex.: Sam Houston State University, Criminal Justice Center.

Stark-Adamec, C. and P. Adamec (1982). "Aggression by Men Against Women: Adaptation or Aberration?" *International Journal of Women's Studies* 5, 1: 42–54.

Stark, E. and A. Flitcraft. (1983). Social Knowledge, Social Policy and the Abuse of Women: The Case Against Patriarchal Benevolence. In D. Finkelhor, R. Gelles, G. Hotaling and M. Straus (eds.), *The Dark Side of Families*. Beverly Hills, Calif.: Sage Publications.

Stark, E., A. Flitcraft and W. Frazier. (1979). "Medicine and Patriarchal Violence: The Social Construction of a 'Private' Event." *International Journal of Health Services* 9: 461–492.

Stebbins, R. (1970). "The Meaning of Disorderly Behavior." *Sociology of Education* 44: 217–236.

Stedman-Jones, Gareth. (1984). *Outcast London.* Toronto: Penguin Books.

Steedman, C. (1984). *Policing the Victorian Community: The Formation of the English Provincial Police Forces.* London: Routledge and Kegan Paul.

Stinchcombe, A. (1964). *Rebellion in a High School.* Chicago: Quadrangle.

Stoddard, E. (1971). Blue-Coat Crime. In L. Radzinowicz and M. Wolfgang (eds.), *The Criminal in the Arms of the Law.* Vol. 2. New York: Basic Books.

Stone, C. (1975). *Where the Law Ends: The Social Control of Corporate Behavior.* New York: Harper and Row.

Storch, R. (1982). "The Policeman as Domestic Missionary: Urban Discipline and Popular Culture in Northern England, 1850–1880." *Journal of Social History* (winter): 481–497.

Stotland, E. (1977). "White Collar Criminals." *Journal of Social Issues* 33: 179–196.

Straus, M. (1976). "Sexual Inequality, Cultural Norms and Wife Beating." *Victimology* 1: 54–76.

——————— (1977). "Societal Morphogenesis and Intra-Family Violence in Cross Cultural Perspective." *Annals of the New York Academy of Sciences* 285: 721–732.

——————— (1978). "Wife Beating: How Common and Why?" *Victimology* 2: 443–457.

Straus, M. and R. Gelles. (1986). "Societal Change in Family Violence from 1975 to 1985 as Revealed by Two National Surveys." *Journal of Marriage and the Family* 48: 1–23.

Straus, M., R. Gelles and S. Steinmetz. (1980). *Behind Closed Doors: Violence in the American Family.* New York: Anchor Books.

Sumner, C. (1976). Marxism and Deviance Theory. In P. Wiles (ed.), *Crime and Delinquency in Britain.* Vol. 2, London: Martin Robertson.

——————— (1981). *Abandoning Deviancy Theory in Marxist Criminology in Britain Since 1975.* Paper presented at the annual meeting of the American Society of Criminology, Washington, D.C.

Sutherland, E. (1939). *Principles of Criminology.* 3rd ed. Philadelphia: Lippincott.

——————— (1940). "White Collar Criminality." *American Sociological Review* 5: 1–12.

——————— (1949). *White Collar Crime.* New York: Holt, Rinehart and Winston.

Sutherland, E. and D. Cressey. (1966). *Principles of Criminology.* 7th ed. Philadelphia: J.B. Lippincott.

Szechtman, S. (1985). "Wife Abuse: Women's Duties — Men's Rights." *Victimology* 10: 253–266.

Taft, D. (1966). *Criminology.* 5th ed. New York: Macmillan.

Tagaki, P. (1979). Death by Police Intervention. In U.S. Department of Justice Report, *A Community Concern: Police Use of Deadly Force.* Washington, D.C.: Publication #JUS–436, January.

Tannenbaum, F. (1938). *Crime and Community.* Boston: Ginn.

Tanner, J., G. Lowe and H. Krahn. (1985). Youth, Unemployment and Moral Panics. In T. Fleming (ed.), *The New Criminologies in Canada.* Toronto: Oxford University Press.

Tappan, P. (1947). "Who is the Criminal?" *American Sociological Review* 12: 96–102.

Taylor, I., P. Walton and J. Young. (1973). *The New Criminology.* London: Routledge and Kegan Paul.

_____ (1975). *Critical Criminology.* London: Routledge and Kegan Paul.

Thiam, A. (1985). "Women's Fight for the Abolition of Sexual Mutilation." *International Social Science Journal* 78: 27–34.

Thompson, E.P. (1975). *Whigs and Hunters: The Origin of the Black Act.* New York: Pantheon.

Toby, J. (1957). "Social Disorganization and Stake in Conformity: Complementary Factors in the Predatory Behaviour of Young Hoodlums." *Journal of Criminal Law, Criminology and Police Science* 48: 12–17.

_____ (1966). "Violence and the Masculine Ideal. Some Qualitative Data." *Annals of the American Academy of Political and Social Science* 364: 19–27.

Tribble, S. (1972). "Socio-economic Status and Self-reported Juvenile Delinquency." *Canadian Journal of Criminology and Corrections* 14: 409–415.

Tross, H. (1977). *A Report on School Vandalism and its Effects on the Ottawa Board of Education.* Ottawa: Board of Education.

Turk, A. (1969). *Criminality and the Legal Order.* Chicago: Rand-McNally.

_____ (1981). Organizational Deviance and Political Policing. In C. Shearing (ed.), *Organizational Police Deviance.* Toronto: Butterworth and Co.

Ursel, Jane. (1984). *Preliminary Report on Wife Abuse.* Winnipeg, Man.: Institute for Social and Economic Research, Faculty of Arts, The University of Manitoba.

Van den Haag, E. (1975). *Punishing Criminals: Concerning a Very Old and Painful Subject.* New York: Basic Books.

Vance, C. (ed.). (1984). *Pleasure and Danger: Exploring Female Sexuality.* London: Routledge and Kegan Paul.

Vaz, E. (1965). "Middle Class Adolescents: Self-Reported Delinquency and Youth Culture Activities." *The Canadian Review of Sociology and Anthropology* 2: 52–70.

Vestermark, S. and P. Blauvelt. (1980). Understanding Violence. In K. Baker and R. Rubel (eds.), *Violence and Crime in the Schools,* Lexington, Mass.: D.C. Heath.

Visano, L. (1985). Crime, Law and State: The Linkage Problem. In T. Fleming (ed.), *The New Criminologies in Canada.* Toronto: Oxford University Press.

Vold, G. (1979). Group Conflict Theory as an Explanation of Crime. In G. Vold, *Theoretical Criminology.* New York: Oxford University Press.

Walker, E. and R. Heyns. (1962). *An Anatomy for Conformity.* Englewood Cliffs, N.J.: Prentice-Hall.

Weber, M. (1954). Law in Economy and Society. In M. Rheinstein (ed.), *Max Weber on Law in Economy and Society.* Cambridge, Mass.: Harvard University Press.

Weiss, R. (1983). Radical Criminology: A Recent Development. In E. Johnson (ed.), *International Handbook of Contemporary Developments in Criminology: General Issues and the Americas.* Westport, Conn.: Greenwood Press.

West, W. Gordon. (1979). Serious Thieves: Lower Class Adolescent Males in a Short Term Deviant Occupation. In E. Vaz and A. Lodhi (eds.), *Crime and Delinquency in Canada.* Toronto: Prentice-Hall.

——————— (1985). *Young Offenders and The State.* Toronto: Butterworth and Co.

West, W. Gordon and L. Snider. (1985). A Critical Perspective on Law in the Canadian State. In T. Fleming (ed.), *The New Criminologies in Canada.* Toronto: Oxford University Press.

Westley, W. (1970). *Violence and The Police.* Rev. ed. Cambridge, Mass.: MIT Press. (Originally published in 1956.)

Wiatrowski, M., D. Griswold and M. Roberts. (1981). "Social Control Theory and Delinquency." *American Sociological Review* 46: 525–541.

Willis, P. (1977). *Learning to Labour: How Working Class Kids Get Working Class Jobs.* Aldershot: Saxon House.

Wilson, E. (1977). *Women and the Welfare State.* London: Tavistock Publications.

Wilson, H. (1980). "Parental Supervision: A Neglected Aspect of Delinquency." *British Journal of Criminology* 20: 203–235.

Wilson, J.Q. (1975). *Thinking About Crime.* New York: Basic Books.

Winnipeg Police Department. (1980). *Report on Vandalism.* Winnipeg: Research and Planning Unit.

Yinger, J.M. (1960). "Contraculture and Subculture." *American Sociological Review.* (October): 628–635.

Young, T. (1981). "Corporate Crime: A Critique of the Clinard Report." *Contemporary Crises* 5: 330–340.

Zeitlin, I. (1984). *The Social Condition of Humanity.* New York: Oxford University Press.

Zimbardo, P. (1982). *A Social Psychological Analysis of Vandalism: Making Sense of a Senseless World."* Centre of Criminology, University of Toronto.

Zimring, F. and G. Hawkins. (1973). *Deterrence.* Chicago: University of Chicago Press.

NAME INDEX

Adamec, P., 158, 167
Allen, S., 90
Andenaes, J., 102

Balbus, I., 67
Ball-Rokeach, S.J., 172
Barnard, C., 114n.3
Beaudry, M., 159
Beccaria, Cesare Bonesana, Marchese
de, 102
Becker, H., 16, 17, 18, 23n.12, 26, 27,
51, 56-57, 59, 61, 63, 80n.12, 105,
184, 205
Bell, B.J., 18, 19
Berk, R., 170, 171
Bierne, P., 67
Birman, B., 198
Bittner, E., 149
Blauvelt, P., 184
Bloch, H., 202, 204
Blumberg, M., 152n.18
Boritch, M., 152n.18
Boritch, H., 142
Bowker, L., 168
Box, S., 26, 47, 84, 88, 96-97, 139,
147-148, 149, 153n.24, 154n.37,
156n.54

Braithwaite, J., 104
Briar, S., 40, 42-43, 203
Burris, C., 170
Burstyn, V., 172, 175-177

Cadieux, A., 158-159, 163, 167
Cavoukian, A., 189, 190
Chan, K., 160
Chambliss, W., 12, 13, 58-59
Chappell, D., 154n.37
Chimbos, P., 160
Choi, A., 198
Christie, N., 196, 208n.12
Cicourel, A.V., 63
Clement, W., 111
Clinard, M., 12, 22n.9, 84, 85-86,
87-88, 89, 93, 96, 98, 101-102,
114nn.7,13, 115n.16
Cloward, R., 12, 33, 34
Cohen, A., 12, 13, 26, 32-33, 34, 41,
45, 79n.5, 193-195, 202, 203
Cohen, P., 191
Cohen, S., 183, 184, 197, 198-199,
204, 208n.12, 209n.20
Colvin, M., 36-37, 48
Comte, A., 79n.9
Cooley, C.H., 57

Corsi, J., 23n.16
Crawford, L., 90
Cressey, D., 61-62, 101

Dahrendorf, R., 73
Davidson, T., 165
Davis, K., 30
Dentler, R., 9
Dietrick, D., 38
Dion, R., 126
Dobash, R., 175
Dobash, R.E., 175
Douglas, J., 50
Dowie, M., 105-106
Downes, D., 30, 37, 47, 77
Dubin, C.J., 89, 93
Durkheim, E., 9, 11, 16, 28, 30, 39,
    49, 79nn.8,9, 100, 101

Edgerton, R., 6, 7, 8
Eitzen, S., 93
Elliott, D., 190
Ellis, D., 39, 198
Engels, F., 64
Ericson, R., 137, 139, 143,
    155nn.40,48
Erikson, K., 9, 16, 17, 55-56, 78n.1,
    80n.12
Erlich, I., 48
Ermann, M.D., 87, 88, 105

Fillmore, C., 104-105
Fitzgerald, M., 203
Fleming, T., 160
Freeman, J., 172
French, M., 165
Friedenberg, E., 151n.4, 182, 201
Fyfe, J., 139

Geis, G., 94, 103, 104
Gelles, R., 159, 164, 166, 168
Gibbons, D., 13
Gibbs, J., 12, 18, 63, 79n.11
Gladstone, F., 130
Glassbeek, H., 84, 95, 108
Goff, C., 88, 103, 104, 108, 109, 110
Goffman, E., 2, 55
Gottfredson, M., 209n.15
Gouldner, A., 23n.15, 78n.2
Graham, C., 154n.37
Greenberg, D., 27, 67, 204-207
Greenglass, E., 172

Greenspon, L., 125
Greisman, H., 18, 78n.1
Gronau, A., 31

Hagan, J., 12, 13, 14, 22n.10, 79n.9,
    183
Haliechuk, R., 125
Hall, S., 20, 68, 70, 77
Harris, M., 127
Heibronner, R.L., 76
Henley, N., 172
Henry, S., 102
Henshel, R., 131, 147
Henton, D., 132
Hepburn, J., 47
Heyns, R., 8
Hibbert, T., 165
Hinch, R., 81n.24
Hindelang, M., 47
Hirschi, T., 12, 26, 27, 37, 40, 43, 47,
    48, 64, 78n.2, 79nn.8,9, 101, 138,
    192-194, 203, 204, 209n.15
Hirst, R., 77
Hobbes, T., 6, 38-40, 49, 79n.8
Hollander, E., 21n.3
Hotaling, G.T., 158
Huizinga, D., 190
Hyman, H., 38

Jaffee, P., 169-170
Johnson, E., 9

Kalmuss, D., 168-169
Kitsuse, J., 16, 17, 23n.13, 38
Kornhauser, R., 40, 47

Lee, J., 127
Lemert, E., 16-17, 18, 38, 51-52,
    58-59, 61, 141
Levens, B., 169
Levy, M.J., 6
Leyton, E., 190-191
Linden, R., 194-195
Lockwood, D., 148
Lundman, R., 87, 88, 105, 139

Maclean, B., 24n.20, 81n.24
Macleod, L., 158, 159, 163, 167
McIntosh, M., 101
McLaren, C., 9
McMullan, J., 81n.24
Malarek, V., 79n.5

Mann, E., 127, 133
Manning, P., 136, 146, 149
Marshall, M., 8, 105, 106
Marx, G., 27, 142
Marx, K., 64-67, 73, 80n.21, 107, 108, 179n.18
Matsudea, R., 64
Matza, D., 34, 36, 79n.6, 191, 203
Mead, G.H., 49-50, 57, 59
Melossi, D., 59-60, 63
Merton, R., 11, 16, 31-32, 33, 96, 97, 114n.12
Messerschmidt, J., 203-204
Miliband, R., 68-70, 81nn.26,30,31, 107
Miller, W., 8, 33, 34, 38, 167-168
Mills, C.W., 59
Monahan, J., 94
Morand, D., 131-132
Morgan, P., 171
Muncie, J., 203
Musgrove, F., 198, 203, 209n.17

Nattrieloo, G., 198
Neiderhoffer, A., 202, 204
Newman, G., 197-198
Newman, J., 197-198
Noble, K., 103
Novaco, R., 94

Ohlin, L., 12, 33, 34

Palmer, J., 171
Panitch, L., 81n.26
Parsons, T., 6
Pauley, J., 36-37, 48
Pearce, F., 13, 107, 108
Pepinsky, H., 139, 171
Piliavin, I., 40, 42-43, 203
Plummer, K., 57
Polsky, H., 30
Poulantzas, N., 68, 71-72, 82n.34, 107, 111, 156nn.54,56
Punch, M., 143

Quinney, R., 12, 13, 14, 22n.9, 85, 86, 88, 146, 156n.50

Rapaport, D., 19
Ratner, R., 30, 81n.24, 155n.48
Reasons, C., 88, 89, 92, 95, 103, 104, 108, 109, 110

Redlinger, L., 136
Reiman, J., 96
Reiner, R., 140, 148-149, 156n.56
Reiss, A., 135
Richards, P., 202
Rock, P., 30, 37, 47, 77
Rowland, S., 95
Rubington, E., 54, 59, 104
Russell, D., 168

Sawadsky, J., 127
Scherer, J., 198
Schrager, L., 84, 88
Schreiber, J., 18
Schulman, M., 179n.11
Schur, E., 168, 171
Shearing, C., 135-136
Sherman, L., 52, 86, 117, 135, 139, 140, 141, 155n.39, 170, 171
Shook, L., 47
Short, J., 84, 88
Silberman, C., 142
Simon, D., 93
Small, S., 159-160
Smandych, R., 110
Smith, M., 163
Snider, L., 84, 88, 89, 108, 109, 110
Sparks, R., 77
Spector, M., 63
Spitzer, S., 13, 26, 67-68
Stachura, J., 179n.11
Stark-Adamec, C., 158
Steinmetz, S., 159, 164
Stoddard, E., 155n.39
Stone, C., 115n.14
Storch, R., 146
Straus, M., 158, 159, 164, 168-169, 178n.1, 179n.10
Sumner, C., 14-15, 77
Sutherland, E., 60, 61-63, 85, 96, 98

Taft, D., 86
Tannenbaum, F., 15-16
Tappan, P., 12
Taylor, I., 12, 30, 37, 59, 66-67
Thiam, A., 165
Thompson, E.P., 77, 82n.36
Thompson, J., 169-170
Thompson, J.D., 86, 114n.3
Toby, J., 40, 203
Tribble, S., 190
Turk, A., 19-20, 73-75, 76, 149-150

Ursel, J., 163

Van den Haag, E., 102
Vaz, E., 190
Vestermark, S., 184
Visano, L., 116n.21

Walker, E., 8
Walton, P., 12, 30, 37, 59, 66-67
Weber, M., 73, 76
Weinberg, M., 54, 59, 104
West, W.G., 15, 63, 110
Westley, W., 135

Wiatrowski, M., 47
Willis, P., 21n.3
Wilson, E., 175
Wilson, H., 44
Wilson, J.Q., 141-142

Yeager, P., 84, 87-89, 93, 98, 101, 102,
    114n.7, 115n.16
Yinger, M.M., 21n.3
Young, J., 12, 37, 59, 66-67
Young, T., 88

Zeitlin, I., 39

SUBJECT INDEX

Abusive violence, 160
Achieved deviant, 79n.11
Adolescence, 206-207
Adolescent, 209n.17
Adolescents, segregation of, 196
Age, social consequences of, 202-203.
    See also Adolescence
Aggressive masculinity, social
    determinants of, 168
Alcoholism, wife abuse and, 173
Ambivalence, 191
Amplification theory, 197, 198-199.
    See also Mass media; Folk devil;
    Moral panic
Amway Corporation, 90
Anomie, concept of, 29, 31
Anomie theory. *See* Social control
    theory; Strain theory
Anomie-at-the-Top, 100-101
Anti-combines legislation, 110. *See
    also* Anti-trust laws
Anti-trust laws, development of
    (U.S.), 107-108
Arrest. *See* Deterrence, arrest as
Ascribed deviant, 55
Attrition, process of. *See* Corporate
    crime, convictions for

Authority, hierarchy of, 101-102
Authority of leadership. *See*
    Corporations, dominant coalition
Authority of position. *See*
    Corporations, dominant coalition

Bail Reform Act, 155n.41
Battered women, 173
Bendectin, 105-107
Black Panthers, 127
Body norms, 2, 55
Bond to society
    elements of, 43-46
    social control and, 48
Bond theory. *See* Social control
    theory
Bureaucracies, schools as, 201
Bureaucrats, detectives as, 143-144
By-laws, as social control, 147

Calgary Stock Exchange, 90
Canadian Charter of Rights and
    Freedoms
    civilian complaints and, 130
    compared to Canadian Bill of
        Rights, 153n.19
    police investigations and, 124-125

Canadian Civil Liberties Association, 125-126, 131
Canadian Security Intelligence Service, 127
Canadian Urban Victimization Survey. *See* Seven Cities Study
Capital punishment. *See* Deterrence, punishment as
Capitalism. *See also* Deviant class
  as cause of crime, 67
  described (Marx), 65-66
Capitalist society
  as criminogenic, 76, 77
  strain and, 31-32
Capitalist state
  instrumentality of, 177
  wife abuse and, 174
Capitalists, 66
Captured state. *See* State, instrumental conceptions of
Career delinquency, causes of, 38
Career delinquent, 57-58
Career deviant, 140. *See also* Labelling, successful; Saints and Roughnecks
Case law, 130
CCLA. *See* Canadian Civil Liberties Association
CIRPA. *See* Citizen's Independent Review of Police Activities
Citizen's Independent Review of Police Activities, 131-132
Civilian complaints
  convictions following, 129-130
  police investigation of, 131-132
Class conflict theory. *See* Conflict theory
Class fraction. *See* Generalized class rule, defined
Class rule. *See* Generalized class rule, defined
Code of Discipline (police), 120
Combines Investigation Act, 92, 103, 104, 109
Conflict crimes. *See* Typologies
Conflict Tactics Scale, 160
Conflict theory
  class, 203-204
  gender, 174-175
  gender-class, 175-177
  generational, 200-203
  group, 73-75, 149-150

instrumental, 107-109, 145-148
integrated (generation-class), 204-207
Marx, 64-66
structural, 109-112, 145, 148-150
Conformity, defined, 21n.3. *See also* Conformity and deviation
Conformity and deviation
  conflict and, 4-5
  contribution to social order of, 9-10
  general theories of, 5
  instrumentality of, 7-9
  moral evaluations in, 4-5
  relation between, 4-10
  universality of, 5-6
  variability of, 6-7
Consensual assumptions, defined, 38
Consensus crimes. *See* Typologies
Corporate assault, rate of, 94
Corporate conduct, regulation of, *See* Regulatory agencies, dual role of
Corporate crime
  amount of, 89-96, 112
  convictions for, 91-92, 109
  defined, 83-87, 112
  economic, 90-93
  effects of, 93, 112
  fines for, 92
  objective vs subjective definitions of, 87-88
  theoretical perspectives on, 96-112
  violent, 94-96
Corporate executives, criminalization of, 75
Corporate violence
  defined, 94
  economic cost of, 96
Corporations
  dominant coalition in, 86, 101. *See also* Minamata
  social control in, 99
  socialization in, 99
Covert facilitation, 142-143
Crime
  defined, 11, 24n.20
  as functional, 11, 28-29
Crime and deviance
  causes of, 66-68
  consensus theories of, 76
  historical approaches to, 76
Criminal Code, 117, 118, 153n.21
Criminality, defined, 20

Criminalization. *See also* Corporate
  executives
  differences in, 73
  rates of, 75
  social conflict and, 73-74
Criminals, defined, 3
Criminogenic, police work as. *See*
  Proactive policing
Criminogenic environment. *See*
  Proactive policing
Criminogenic subculture. *See*
  Subculture, criminogenic
Cultural norms, 74, 166
Cultural theories. *See* Wife abuse,
  theoretical perspectives

Deaths. *See* Work-related deaths
Definitions
  consequences of, 210
  evaluation of, 17-20, 88
  objective and subjective evaluated,
    88
  political character of, 211-212
  political use of, 157
  technical use of, 157
Delegated vigilantism, 148
Delinquency. *See also* Career
  delinquency; Parental
  supervision; Teachers
  cause of, 62
  class and. *See* Saints and
    Roughnecks
  commitment to, 79n.6
  defined, 12, 14-15
  schools and, 202
Delinquent. *See* Career delinquent;
  Juvenile delinquent
Delinquent behaviour, described,
  42-43
Delinquent subculture. *See*
  Subculture, delinquent
Dependency
  objective, 168
  subjective, 168
  theory. *See* Social control theory
  and violence, 172
Deterrence. *See also* Corporate crime,
  convictions for arrest as, 170-171
  effectiveness of, 103-104
  general, 103
  punishment as, 48
  specific, 103

Deterrence theorists, orientations of,
  140
Deterrence theory. *See* Social control
  theory
Deviance. *See also* Primary deviance;
  Secondary deviance; Sexual
  deviance
  criminal/non-criminal,
    differentiated, 83-84
  defined, 4, 20, 55, 78
  objectively, 10-15
  subjectively, 15-17
  forms of (Edgerton), 6, 7
  historical approach to, 211
  psychological definitions of, 11
  psychological theories of, 133, 150.
    See also Rotten apple theory
  as reaction to social control, 51
  social control and, 56. *See also*
    Career delinquent
  sociological study of, 16, 37, 63
  theories of. *See* Conflict theory;
    Interactionist perspective;
    Social control theory; Strain
    theory
Deviance matters, defined, 22n.11
Deviant, defined, 3.6. *See also*
  Achieved deviant; Ascribed
  deviant; Career deviant; Double
  deviant; Occasional deviant;
  Reactive deviant
Deviant acts, defined, 12
Deviant behaviour, defined, 12,
  23n.13
Deviant class, capitalism and
  production of, 68
Deviations, classified (Hagan),
  22n.10
Differential association theory. *See*
  Interactionist perspective
Domestic homicide, 161
Dominant class, hegemonic fraction
  in, 111-112
Dominant coalition. *See*
  Corporations, dominant coalition
Dominant fraction, 109
Double deviant, 2, 141
Dramatization of evil, 15
Drift, 34
Drug law enforcement. *See* Proactive
  policing
Drug problem, 141-142

Drug squad. *See* Royal Canadian Mounted Police

Economism, 156n.56
Elites. *See* Ruling class, defined, elites; State elites
Entrapment. *See* Covert facilitation
Ethnography, 62-63
Existential norms, 6
Expressive crimes. *See* Typologies

Family, social control in the, 41-42. *See also* Stake in conformity
Family Violence Research Programme, 166
Feathering and flocking, 45-46, 191-196
Federal Drug Agency (U.S.), 105-106
Firearms, police use of, 139
Fisheries Act, 115n.19
FLQ, 127
Folk devil, 198-199
Force, unauthorized use of, 148
Formal organizations, corporations as, 97
Functional theory. *See* Interactionist perspective
Functionalist theory, essentials of, 22n.7

Game, society as, 49
Gender, concept of, 172
Gender-class conflict theory. *See* Conflict theory
Gender classes, concept of, 175-176
Gender norms, 172
Gender roles. *See* Roles, stratification of
Genderic state, 176-178
Generalized class rule, defined, 70
Generational conflict theory. *See* Conflict theory
Gerontocratic rule, 182
"Grasseaters." *See* Reactive deviant
Grounded labelling theory. *See* Labelling theory
Group conflict, conditions for, 74
Group conflict theory. *See* Conflict theory
Gynaephobia, 167

Hazardous practices, 92-93

Hegemonic fraction. *See* Dominant class, hegemonic fraction
Heroin addiction, control of, 141-142
Historical analysis. *See* Sociology, historical approach
Historical sociology. *See* Sociology, historical approach
Homicide. *See* Domestic homicide; Spousal homicide

Ideological orientations, 150
Incidence estimates, defined, 179n.10
Individuation, process of, 100-101. *See also* Bureaucrats, detectives
Inequality, as cause of crime, 67
Interactionist theorists, shared attributes of, 50-51
Interactionist perspective
 differential association, 60, 61-62, 80n.16
 functional, 55-56
 labelling, 53-55, 197-198
 grounded, 59-60
 self, 140-141, 151
 societal reaction, 51-52, 56-59, 172-173
 symbolic, 49-50
 transactional, 198-199
Instrumental crimes, *See* Typologies
Intra-class conflict, 70
Ironical effects. *See* Social control, ironical effects
Irony. *See* Social control, irony

Judges Rules, 117, 134
Juvenile delinquents, defined, 12

Keable Commission, 126
Kenora, 125-126
Kentville, N.S., 119-121

Labelling process, 53, 104-105
Labelling, successful, 54-55. *See also* Social definitions
Labelling theory. *See* Interactionist perspective
Labour
 appropriation of, 176, 179n.18
 division of, 176
Law
 administrative, 113n.1
 civil, 113n.1

criminal, 113n.1

Laws, origin and function, 72

"Left handing." *See* Search warrants, forged

Legal norms, 3, 10-11, 74-75

Loners, 101, 138. *See also*
Adolescents, segregation; Bond to society, elements, bureaucrats, detectives; Vandalism, lonely students; Individuation process

Lumpen proletariat, 146

McDonald Commission, 126

Masculine dominance
concept of, 175
state and, 177

Masculinity. *See* Aggressive masculinity

Mass media, 198-199

Materialism. *See* Social change, materialist account

Maturational reform. *See* Strain theory

"Meateaters." See Double deviant

Methadone Maintenance Program, 141-142

Metropolitan Toronto, 121-124, 137, 147, 188

Minamata incident, 87-88

Minneapolis Domestic Violence Experiment, 170

Montreal, 127-128

Montreal Urban Community Police Department, 127

Moral drama
interaction as, 105-106
labelling process and, 53

Moral panic, concept of, 198-199

Normative norms, 6

Normative violence, defined, 159, 172

Norms. *See* Body norms; Cultural norms; Existential norms; Gender norms; Legal norms; Normative norms; Social norms; subcultural norms

Nova Scotia Police Commission (NSPC), 119-121

Occasional deviant, 140. *See also* Reactive deviant

Occupational crime, defined, 86. *See also* White-collar crime

Occupational health and safety, 94, 115n.18

Occupational Health and Safety Act (Ontario), 103

Ontario Provincial Police, 126

Ontario Task Force on Vandalism, 182-183

Ontario Task Force Report on Vandalism, 188

Organizational theories. *See* Social control theory

Parental control. *See* Vandalism, parental control

Parental supervision, delinquency and, 44-45

Parental violence, 166-167

Patriarchy, defined, 173, 174, 175

Peer group, deviance and, 138-139.
See also Feathering and flocking; Social control; Subculture

Plea bargaining, 153n.21

Police
civilian complaints against, 122-124
legal status of, 130
regulation of. *See* Canadian Civil Liberties Association; Code of Discipline; Criminal Code; Judges Rules; Police Act; Police Complaints Board; Public Complaints Board; Public Complaints Commissioner
relative autonomy of, 140, 148-149

Police Act, 117

Police Complaints Board, 129

Police deviance
amount of, 119-128
defined, 117-118
social determinants of, 133-134
theoretical perspectives on, 133-150

Police investigations. *See* Canadian Charter of Rights and Freedoms

Policing. *See also* Proactive policing
as functional, 30-31, 78n.4
historical analysis of, 146-147, 156n.51
as political, 149-150

Pornography, as functional, 30-31

Positivism, in sociology, 79n.9
Power, illegal use of, 153n.19
Prevalence estimates, defined,
    179n.10
Primary deviance, 16, 51-52
Proactive policing, 136-137
Process theory, 61
Prostitution, as functional, 30-31
Public Complaints Board, 122
Public Complaints Commissioner,
    121-125, 128-132
Punishment. *See* Deterrence,
    punishment; Social control,
    punishment

Quebec Provincial Police, 127

Rape. *See* Conformity and deviance,
    variability
Reactionary crimes. *See* Typologies
Reactive deviant, 140
Repressive crimes, *See* Typologies
Regulatory agencies, dual role of,
    110-112
Relative autonomy, concept of, 148
Relatively autonomous state, 110-112.
    See also State, structural
    conceptions
Role differentiation, concept of, 174
Roles, stratification of, 174
Rotten apple theory, 121, 133, 150
Royal Canadian Mounted Police
    Drug Squad, 128
    G-section, 126-128
Ruling class. *See also* Dominant class,
    hegemonic fraction; Generalized
    class rule, defined
    defined, 69
    elites in, 81n.28

Saints and Roughnecks, 58-59
Schools, social class system and,
    203-204. *See also* Delinquency,
    schools; Vandalism, schools
Search warrants, forged, 143-144,
    155n.42
Secondary deviance, 16, 52-53
Secondary deviant, 141
Security Intelligence Review
    Committee, 127
Self-labelling. *See* Labelling theory

Self-reporting. *See* Vandalism, self-
    report study
Seven Cities Study, 162-163, 187
Sexual deviance, 47-48
Sexual harassment, 85
Shelter theorists, 173
Situational social control theory, 42
Skinner Box, 140
Social change
    general class-conflict theory of
        (Marx), 64-66
    materialist account of, 65-66
Social class. *See* Schools, social class
    system
Social classes, formation of, 179n.18
Social control. *See also* Bond to
    society; By-laws; Career
    delinquent; Corporations; Family
    deviance and, 34-35
    function of, 40
    ironical effects of, 141-142
    irony, 171
    peers and, 41-42
    punishment as, 39
    as reaction to deviance, 51
Social control theorists, shared
    attributes of, 40
Social control theory
    anomie, 100-101
    bond, 43-47, 101-102, 138-139
    dependency, 168-169
    deterrence, 102-104, 139-140, 150,
        169-171
    organizational, 101
    subcultural, 41-43
Social definitions, labelling process
    and, 53-54
Social determinants. *See* Police
    deviance, social determinants
Social deviations, 13-14
Social diversions, 13-14
Social dynamite, 13
Social groups. *See* Society, structure
    of
Social junk, 13
Social norms, 2, 6, 10, 74
Social order, basis of, 28
Social process
    defined, 25-26
    deviance and, 16
Social structure, defined, 25
Socialism, described (Marx), 65

Violence. *See also* Conformity and
    deviance, variability; Force,
    unauthorized use; Power, Illegal
    use
  abusive, 160
  corporate, 94
  normative, 159, 172
  police subculture and, 134-135
  spousal, 158, 166
Vocabularies of motives, 59-60,
    80n.15
Vulgar Marxism, 81n.31

White-collar crime, defined, 85-86
Wife abuse

amount of, 160-165
backlash thesis of, 168
cross-cultural data on, 164-165
definitions of, 157-160
  gender-neutral, 159-160
feminist scholars and, 159
historical analysis of, 171
politics in defining, 160
spousal violence and,
    distinguished, 158-160
state policies and, 175
theoretical perspectives on,
    166-177
Wife assault, amount of, 162-163
Work-related deaths, statistics, 95